W9-ABZ-360

Lucia Boldrini's study examines how the literary and linguistic theories of Dante's treatises and the poetics of the *Divine Comedy* helped shape the radical narrative techniques and linguistic inventiveness of Joyce's last novel *Finnegans Wake*. Detailed parallel readings raise diverse issues such as the question of Babel, literary creation as excrement, the complex relations between literary, geometrical and female forms. Boldrini places Joyce's work in the wider context of other modernist writing's relation to Dante, thereby identifying the distinctness of Joyce's own project. She considers how theories of influence and intertextuality help or limit the understanding of the relation. Boldrini shows how, through an untiring confrontation with his predecessors, constantly thematised within his writing, Joyce develops a 'poetics in progress' that informs not only his final work but his entire *oeuvre*. This book will appeal to scholars and students interested in Joyce, Dante and questions of literary relations.

LUCIA BOLDRINI is lecturer in English at Goldsmiths College, University of London. She has published on Joyce and Dante, Robert Browning and literary theory. She is the author of *Biografie fittizie e personaggi storici: (Auto)biografia, soggettività, teoria nel romanzo inglese contemporaneo* (1998) ('Fictional Biographies and Historical Characters: (Auto)biography, Subjectivity, Theory in the Contemporary English Novel').

JOYCE, DANTE, AND THE POETICS OF LITERARY RELATIONS

Language and Meaning in *Finnegans Wake*

LUCIA BOLDRINI

CAMBRIDGE
UNIVERSITY PRESS

PR
6019
.09
F562
2001

PUBLISHED AT THE PRESS SYNDICATE OF THE UNIVERSITY OF CAMBRIDGE
The Pitt Building, Trumpington Street, Cambridge, United Kingdom

CAMBRIDGE UNIVERSITY PRESS
The Edinburgh Building, Cambridge CB2 2RU, UK   www.cup.cam.ac.uk
40 West 20th Street, New York NY10011–4211, USA   www.cup.org
10 Stamford Road, Oakleigh, Melbourne 3166, Australia
Ruiz de Alarcón 13, 28014 Madrid, Spain

© Cambridge University Press 2001

This book is in copyright. Subject to statutory exception and to the provisions of relevant
collective licensing agreements, no reproduction of any part may take place without the
written permission of Cambridge University Press.

First published 2001

Printed in the United Kingdom at the University Press, Cambridge

Typeface 11/12.5pt Baskerville   *System* 3B2   [CE]

A catalogue record for this book is available from the British Library

Library of Congress Cataloguing in Publication data
Boldrini, Lucia.
Joyce, Dante, and the poetics of literary relations: language and meaning in
Finnegans Wake /Lucia Boldrini.
p.   cm.
Includes bibliographical references and index.
ISBN 0 521 79276 2 (hardback)
1. Joyce, James, 1882–1941. Finnegans Wake.
2. Joyce, James, 1882–1941 – Knowledge – Literature.
3. Dante Alighieri, 1265–1321 – Influence.
4. English fiction – Italian influences.
5. Joyce, James, 1882–1941 – Technique.
6. Influence (Literary, artistic, etc.)
PR6019.09F562   2001
823'.912–dc21   00–062143

ISBN 0 521 79276 2 hardback

44876910

*For my parents, Luciano and Luciana Boldrini,
and for John and Catherine Robinson.*

Contents

Acknowledgements

This book is the result of several years of study, and more teachers, friends and colleagues deserve my thanks than I can acknowledge here. To many I owe more than academic gratitude: Klaus Reichert, whose seminar on *Finnegans Wake* at the University of Pisa in 1988–9 lit the spark; Paola Pugliatti and especially Elsa Linguanti for their encouragement and affection; Valeria Raglianti Biagioni, who pushed me, and Dirk Vanderbeke, who listened when I had nothing yet to say; then Jane Everson, who listened even when I had too much to say, and patiently waited for me to get back on the straight way – and for some years, simply waited; Kelvin Everest first, then Martin Stannard, who also had to wait; the Leeds James Joyce Research Group, who heard the early, eager ramblings of this work, and more recently helped put a full stop to it; Fritz Senn, for his unfailing support; and Laurent Milesi, who made all the difference.

Very special thanks go to my parents, who made it all possible, and John and Catherine Robinson, who know that, after all, I owe it all to them. And John, of course, for his patience with the too many late evenings and working weekends.

I also wish to give my thanks to the British Library for the permission to reproduce the diagram from the Frankfurt 1591 print of Giordano Bruno's *De monade, numero et figura* (532 b29), and the Library's staff for their helpfulness.

Abbreviations

Conv	Dante, *Convivio*, ed. G. Busnelli and G. Vandelli. Florence: Le Monnier, 1964.
'DBVJ'	Samuel Beckett, 'Dante. . . Bruno. Vico. . Joyce'. In *Our Exagmination* (see below).
Dve	Dante, *De vulgari eloquentia*, ed. A. Marigo. Florence: Le Monnier, 1957.
Exag	Samuel Beckett et al., *Our Exagmination Round His Factification for Incamination of Work in Progress*. London: Faber, 1951.
FW	James Joyce, *Finnegans Wake*. London: Faber, 1950.
Inf	Dante, *Inferno. La Commedia secondo l'antica vulgata*, ed. Giorgio Petrocchi. Testo della Società Dantesca Italiana, Milan: Mondadori, 1966–8.
Purg	Dante, *Purgatorio. La Commedia secondo l'antica vulgata*, ed. Giorgio Petrocchi. Testo della Società Dantesca Italiana, Milan: Mondadori, 1966–8.
Par	Dante, *Paradiso. La Commedia secondo l'antica vulgata*, ed. Giorgio Petrocchi. Testo della Società Dantesca Italiana, Milan: Mondadori, 1966–8.
*JJ*II	Richard Ellmann, *James Joyce*. Oxford: Oxford University Press, 1982.
Letters I, II, III	*Letters of James Joyce*, vol. I ed. Stuart Gilbert. London: Faber, 1957; vols. II and III ed. Richard Ellmann. London: Faber, 1966.
P	James Joyce, *A Portrait of the Artist as a Young Man*, ed. Chester G. Anderson. Harmondsworth and New York: Penguin, 1968.
SH	James Joyce, *Stephen Hero*, ed. Theodore Spencer. London: Paladin, 1991.

SL   *Selected Letters of James Joyce*, ed. Richard Ellmann. New York: Viking, 1975.

U   James Joyce, *Ulysses*. London: Bodley Head, 1960.

VN   Dante, *Vita Nuova*, ed. Edoardo Sanguineti. Milan: Garzanti, 1977.

All translations from Dante's works are mine unless otherwise indicated.

Introduction: In the Wake of the Divine Comic

L'acqua ch'io prendo già mai non si corse;

        . . .

Voialtri pochi che drizzaste il collo
per tempo al pan de li angeli, del quale
vivesi qui ma non sen vien satollo,
    metter potete ben per l'alto sale
vostro navigio, servando mio solco
dinanzi a l'acqua che ritorna equale.[1]

(Par II, 7; 10–15)

Skim over *Through Hell with the Papes* (mostly boys) by the divine
comic Denti Alligator

(FW 440.05–6)

In canto xxv of the *Inferno*, abandoning his (often only nominal)
deference towards the *auctoritates* of the literary past and the mask of
the unworthy follower ('io non Enea, io non Paulo sono'; 'I am not
Aeneas, I am not Paul', *Inf* II, 32), Dante tells of the complex and
terrible metamorphoses to which the thieves are subjected, and
underscores his poetic invention by bidding Lucan and Ovid be
silent, because the changes they described in their works could not
stand comparison with what Dante is now witnessing – or, as we are
to understand, with his own superior inventiveness:

Taccia Lucano omai là dov' e' tocca
del misero Sabello e di Nasidio,
e attenda a udir quel ch'or si scocca.
    Taccia di Cadmo e d'Aretusa Ovidio,
ché se quello in serpente e quella in fonte
converte poetando, io non lo 'nvidio . . .   (*Inf* xxv, 94–9)

(Let Lucan now be silent, where he tells of the wretched Sabellus and of
Nasidius, and let him wait to hear what is now being fired. Of Cadmus and
Arethusa let Ovid be silent, for if he converts by his poetry the one into a
serpent and the other into a fountain, I do not envy him . . .)

I

Dante's boastful self-appraisal in this literary duel ('scocca' describes the moment the arrow is fired from the bow) achieves a double result: the poet acknowledges two of his main sources of inspiration, Lucan and Ovid, and, at the same time, marks his departure from the pagan models he is imitating and their mythical subject-matter. The principal issues are thus that of originality, understood both as temporal anteriority and as novel treatment of one's poetic material, and that of the competition with one's sources and models in order to surpass or defeat them; what is really at stake, then, is the assertion of one's own rights to authorship, the victorious reversal of Harold Bloom's notion of anxiety-laden influence into an appropriation and metamorphosis of the earlier poet, guided by an awareness of the superiority of one's poetic weapons. But those who live by literature die by literature, and Dante's success in his competition with his predecessors has transformed him into a model to be appropriated and transformed to new ends by his successors.

Joyce's relationship with Dante is to an extent comparable to the one thus sketched by Dante: by inscribing Dante's literary theories and techniques into his text, appropriating (thieving) and transforming (metamorphosing) them for his own purposes, Joyce can be said to be implicitly proclaiming his own 'Taccia Dante'. By means of this silent silencing, however, Joyce also allows Dante's voice to resound through his work, acknowledging his source and giving a clue to one of the many (and always insufficient) poetic, structural and exegetical models for *Finnegans Wake*.

Joyce started reading Dante already when he was at school, and his interest in the Italian poet never lapsed.[2] Of course, Joyce was not alone: while, apart from Milton's *Paradise Lost*, the seventeenth and most of the eighteenth centuries had shown scant interest in Dante's works,[3] Blake's illustrations of the *Commedia*, the medievalism of the Romantics, or even more specifically, the German Romantics' writings on Dante, introduced by Coleridge into Britain, are just three instances of the Florentine's increasing prominence in the landscape of past literary masters from the late eighteenth century. Coleridge, Hunt, Shelley, Byron, all read Dante, wrote on him and borrowed from his works. Whereas the Romantics' picture of the medieval poet was often of a proud, solitary and cheerless figure and their concern was mainly with the dark but lively *Inferno*, later in the nineteenth century Dante became for Ruskin the 'central man of all the world . . . representing in perfect balance the imaginative, moral and intellectual faculties, all at their highest',[4] while Rossetti and the Pre-Raphaelites promoted an image of Dante and of his work as both highly sensual and spiritual, focusing on the poet's love and on the figure of Beatrice, and often privileging the *Vita Nuova*, which had generally been neglected until then.[5] In the early decades of the twentieth century, Dante was a main source of inspiration for the modernists, to the extent that it has been claimed that 'Dante has dominated the imagination of [Yeats, Pound, Eliot, Beckett, Stevens, Auden] as has no other writer',[6] while another critic has argued that 'One of the ways we could describe an aspiration of virtually all the major modernist writers in English is that they were all trying to write the *Commedia* of the twentieth century . . . there is a sense in which Yeats, Wyndham Lewis, Beckett, and Eliot, in addition to Pound and Joyce, were simply imitating *the* Italian, Dante Alighieri.'[7]

Why was Dante so central to the modernist project of 'making it new' (to use Pound's slogan), and why was he so relevant, in particular, to Joyce's radically new narrative technique in *Finnegans Wake*? With Dante, the Italian language achieved a semantic and lexical flexibility and range that were unthinkable before him. Bare mathematical statistics show the scope of Dante's linguistic innovation. The linguist Bruno Migliorini points out that the vocabulary of the Italian language increased from 4,000–5,000 words at the turn of the first millennium to 10,000–15,000 around 1300.[8] Compared with this 'common language', the extension of Dante's lexicon is stunning: nearly 28,000 words, a figure that becomes even more striking if we consider the lexical range of contemporary Florentine poets: Dante's friend Guido Cavalcanti, for instance, used just over 800 words in his poetry. It is not surprising then that Dante should have earned the reputation of 'father' of the Italian language, a claim which Joyce characteristically acknowledged while simultaneously pointing both to the 'distortion' inherent in Dante's technique and in his own treatment of language, and, implicitly, to the 'metamorphosis' and 'distortion' to which his 'model' will also be subjected: 'May Father Dante forgive me', he is reported to have said, 'but I started from this technique of deformation to achieve a harmony that defeats our intelligence, as music does';[9] nor is it surprising that Dante should be the author to whom modernists turned in their project of renewing literary language.

As we shall see in chapter 4, Dante's impressive expansion of the vernacular was not due to some kind of 'baroque' exhibitionism, but it was in fact both justified and necessary on account of his programme, famously stated at the end of the *Vita Nuova* (his autobiographical *Künstlerroman*, to use a modern term), to go beyond the immediate perceptual reality in order to say what had never been said by anyone before – in order, that is, to express the *novum*, the divine, the ineffable (*VN* XLII). Joyce's trajectory too may be said to be informed by a poetics of the *novum*: it appeared at least as early as his own autobiographical *Künstlerroman*, *A Portrait of the Artist as a Young Man*, cut short like the *Vita Nuova* exactly when Stephen announces his intention to forge the 'uncreated conscience of [his] race' (*P* 253). It is also central in the *Wake*'s (in)ability to tell in 'nat language' (*FW* 83.12, night language, not language), through techniques that can be profitably aligned with the (im)possibility of representing the ineffable in the *Paradiso* – the 'something itself' ('DBVJ' 14) that is its subject.

But this is Dante the poet. In the first three chapters of this book I argue that Dante the theorist, concerned with a diachronic and synchronic study of the language and with the signifying structure of the polysemic text, was an equally powerful model that Joyce confronted in his construction of *Finnegans Wake*.

Several of Dante's works, including his treatises *De vulgari eloquentia* and *Convivio*, were available to Joyce in Dublin in either Marsh's or the National Libraries. Given the young Joyce's propensity for delving outside the mainstream literary canon (reflected in Stephen's spending his time among the dark and dusty tomes of Marsh's Library to read medieval books of the Italian Trecento, *SH* 181, and the fading leaves of Gioacchino da Fiore's prophecies,[10] *U* 49) or for putting the mainstream into the service of his semi-heretic, or at least very individualistic, aesthetics, it would not be out of character if already at this early stage he had at least browsed through these less canonical, generally less well-known works by the Florentine.

I have found no clear evidence in Joyce's earlier writings of any direct uses of Dante's linguistic and literary theories; at this point, for Joyce too, Dante is still very much the poet of the *Vita Nuova* and the *Commedia*. This lack of explicit evidence should not suggest however that Joyce would not have been aware of the existence of these works and their contents. As his curriculum included the history of Italian, it is more than likely that mention would have been made of the *questione della lingua* ('the question of the language'), an issue which in Italy – a nation politically divided until the nineteenth century and in which regional differences and desire for national unity have always constituted motives of tension – flared up especially in the Cinquecento and the Risorgimento.[11] In the Cinquecento in particular Dante's position became a motive for fierce debate from the moment Giorgio Trissino rediscovered and then printed a manuscript of the *De vulgari eloquentia* and brought it to the attention of his contemporaries, including Francesco Bembo (whose statement on the *Divine Comedy* appeared in one of the papers that Joyce had to take for his honours examination,[12] and whose *Prose della vulgar lingua* existed in Marsh's Library in manuscript form) and Machiavelli, who pointed out the contradictions between the treatise and Dante's practice in the *Commedia*, thus casting doubt on the attribution of the treatise, to the point that some scholars even accused Trissino of forging the work. (An Italian translation of Dante's *De vulgari eloquentia* published in Venice in 1644 and opening the first of six tomes of a large work collecting various works on the Italian language by Trissino, Bembo and several other scholars who intervened in the *questione della lingua* was also available in Marsh's Library; the National Library, apart from a number of editions and translations of the *Commedia*, also had a translation of the *De vulgari eloquentia* by Ferrers Howell[13] and at least one of *The Banquet* (*Il Convito*) by Katharine Hillard, also containing the 'Epistle of Dante to Can Grande' in the appendix.[14])

Joyce's life on the Continent and the ten years he spent in Trieste would have made all of Dante's works available to him. Scholarly interest in the *De vulgari eloquentia* in particular had been sparked anew in Italy by the Risorgimento, when the *questione della lingua* and Dante's position within it – debated, among others, by Alessandro Manzoni – was once again brought into focus and linked to the political issue of Italy's struggle for independence and unification, issues that the Triestine *irredentisti* would take up again.[15] In the last decades of the nineteenth century and the first of the twentieth publications on the *De vulgari eloquentia* and Dante's other treatises continued to increase.[16] In 1916 a new manuscript of the *De vulgari eloquentia* was discovered in Berlin, and it kindled again discussions on this much debated treatise, on Dante's linguistics and on the authorship of some of his works, including the *Epistle to Can Grande*.

Nino Frank claimed that Joyce's interest in Dante declined and finally ceased as he wrote *Finnegans Wake* ('Dante's importance was to recede, and only Vico's philosophy, with its "turn" and "return," would remain part of the inspiration of *Finnegans Wake*'[17]), but I would argue on the contrary that Joyce's understanding of the way he could rely on and exploit Dante's works culminated with the *Wake*, and that it is possible to speak of a specifically 'Dantean poetics' of *Finnegans Wake*. By this I am certainly not trying to suggest that Joyce's use of Dante in his earlier works was 'immature' or that his 'understanding' of the medieval poet was limited. It has been pointed out that 'The Sisters' opens with a reference to the portal of Hell in the *Inferno*,[18] and I have argued elsewhere that, from the start, the Dantean subtext enables Joyce to confront the aesthetic and ethical implications of his literary practice through a use of textual references that is already much more problematic than simple parody, the borrowing of a structure or a humble following in literary footsteps, and that this confrontation already implies – as is the case in all of Joyce's works, up to and including *Finnegans Wake* – a reflection on the nature of the relationship between the modern author and his precursors.[19]

Mary Reynolds has demonstrated in *Joyce and Dante* how subtly Joyce wove references to Dante into all his books, in order to both shape and give depth to themes as different as love, father-figures, rebirth. Yet Reynolds's thematic approach finds more suitable ground in Joyce's work up to *Ulysses*, whereas *Finnegans Wake* is discussed in general, though very perceptive, terms. As I have said, I believe that it is precisely in the *Wake* that Joyce's use of Dante becomes most pervasive and far-reaching. In the work of the Italian, Joyce could find an unprecedented and unequalled complex semiotic, structural and linguistic programme, and if plurality and polysemy are two of the main structural and thematic aspects of the *Wake*, then Dante is the obvious antecedent to look at, not only in order to go back to his works but also to parody them, 'thieve' from them, 'metamorphose', surpass and 'silence' them.

Polysemy, or plurality of meanings, and linguistic plurality will accordingly be the focus of the first three chapters of this book. Dante was the first to design and apply to his own poetry a fully-fledged model of literary interpretation, which he based on the exegetical theory of the four meanings of Scriptural writing. Admittedly, the system did not work too well; as I shall argue in chapter 1, its application and parody in *Finnegans Wake* also exposes its contradictions and ultimate failure. This is not to say, of course, that Joyce was exploiting a failed model in a facile show-off of literary superiority; on the contrary, the adoption of the model also involves a reflection on the nature of signification and on the deviations and distortions that the writer must face in order to achieve polysemy. If for Harold Bloom the only way forward for the later poet is to misread the precursor, and thus to be condemned to suffer from the anxiety of the latent 'guilty' knowledge of this misreading even as the process allows the successor to achieve his own greatness,[20] Joyce's fully conscious recycling of Dante (as well as of any other writer) shows, rather, how it is in fact the precursor that already contains, or even determines, the possibility, for the later poet, to distort his works; the operation should therefore be described not so much as 'misreading' but as a reading between the lines which will expose *any* model's limitations. This also involves an awareness of one's own unstable position, as the silencing of the earlier writer always entails the possibility of being 'silenced' in turn in the future: Dante's 'Let Ovid be silent' is counterbalanced in the following canticle by Oderisi da Gubbio's warning about the futility of taking pride in one's own artistic supremacy:

> Credette Cimabue ne la pittura
> tener lo campo, e ora ha Giotto il grido,
> sì che la fama di colui è scura.
>   Così ha tolto l'uno a l'altro Guido
> la gloria de la lingua; e forse è nato
> chi l'uno e l'altro caccerà dal nido.   (*Purg* XI, 94–9)

(Cimabue believed that he held the field in painting, and now Giotto has the cry, so that the former's fame is dim. Thus has the one Guido taken from the other the glory of the language; and he perhaps is born that shall chase the one and the other from the nest.)

Another will always come who will overturn, displace and replace the present prevailing model – a movement that any reader of Joyce will also recognise as typical of the pattern of supersession at work in literary as well as family genealogies in *Finnegans Wake*. Interestingly the last sentence in the lines above – 'he perhaps is born' – has been interpreted as referring to Dante himself, whose name has displaced that of the two Guidos (Guinizzelli and Cavalcanti); but this also entails that Dante is guilty of the sin of pride at the same time as he describes both its futility and how it is punished and expiated. Although this apparent contradiction can be explained by saying that, in this context, Dante may be showing that he is conscious of his own supremacy now, but also of his inevitable later displacement, one can only be struck by the frequency and the extent to which Dante's pride informs so much of his writing, a point I shall come back to in chapters 2 and 3.[21]

The same process of 'thieving' and 'metamorphosing' applies to the issue of linguistic plurality: Dante's account of the Babel episode in the *De vulgari eloquentia* (which I shall examine in chapter 2) and then, in the second part of the first book of treatise, his quest for, or rebuilding of, an 'illustrious' language (which I shall discuss in chapter 3), may have suggested to Joyce possible ways of exploiting the theme of Babel and provided a structural model of linguistic construction, but they also offered a system to be parodied and distorted into a principle for organising the plot (e.g. in the pattern that relates linguistic, alcoholic and excremental distillation – see chapter 3) and for composing the *Wake*'s protean and highly unusual 'characters' (e.g. HCE as a language that rises and declines, itself to be declined and articulated in various forms). Joyce's treatment of Dante's linguistic history also allows the reader to look back at Dante as a Nimrod figure proudly attempting to reverse history by achieving what had been denied to his Biblical/mythical precursor.

I must clarify at this point that although this book aims to offer primarily a reading of Joyce rather than of Dante, the obscure words of *Finnegans Wake* may also throw unexpected light on aspects and implications of Dante's works that have not been given much attention, or bring into focus startling conclusions that many eminent Dantists have found difficult to accept. As I shall argue in the next three chapters, for instance, it is difficult to be aware on a first reading of the treatises of the extent to which Dante's project of linguistic redemption in the *De vulgari eloquentia* brings him perilously close to the sin of pride symbolised by the tower of Babel which he endeavours to redress, but if one goes back to the treatise and reads it in conjunction with the *Wake*'s fusion of different roles (HCE and Shem, the language and the tower, the hunter and the hunted, linguistic synthesis or distillation and technique of characterisation), one arrives at an almost perverse image of a Dante who is both saviour and sinner, builder of the Tower and redeemer of Babel. To give another example, the impasse of Dante's theory of polysemy in the *Convivio* is generally read as a flaw which contributed to its abandonment, and contradictions are pointed out between the

Convivio's view of the superiority of Latin on the one hand and the *De vulgari eloquentia*'s defence of the vernacular as more noble on the other. However, if one rereads the *Convivio* and the *Epistle to Can Grande* through the prism of Joyce's last novel, one realises that Dante's contradictions and paradoxes are in fact productive, that they prove to be instrumental to Dante's project instead of limiting its validity, and that only when a later writer takes them up and pursues their implications can the reader perceive what new paths Dante's 'limits' had opened up for him and his successors. It is therefore to Joyce's credit that he did not try to speak in the 'true dantescan voice' and steered clear of the broad avenue of 'easy' imitability that, according to Eliot's questionable view, Dante's universal language allowed,[22] but looked instead for the untrodden paths, taking up the challenge of the 'deep salt' and of the waters that have never been 'coursed' before, or of the 'wake' that has 'turn[ed] smooth again' (see the first epigraph to this introduction), also accepting the nourishment of Dante's 'sacred' poetry (his own 'pan de li angeli'). By following this 'uncoursed wake', Joyce may in fact have been the best imitator of Dante among the modernists, as Reed Way Dasenbrock has written[23] and the 'sole disciple of Dante' who can repeat the poet's experience in the writing activity itself, as Jacqueline Risset has observed in her fine commentary on Joyce's Italian translation of the ALP chapter.[24] It may be useful at this point to briefly sketch what I see as the main differences between the relationship that Joyce on the one hand, and Pound and Eliot on the other, established with Dante.

Despite Pound's claim that the poet must consciously imitate in order to be independent from his models and sources of inspiration,[25] the reverence with which Dante is always treated by both Pound and Eliot – the latter being the poet on whom the former bestowed the title of 'true dantescan voice'[26] – may suggest that a real independence was never really achieved, and that Dante always remained the standard of excellence to which the modern poet could only aspire. Notwithstanding their proclaimed anti-Victorianism, it is very much to a Ruskinian view of the 'centrality' of Dante within an organic and unified Middle Ages that both poets subscribe, as Eliot's deploring of the modern 'dissociation of sensibility' also shows.[27] The notion that imitation is only a stage in the poet's development and in his search for the 'lost' roots of our decaying modern culture is somewhat belied by both Eliot's and Pound's adoption of Dante to confirm, support or justify their ideologies,[28] and by their all-too-faithful linear rewriting of the Hell–Purgatory–Paradise sequence (cf. the *Cantos*, to a large extent structured on the *Commedia*, as the project of a 'restorative' epic of the crumbling modern world which would thus be cured of its ills by the messianic poet; and Eliot's sequence from the '*Inferno*' of *The Waste Land* – or, earlier, 'Gerontion' – to the unified final vision of 'Little Gidding' in *Four Quartets*, where the lines 'the tongues of fire are in-folded / Into the crowned knot of fire / And the fire and the rose are one'[29] clearly evoke the vision of God and of the rose of the blessed in the last cantos of Dante's *Paradiso*).

Joyce's use of Dante (as of any other source) is rarely informed by the deference shown by his two contemporaries. Although it has been claimed for instance that the structure of the short story 'Grace' is indebted to that of the three *cantiche* of the *Divine Comedy*,[30] even here the model is ironised, its inadequacy as a linear plot of 'salvation' exposed. Joyce's eclecticism, and the relevance that Vico's cyclical pattern acquired in his last work, enabled him both to forgo the teleology of the *Inferno*-to-*Paradiso* pattern (or, for that matter, the opposite view of contemporary culture as being in a process of ineluctable decline that required messianic intervention) and to play off any model against any other, so as to show that if they can all be equally valid, they are also equally 'debunkable'. If Dante was a source for Joyce, he was, as I have suggested above, one which encouraged plurality, and this would already be enough to offset the priority of any single model – including Dante himself – and undermine its univocal use. It is this radically eclectic and playful relationship to 'parent' texts that best distinguishes Joyce's literary practice from that of his fellow-modernists. After all, the quotation from *Finnegans Wake* I have chosen for my second epigraph shows what kind of (comic) operation Joyce performs on Dante: the reference appears to be to *Inferno* XIX, where a pope, soon to be followed by others, is thrust head down into a hole in the ground with his feet sticking out and kicking up in the air. Joyce's 'Papes' echoes the distorted words uttered by Pluto in *Inf* VII, 1 (where the word 'pape', in turn evoking both 'pope' and 'father', is associated with 'Satan') and thus creates a further pun that would have undoubtedly delighted Dante. If we apply this image back to the *Wake*, Joyce may be said to be turning Dante and his works (and the literary canonical tradition) upside down in a comic and irreverent parody; yet Dante, who displays traits that may associate him to Lucifer, is himself a divine 'father' and poet who produced an imperishable and divine 'comedy'.

Joyce's use of earlier writers also points to the necessity to reconsider the theoretical frame within which the critic must work. The reader cannot be bound by any single model of literary interrelationship, whether one wants to call it imitation (as the conscious practice of literary borrowing and transformation, in the sense described by Pound – not dissimilar from the Renaissance concept and practice – and adopted by Dasenbrock[31]), influence (as in Harold's Bloom's theory, to cite the best known but also the most controversial), or intertextuality (as in the original theoretical programme, outlined in particular by Kristeva and Barthes, of a textual relationship which reverses or rejects the traditional critical model of literary-historical filiation). It is Joyce's practice in the first place that invalidates any such neat categories, and while all these theories will offer insights into the *Wake*'s relationship with Dante or any other writer, none will suffice on its own.

Dasenbrock has convincingly defended the case for the use of the term 'imitation', and to a large extent I share his claim that literature is made by conscious agents whose imitations are deliberate and intentional acts.[32] To be more precise, I agree with the assumption that the writer makes conscious choices; but I cannot share Dasenbrock's hostility towards the concept and what he calls 'the language of intertextuality',[33] which in his case goes as far as banning the words 'intertextuality' and even 'text' from his book. Indeed, *Finnegans Wake* probably best demonstrates Barthes's claim that the text is a tissue of quotations whose nature therefore is to be always already an intertext,[34] and that it is an autonomous entity cut loose from the intentionality of its author, programmed in such a way as to generate unpredicted meanings and textual connections that the reader has every right to discover or to establish in his/her own 'writing' of the text (to take up Barthes's distinction between the 'readerly' and the 'writerly' text, which arose in conjunction with the emergence of the concept of intertextuality[35]). I have already suggested above that reading Dante's works through the *Wake* enables us to discover in them aspects that a non-intertextual, traditional source study would not reveal, and it is especially in the fourth chapter, where I discuss Dante's and Joyce's attempts to deal with the problem of the ineffable and of the unspeakable, of what cannot but also ought not to be said, that I shall try to 'write' the *Wake* and the *Paradiso* at the same time as I read them, so that the critical discourse becomes an intertextual *parcours* that weaves the two texts together in a 'single' one spanning several centuries and in which, from this perspective at least, chronology is ultimately irrelevant.

But the theory of intertextuality banishes the link of textual filiation from its vocabulary, whereas in reading Joyce's works one cannot but notice the omnipresence of the father/son theme, often expanding into the theme of generation as well as into an exploration of family relationships more at large, and which operates also at the level of the literary relationship ('May father Dante forgive me') and would therefore seem to require the critic to turn to Bloom's oedipal framing of the theory of influence. However, Bloom's oedipal conflict can rarely be resolved victoriously for any successor, and his claim that poetic influence may make poets more, not less original (though not necessarily better)[36] is somewhat belied by his later statement that the dynamics of influence inevitably leads to the 'diminishment' and 'decline' of poetry.[37] In *Finnegans Wake* the son always displaces the father, even if it is only in order to be displaced again in turn; thus the burden of the oedipal link – 'anxiety' – seems to fall always on the father/precursor rather than on the son/successor, while the process of appropriation and distortion (thieving and metamorphosis, to return to the context of *Inferno* xxv) proves to be always an intentional and fully conscious one. I shall return to this confrontation in chapter 3, in the context of my analysis of the father/son battle of Sebastopol, a battle which also affects and informs the treatment of the earlier text and which therefore seems once again – even in its setting, 'the battle' – to evoke Bloom's framing of the theory.

Bloom's model of literary influence cannot work for Joyce on at least another account. Bloom's interest lies in poets as poets – or strong poets as strong poets, and strong poets' poems as strong poets' poems; even when he can state that his theory concerns 'relationships *between* texts' (rather than texts on their own, and than poets as individuals),[38] it still remains true, as Jay Clayton and Eric Rothstein have pointed out, that Bloom's theory is absolutely non-referential and that for him the subject-matter of the poems is only the 'backdrop' for the acting out of the 'central drama of poetic influence'.[39] Joyce's imitation/displacement of his precursors, including of course Dante, is on the contrary played out and fought on the battleground of specific literary structures, themes, stylistic and linguistic choices, and is therefore always referential and rooted in the nature of the subject-matter. It is first and foremost on the ground of the form, content and poetics of Dante's texts, and not from under the shadow of his towering figure, that Joyce engages with his predecessor in order to elaborate his own linguistic poetics in *Finnegans Wake*.[40]

This leads me to two related points: the first is that Joyce's use of earlier texts always entails a reflection on the process of writing and of textual creation as well as on his own relationship with his sources: the reasons for and the implications of a certain choice, the positioning of himself and of his texts within a specific literary tradition and within literary history, i.e. *in relation to* and *as a relation of* other writers (I shall come back to the thematisation of the literary in the context of familial relations, especially in chapters 3 and 4); this process is part of the elaboration of a poetics 'in progress', a poetics, that is, continually worked out as the texts are written, subject to permanent revision and which implies that no work stands on its own in the writer's *oeuvre*. Secondly, when I say, as I did earlier, that it is possible to speak of a specifically 'Dantean poetics of *Finnegans Wake*', I am suggesting not that the *Wake* was written according to a notion of poetics arrived at, practised or theorised by Dante and which Joyce adhered to, but that there is *a* poetics of *Finnegans Wake* (a conception of the relationship between language and literature, and between theme, structure and style, as well as of the scope of the literary work, and of how a text signifies) which is comparable to the poetics of Dante's works (also constantly 'in progress') and which I believe Joyce recognised and actively engaged with by reading and 'raiding' Dante, 'writing' Dante, exploiting both the words and the gaps left by his texts, in a process best expressed by the words of *Finnegans Wake* itself: 'The prouts who will invent a writing there ultimately is the poeta, still more learned, who discovered the raiding there originally' (*FW* 482.31–2). The poet's invention of language ultimately coincides with a practice of writing as reading, and of reading as plundering, thieving and metamorphosing of his sources.[41] Yet this is only one possible path, one of the many poetics of *Finnegans Wake*; the *Wake*'s plurality of inspirations/raidings are another reason why Bloom's theory is ultimately inadequate for Joyce: no son will suffer from any oedipal anxiety when he has too many fathers.

This eclectic conception of literary interrelations – or, more specifically, this poetics of literary relations – also enables the critic to avoid the trap Beckett warned his readers of in his 1929 essay 'Dante. . . Bruno. Vico. . Joyce': the danger of the 'neatness of identifications', of trying to 'stuff' the work of one into the 'pigeon-hole' of the other ('DBVJ' 3–4), or into rigid categories devised by the critic him/herself. Although Beckett was the first to deal at some length with Joyce's use of Dante in his jocoserious and often out-rageous essay, the importance of 'Dante. . . Bruno. Vico. . Joyce' lies not so much in its chronological priority or in its content but in its technique: as in the case of the typically modernist unreliable narrators, Beckett's unreliable critic may not tell the truth, but can still tell us a lot on Joyce's unreliable imitations. Reading Beckett on *Work in Progress* is probably the best introduction to reading *Finnegans Wake,* and that is why I have chosen to enter the forest of Joyce's relationship(s) with Dante by the crooked path of Beckett's essay.

Prelude: 'Bethicket me'; or, Looking for the straight way in the wood of Samuel Beckett's obliquity of exagmination

> 'You is feeling like you was lost in the bush, boy? You says: It is a puling sample jungle of woods. You most shouts out: Bethicket me for a stump of a beech if I have the poultriest notions what the farest he all means'
>
> *(FW* 112.03–6)

Samuel Beckett's 'Dante. . . Bruno. Vico. . Joyce', the first of the twelve essays collected under the curious title *Our Exagmination Round His Factification for Incamination of Work in Progress*, is the earliest critical attempt to deal with the importance of Dante's works for Joyce's *Finnegans Wake*. The essays, published ten years before the book they introduced or 'exagmined', will have to be taken with a good degree of scepticism: for one thing, the author of what was then known as *Work in Progress* was still able to modify parts of the text and to parody his own 'twelve apostles' (*JJ*II 613), for instance by transposing the title of the collection into his novel (see *FW* 497.02–3) and by referring to them in a patronising and tongue-in-cheek tone (e.g. *FW* 369.06–7). More importantly, as the function of the *Exagmination* was to advertise Joyce's 'unreadable' new novel, the tone of the essays is seldom balanced or objective, and the essays must celebrate (some of) the main innovative features of *Work in Progress*, make its readers curious, enthusiastic, irritated, even angry – anything but indifferent.[1] The overall message is that, even if *Work in Progress* is no ordinary book, it is a readable, highly original and amusing one, and the point repeated throughout the collection is that the obstacles that stand between readers and their comprehension of the work are not in the book itself but in their mental attitude. Given the premises of this militant campaign, the essays will have to operate, and therefore be read, according to particular strategies; they contain most of the information about their topic but the presentation is often indirect, inexplicitly suggested, sometimes even misleading so that the reader can get its full impact only after careful deciphering of the 'explanatory' essay as well as of *Work in Progress*. We shall see that Beckett's piece is an outstanding example of this technique, and the best guide for the pilgrim lost in the dark forest of Joyce's work, the bewildering jungle of words described in the epigraph to this chapter (I shall return to this point in chapter 3).

Joyce himself orchestrated the production of the *Exagmination*. He asked the twelve critics to collaborate, suggested subjects for their essays, perhaps also recommended some of the arguments they should use and the features of *Work in Progress* to which he wanted to draw the readers' attention; Joyce's words in his letter, that he did stand behind his twelve 'Marshals' directing them as to the lines of research they should follow (*SL* 345[2]), conflate the parallel purposes of explaining and researching his difficult work, and the militant campaign that his 'marshals' were undertaking on his behalf. Some of the strategies used by Beckett are indeed typically Joycean: the attribution of an allusion to a 'wrong' text or writer while the 'right' source is mentioned a few lines away in a different context;[3] deliberate 'mistakes' and slight misinterpretations, hints dropped but never clarified. The problem is encapsulated by Suzette Henke at the beginning of her review of the *Exagmination*: 'How does one conceal and reveal at the same time, leaving clues to "authorial intention" but obscuring the origins of a commentary that never allows itself directly to comment on the text or its origins?'[4]

'The twelve unwary disciples', Henke writes, 'were marshaled by an author who, like Christ and Averroës, spoke in riddles and parables while destabilizing traditional cognitive formulas.' But Henke makes the 'disciples' more naive or ingenuous than they probably were: 'Little did those first brave exagminers suspect that they were analyzing incaminated chapters.'[5] I suspect that Beckett, for one, was aware of the rules of the game he was playing at with (for) the 'master', and often put them into practice as well: the tone of 'Dante. . . Bruno. Vico. . Joyce', scornful, ironic, tongue-in-cheek throughout, speaks for itself – which is what makes this combination of suggestions from the master, critical insight, advertisement and youthful arrogance such a good introduction to *Finnegans Wake*. The critical danger is indeed the temptation to find neat, straightforward identifications ('DBVJ' 3), and Beckett will let his readers meet no such dangers on their way. From the opening sentences of the essay we realise that Beckett too is playing games with his readers: 'The conception of Philosophy and Philology as a pair of nigger minstrels out of the Teatro dei Piccoli is soothing, like the contemplation of a carefully folded ham-sandwich' ('DBVJ' 3). As Massimo Verdicchio has pointed out, Beckett's near-nonsense is not wholly out of place, and Dante's *Convivio*, or *Banquet*, is the ironic antecedent evoked here, insofar as Beckett is stressing the dangers inherent in a 'carefully folded analogy'[6] that would lead either to distorting the work of one writer to fit the system of the other, or to the reduction of literary criticism to dry, unimaginative book-keeping ('DBVJ' 3–4).

The danger to be avoided by any reader approaching the *Exagmination* is to expect to find in 'Dante. . . Bruno. Vico. . Joyce' neat identifications of what in Joyce's work derived from each of the three Italian authors. As with *Work in Progress*, the reader must be able to pick up the hints and clues hidden beneath the surface of Beckett's text. Beckett, Henke points out, had inherited the weapons Joyce had bestowed on his character Stephen: cunning, exile and silence.[7] In the following pages I shall therefore *exagmine* some of Beckett's silences and cunning techniques, as well as make some references to the question of exile, on the subject of Joyce and Dante.

A good part of Beckett's essay is devoted to Vico, whereas Bruno gets a lesser share of the critical argument which, moreover, always remains quite general whenever the heretic philosopher is concerned: Beckett only mentions the coincidence of opposites (originally in fact not a Brunonian concept), after stating that at this point 'Vico applies Bruno – though he takes very good care not to say so' ('DBVJ' 5–6) – an assertion which is, at the very least, debatable. Equally debatable statements are made concerning Dante. According to Linda Ben-Zvi, Beckett had been familiar with Dante's works since his youth, whereas he was less acquainted with Bruno and Vico at the time of writing the essay.[8] If questionable interpretations regarding the two Neapolitan philosophers *may* therefore be attributed to hasty reading or misinformation (though I wouldn't too quickly discard the possibility of Beckett's cheekily devious treatment of his sources in this case either), 'mistakes' about Dante are more likely to be due either to a frankly wrong reading of the medieval poet or to deliberate cover-ups (as in detective fiction) meant to disseminate through the text oblique clues that only the cunning reader will be able to pick up.

One would normally expect a title to be chosen to reflect and sum up what the essayist deals with in his text, but Beckett introduces the section on Dante with a dismissive 'To justify our title' ('DBVJ' 17), as if he had to deal with Dante because the 'essay topic' (perhaps imposed by the 'master'?) required it. Despite this apparently casual, almost apologetic remark, the section on Dante covers about a quarter of the text, which after all is exactly its due in an essay dealing with four authors. Beckett mentions most of Dante's works: the *Divine Comedy*, the two theoretical treatises *De vulgari eloquentia* and *Convivio*, from which he also cites the titles of two *canzoni*, and the *De monarchia*, briefly referred to as the book that upset the Church and was burnt in public as heretical. Thus most of Dante's work is invoked as relevant to Joyce's, more than satisfactorily 'justifying' the title, in fact suggesting that Dante's entire production, and not just some basic concepts as in the case of Vico and Bruno, needs to be taken into account.

Beckett starts his discussion of Dante and Joyce from the two writers' attitudes towards the 'worn out and threadbare' conventions of the literary language of their times and their rejection of any 'approximation to a universal language' – Latin and English, in medieval and in modern times respectively – ('DBVJ' 17–18; but see also William Carlos Williams's similarly worded defence of Joyce's literary quest to 'save the world' from 'the static, worn out language' of literature.[9] That Joyce casts himself, or is cast by his 'apostles', in the role of 'saviour of the language' recalls one of the functions that Dante implicitly attributes to himself in the *De vulgari eloquentia*, as well as the overtones of spiritual innovation of the *Convivio*; both of these aspects will be discussed in later chapters). In particular, Beckett exalts the linguistic anti-municipalism of the *De vulgari eloquentia*, and props up this point by choosing two *ad hoc* excerpts from Dante's treatise, the former attacking 'the world's Portadownians', the second disparaging the Tuscan dialect as a hideous and foul form of speech ('DBVJ' 18). (If, as Henke suggests, Beckett's inheritance includes exile together with cunning and literary silence, it may be worth pointing out here that the first of Beckett's two quotations, from *Dve* i.vi, 3, introduces in the original Dante's tirade on exile; in referring to it, Beckett may be indirectly drawing attention to the fact that Joyce too was an expatriate – as was Beckett himself – and that this similar biographical condition bears some weight on their literary relationship.)

Beckett then 'concludes' that Dante formulated the theory of an illustrious language refined and purified from any vulgar trait, assembling only the purest elements from each dialect in order to construct a 'synthetic language that would at least possess more than a circumscribed local interest', as if this was a consequence of his 'complete freedom from civic intolerance' ('DBVJ' 18). That the *De vulgari eloquentia* postulated the need for an artificial, 'synthetic' language – a refined and immutable version of the common vernacular – was one of the predominant interpretations at the time of Beckett's essay, although several critics would dispute it[10] (indeed, as I shall point out below, Vico had also criticised this view); the statement that follows – that Dante not only theorised but actually employed his 'synthetic' language in the *Divine Comedy* and that he 'did not write in Florentine any more than in Neapolitan' ('DBVJ' 18) – is rather more difficult to accept without qualifications. It is true that in the *De vulgari eloquentia* Dante elaborates the theory of a supra-municipal, illustrious vernacular, but he *did* write the *Divine Comedy* in an illustrious form of Florentine: he coined new words, used archaic expressions, Italianised Latin, French or Provençal, but the skeleton of the poem was and remained Florentine; and if Beckett was not aware of this, Joyce, with his very good knowledge of Italian and Italian dialects, of Florentine and of Dante,[11] certainly would have been. Why, then, this notion of a *Commedia* written no more in Florentine than in Neapolitan? And why Neapolitan in particular? Interestingly, the idea of the presence of Neapolitan in the *Commedia* has been repeated by Joycean scholars whereas, as far as I am aware, it is not to be found in the writings of Dantean critics – Beckett would no doubt have been pleased to know that he must be responsible for the groundless myth of a semi-Neapolitan *Divine Comedy*. It is clear that Neapolitan finds its way into Beckett's essay not because it had something to do with Dante, but because it had a lot to do with Bruno and Vico, who came from Naples or its neighbourhood. Beckett in other words uses Neapolitan to create a further link between the three authors, and this looks very much like one of the many indirect clues that the reader is invited to unmask.

Beckett's next obliquity is about Dante's Latin readership (needless to say, and unlike what Beckett writes, the language *commonly* spoken in Italy in Dante's time had not been Latin for several centuries), and he reports the anecdote that Dante had actually begun the *Commedia* in Latin, but that he had then changed his mind and substituted the '"barbarous" directness' of the vernacular '*Nel mezzo del cammin di nostra vita*' for the 'suave elegance of: "*Ultima regna canam, fluido contermina mundo*"' ('DBVJ' 19). The anecdote of a *Commedia* originally in Latin derives from Giovanni Boccaccio's *Vita di Dante*,[12] but Beckett does not reveal his source; instead, he fuses it – once again carefully avoiding any explicit acknowledgement of the provenance of the idea – with Vico's interpretation of Dante as the poet of barbarity and directness. Vico writes that the *Divine Comedy* must be read 'as a history of the period of barbarism in Italy, as a source of the fairest Tuscan speech, and as an example of sublime poetry'.[13] Beckett lifts the 'barbarity' from Vico, but ignores his emphasis on Dante's 'fair' Tuscan idiom in order to highlight (whether deviously or wrongly) the *Commedia*'s alleged medley of dialects. In fact, Vico had explicitly denied this reading of the poem, denouncing the notion that 'Dante gathered together the speech of all the various Italian dialects' as 'false', and expressing his scepticism that Dante may have learned in his lifetime 'the vulgar speech of so many communities', or that he may have derived from them 'the abundance of forms he needed and employed to express his thought in the *Comedy*'.[14] Even disregarding Vico's caveat, we know that Dante did not put the theory of the 'synthetic language' of the *De vulgari eloquentia* into practice when it came to writing the 'sacrato poema' ('sacred poem', *Par* XXIII, 62); Beckett is thus forced to make the 'barbarism' of the vernacular poem (a barbarism which, for Vico, is also linked to Dante's achievement as the poet of the sublime) rest on the improbable 'directness' of a patchwork of *vulgares* as opposed to the stiffness of a polished but 'worn out and threadbare' Latin.

Although Beckett withholds the information that Boccaccio is the source of the anecdote on a Latin *Commedia*, he mentions the Italian writer at the end of the same paragraph in a bizarre sentence apparently disjointed from the rest and meant to confirm that the the 'barbarous directness' of the *Commedia* had a similar effect on Dante's Latin audience as Joyce's 'barbarous' writing now has on English ears: 'Boccaccio did not jeer at the "*piedi sozzi*" of the peacock that Signora Alighieri dreamed about' ('DBVJ' 19). Hasn't Beckett just defined Dante's language as an idiom assembled from 'the purest elements from each dialect', that '*could* have been spoken by an ideal Italian' ('DBVJ' 18), just as the language of *Work in*

Progress could reasonably be spoken by an 'international phenom-enon' ('DBVJ' 19)? Yet the first example that he can provide of this purity of idiom is the none too illustrious '*piedi sozzi*' ('dirty feet'), which surely places greater emphasis on the 'vulgar' and 'barbarous' side of the language than on its 'purest elements'. Beckett's parallel between Dante's synthetic vernacular and the language of Joyce's *Work in Progress* does not hold: the language of the *Wake* would have puzzled any contemporary 'international phenomenon' much more than Dante's *Divine Comedy*, whose (largely Florentine) idiom would have been comprehensible to most despite its amazing inventiveness. A clue to this odd mixture of Boccaccio and Vico, of sublimity and 'dirty feet', is in fact left by Beckett himself: in his *Vita di Dante* Boccaccio reports a dream that Dante's mother ('Signora Alighieri') allegedly had when she was pregnant: among other oneiric-alle-gorical elements, Dante is cast as a peacock, a symbol for poetry but whose feet, Boccaccio points out, are notoriously dirty. Boccaccio explains that the peacock has four features in common with the poet and the *Commedia*: first, it has angelic feathers, and has one hundred eyes therein; second, it has dirty feet and walks quietly; third, it has a horrible voice; and fourth, its flesh is scented and incorruptible. These characteristics also belong to the *Commedia*: its moral and theological meaning is incorruptible, its feathers are like those of the angels because of the beauty of the historical meaning of the pilgrimage, and its great variety is like the hundred eyes of the peacock; its feet are dirty because feet are what the rest of the body rests on, and the *Commedia* rests on the vulgar tongue and walks quietly because of the humbleness of its style; finally, its voice has a horrible sound because of Dante's harshness against the sins of men.[15] It is quite telling that Beckett should obliquely refer to a text whose meaning he obscures in order to prove the need to interpret and unravel the hidden meanings of a dream about beauty and vulgarity and thus underscore their relevance for interpreting the 'dream itself' of *Work in Progress* ('[Joyce's] writing is not *about* something; *it is that something itself*', 'DBVJ' 14).

Beckett's next step is to quote from the *Convivio* a fitting definition of the 'monodialectical arcadians' who cannot understand Joyce's new novel, and an excerpt praising in terms of spiritual enlightening the formal innovation of the Italian vernacular which also celebrates the innovative style of *Work in Progress* ('DBVJ' 19).[16] The *Convivio* is mentioned, that is, not for its polysemic and stratified conception of textual meaning which, as I shall argue in chapter 1, is taken up and exploited – indeed, exploded – in the *Wake*, but in order to continue the offensive against the unsympathetic readership, thus showing (mongering?) a further analogy between the two writers which has the effect of casting the medieval poet into the role of a *figura* for the modern writer.[17] Intriguingly, though the fourfold method of allegorical interpretation is not mentioned by Beckett, both the allusions to Boccaccio's story of Mrs Alighieri's dream and the later references to two of the *canzoni* that the *Convivio* explains through the four levels of meaning evoke this system of medieval polysemy. Beckett also offers further evidence of Dante's role in the development of Joyce's poetics when he emphasises the aptness of the word '*intendere*' (from the *canzone* '*Voi che, intendendo, il terzo ciel movete*') to describe the 'esthetic vigilance' that enables the reader to perceive the merging of meaning and form ('DBVJ' 14). The most satisfactory English word for this 'esthetic vigilance' is, Beckett says, 'apprehend', in the sense used by Stephen in *A Portrait* when he explains to Lynch his Aquinian theory of art and beauty (I shall come back in chapter 3 to the question of how Stephen's Aquinian theory may also be linked to Dante's definition of the 'illustrious vernacular').

After this attack, Beckett goes back to the *De vulgari eloquentia* to point out a 'curious mistake' ('DBVJ' 20) made by Dante when he writes that the Bible is wrong in saying that Eve was the first speaker because the first to use the God-given language must have been Adam. The entire passage about Dante's wrong reading of the Bible is in brackets, and it is only loosely connected with the rest of Beckett's argument. I shall come back in chapter 2 to the questions raised by Dante's inversion and Beckett's comments, but I would like to suggest here what one of the motives behind Beckett's *curious* argument might be: as Dante finds a precedent for his linguistic invention in the Bible and criticises it by (partly) inverting it, similarly Joyce finds one of his major antecedents in Dante's history of the creation and decay of language which he exploits and often subverts. After this bracketed digression, Beckett goes back to his major theme, the generally hostile reception of *Work in Progress*. The relationship between the passage in brackets and its context is not immediately evident, and, to paraphrase Stephen Dedalus, the reader has to look within, behind, beyond or above the lines of Beckett's work in order to find an invisible allusion which has been refined nearly out of existence and thus unveil its relevance to the relationship between Dante and Joyce.

Beckett recalls how Dante's work was regarded as blasphemous for its attack on the papacy and the clergy; was burnt as heretical (the *De monarchia*), and continued to be criticised for years, even centuries, for its 'mighty vindication of the "vulgar"' ('DBVJ' 20). Then, with another very loosely connected digression, Beckett points out that the concern with numbers may offer another motive of comparison ('DBVJ' 21), and goes on to explain the importance of number three in Dante and number four in Joyce. Interestingly, Joyce allegedly used almost the same words in a conversation with Adolf Hoffmeister, and very similar words appear again in Padraic Colum's memoir of Joyce.[18] This provides us with yet another clue that Beckett's argument may be a repetition of Joyce's suggestions or favourite points made in conversations with his friends – or that the osmosis was not only between the 'master' and the 'disciples' but also among acquaintances and/or 'disciples' who copied each other's words and produced a wealth of (perhaps occasionally spurious, and cheekily perpetuated) Joycean anecdotes.

The essay is finally wrapped up by a 'last word about the Purgatories' ('DBVJ' 21) and about the differences and analogies between the function and structure of Dante's Purgatory and the 'purgatorial' quality of *Work in Progress*. On his last page Beckett asks a puzzling question to which he gives an equally puzzling answer: 'And the partially purgatorial agent? The partially purged' ('DBVJ' 22). At one level, the suggestion is that *Work in Progress* stages a world of transience in which nothing and nobody ever reaches a condition of stability, whether of eternal bliss or eternal penance (like the souls in Dante's Paradise and Hell, for instance) or of coming to the final destination (like the 'letter' in the *Wake*). Translating the *Divine Comedy* into terms that evoke Bruno's philosophy more than Dante's poetics, Beckett writes: 'Hell is the static lifelessness of unrelieved viciousness. Paradise is the static lifelessness of unrelieved immaculation. Purgatory is a flood of movement and vitality released by the conjunction of these two elements' ('DBVJ' 22). But the 'purgatorial aspect of the work' is explained by Beckett in Vichian terms too: 'There is an endless verbal germination, maturation, putrefaction, the cyclic dynamism of the intermediate' ('DBVJ' 16).[19] Everything, that is, keeps turning and returning, each time in different guises, and the condition of language as well as the content of the book is most similar to that of the souls subjected to the penance of Purgatory, where suffering and joy coexist in the penance of the present and the vision of the future ('absolute progression and a guaranteed consummation', 'DBVJ' 22) – a future which is however ever-deferred, never achieved (forever only 'partially' realised, as Beckett's 'endless' betrays), condemning to eternity the process of mutation itself (a Brunonian notion). But in the Purgatory evoked by Beckett the penance is in the endless waiting, in looking back to the past and ahead to an unknown future (or vice versa, in a further Brunonian overtone: 'movement is non-directional – or multi-directional, and a step forward is, by definition, a step back', 'DBVJ' 22). This theme will engender Vladimir, Estragon and the ever-postponed coming of Godot in Beckett's own work; in the 1929 essay on Joyce, it leads Beckett to transfigure Dante in terms of Bruno and Vico and eventually to refine him out of existence and beyond recognition. According to this Wakean 'purgatory' (but is it Joyce's or Beckett's?),

Vice and Virtue [Dante] – which you may take to mean any pair of large contrary human factors [Bruno] – must in turn be purged down to spirits of rebelliousness. Then the dominant crust of the Vicious or Virtuous sets, resistance is provided, the explosion duly takes place [Vico's thunder] and the machine proceeds [Vico's cyclical history]. And no more than this; neither prize nor penalty [certainly not *Dante*'s Purgatory]; simply a series of stimulants to enable the kitten to catch its tail [perhaps *Work in Progress*, but no longer Vico]. ('DBVJ' 22; my interpolations)

'Dante. . . Bruno. Vico. . Joyce' can certainly throw light on the relationship between Joyce and Dante, and especially on the way in which Joyce draws material from Dante and transforms it – but only if Beckett's method of twisting his references is heeded as much as, if not more than, what he says: one must beware of Beckett's (and/or Joyce's) obscuring techniques and try to detect and decipher the clues left in the text. One must also beware of what Beckett does not say – for instance, that Vico knew Dante and wrote about him. What Beckett says instead is that 'Vico applies Bruno – though he takes very good care not to say so' ('DBVJ' 5–6); what the reader will most probably infer is that Beckett applies Joyce – though he takes very good care not to say so.

The danger is in the neatness of identifications. No danger in Beckett's essay of such neatness. Nor is there danger, whether in

'Dante. . . Bruno. Vico. . Joyce' or in *Work in Progress*, of a 'distortion in one of two directions' to satisfy the abhorred 'analogymongers': to 'wring the neck of a certain system in order to stuff it into a contemporary pigeon-hole' or, alternatively, to 'modify the dimensions of that pigeon-hole' ('DBVJ' 3–4). As we shall see in the following chapters, the danger of distortions is welcomed, rather than rejected, by James Joyce as it is by Samuel Beckett, and necks are wrung in more than one or two directions, so as to preempt any chance of filling any pigeon-hole. In fact, of Dante's, Bruno's and Vico's poetical or philosophical conceptions on the one hand and Joyce's invention on the other, which would be the system to be stuffed into what plastic pigeon-hole? Does analogymongering take the form, for the comparative critic, of tailoring Joyce's work to fit the more manageable pigeon-hole of the systems of its three Italian models, or, on the contrary, of attempting to fit the models of the past into the much more complex system of the modern master? Perhaps both alternatives are a real critical risk, or perhaps neither of them is: analogymongering would be book-keeping, and literary criticism, Beckett warns us, is neither the one nor the other. What then about literary practice? The answer, as Beckett has obliquely taught us, also involves performing operations on the plasticine of Dante's theories and poetics ('thieving' and 'metamorphosing'), and wringing their necks. But the chief neck-wringer was Joyce himself – the 'dreamskhwindel' who, by constructing an elaborate swindle through the dream of *Finnegans Wake*, necklassoes (*FW* 426.27) his inspirational and antagonistic models, and I hope that the analogies traced in the pages that follow will not be mere book-keeping but an illumination of some aspects of the 'attractive parallel between Dante and Mr Joyce in the question of language' ('DBVJ' 18).

CHAPTER I

Working in layers

spell me how every word will be bound over to carry three
score and ten toptypsical readings

(*FW* 20.14–15)

(if you can spot fifty I spy four more)

(*FW* 10.31)

Dante's poetic work, from the *Vita Nuova* to the *Divine Comedy*, is
informed by recurrent concerns that also provide the conceptual
foundations for the *Convivio* and the *De vulgari eloquentia*, the two
treatises begun in the early fourteenth century but left unfinished,
sacrificed perhaps to the more urgent need to compose the *Commedia*.
These concerns are the relationship between everyday and literary
language, and the exploration of the medium of poetry for producing
meanings which everyday language cannot convey; and the issue of
the semantic capabilities (or limits) of language as a means of
representation and communication of the multiplicity of reality. At
the centre of this life-long reflection stands the nature and status of
the vernacular, the language commonly spoken in Dante's time and
which everybody could understand but which had never been used
before in 'high' literature or for theoretical enquiry, and which was
therefore still in its youth, waiting to be fashioned as a mature idiom.
For Dante, the elevation of the Italian vernacular to the status of a
noble and flexible language was the main task of the poet; the
Convivio, written in Italian between 1304 and 1307, can be regarded
as one of the steps taken in the fulfilment of this programme. Aware
of the 'revolutionary' implications of writing a doctrinal work in
vernacular at the beginning of the fourteenth century, Dante
devoted the greater part of the first book of the treatise to a personal
and philosophical justification of his linguistic choice and to the
praise of the Italian vernacular language, and his object takes on
clear tones of linguistic and spiritual salvation when he describes his

26

own vernacular as the rising of a 'new light, new sun' (*Conv* I.xiii, 12).
As I explained in the 'Prelude', this is the passage that Samuel
Beckett selects to describe the language of *Work in Progress* and its
remedial scope for the contemporary 'worn out and threadbare'
literary language. In the following pages I shall discuss what other
features of the *Convivio*, beside this telling but general analogy (but
Beckett would probably prefer us to use 'point of comparison',
'DBVJ' 21, or 'attractive parallel', 18), can offer the critic one of the
surely infinite possible threads through the labyrinth of the *Wake*. To
this end, it will be useful to start from a preliminary discussion of the
most important element of Dante's treatise for this study: the
hermeneutic theory of the four levels of meaning.

Dante wrote only four of the fifteen books that he had originally
planned for the *Convivio*. The first is an introduction to the whole
treatise, and it explains the purpose of the work and Dante's reasons
for preferring the vernacular tongue over Latin; each of books II, III
and IV begins with a *canzone* which is then illustrated according to the
interpretative method expounded at length in book II. The *Convivio* is
thus both a commentary on poetry and a commentary on the
commentary, and Dante's originality in the treatise is perhaps shown
at its best in this meta-critical scope. The poems, he declares, are
'polysemous', and they must therefore be illustrated through four
senses: literal, allegorical, moral and anagogical. The subdivision of
a text into levels of meaning was an established tradition in the
Middle Ages, but the distinction into the four senses listed and
analysed by Dante had until then been applied only to Biblical texts.
Dante wrote the *Convivio* at the height of a long and rich exegetic
tradition. A. J. Minnis has shown that although literary theory had
developed independently, in the Middle Ages it was subordinated to
Scriptural exegesis and had received great incentive from the study
of the Bible, thus giving rise to much of the most sophisticated
literary theory of the later medieval period.[1] In the thirteenth and
fourteenth centuries, classical authors, including the pagan ones,
were invested with the status of literary and moral *auctoritates*, and
their works were believed to hold important teachings which detailed
analysis would reveal and make explicit. The distance between
Scriptural and secular texts was thus being progressively reduced,
although pagan writers were still naturally seen as inferior to the
Christian ones in the hierarchy of the *auctoritates*, and secular writers

as inferior to the prophets of the Bible, whose word must ultimately be attributed to God's inspiration.

It is at this moment, when the gap between the literary and the religious text is closing up, that Dante writes the *Convivio*. The treatise is thus part of a more general and open debate, but Dante's originality lies in that for the first time a secular writer dared to transfer the method and terminology of Biblical exegesis to poetry – his own love poetry (and love poetry was generally considered as a 'low' literary genre) – in a move that goes beyond the merely terminological or even methodological borrowing and ultimately implies the elevation of the poems to the same level as Holy Writ:

Dico che, sì come nel primo capitolo è narrato, questa sposizione conviene essere litterale e allegorica. E a ciò dare a intendere, si vuol sapere che le scritture si possono intendere e deonsi esponere massimamente per quattro sensi. L'uno si chiama litterale, e questo è quello che non si stende più oltre che la lettera de le parole fittizie, sì come sono le favole de li poeti. L'altro si chiama allegorico, e questo è quello che si nasconde sotto 'l manto di queste favole, ed è una veritade ascosa sotto bella menzogna: sì come quando dice Ovidio che Orfeo facea con la cetera mansuete le fiere, e li arbori e le pietre a sè muovere; che vuol dire che lo savio uomo con lo strumento de la sua voce faria mansuescere e umiliare li crudeli cuori, e faria muovere a la sua volontade coloro che non hanno vita di scienza e d'arte: e coloro che non hanno vita ragionevole alcuna sono quasi come pietre . . . Veramente li teologi questo senso prendono altrimenti che li poeti; ma però che mia intenzione è qui lo modo de li poeti seguitare, prendo lo senso allegorico secondo che per li poeti è usato.

Lo terzo senso si chiama morale, e questo è quello che li lettori deono intentamente andare appostando per le scritture, ad utilitade di loro e di loro discenti: sì come appostare si può ne lo Evangelio, quando Cristo salio lo monte per transfigurarsi, che de li dodici Apostoli menò seco li tre; in che moralmente si può intendere che a le secretissime cose noi dovemo avere poca compagnia.

Lo quarto senso si chiama anagogico, cioè sovrasenso; e questo è quando spiritualmente si spone una scrittura, la quale ancora sia vera eziandio nel senso litterale, per le cose significate significa de le superne cose de l'etternal gloria, sì come vedere si può in quello canto del Profeta che dice che, ne l'uscita del popolo d'Israel d'Egitto, Giudea è fatta santa e libera. Chè avvegna essere vero secondo la lettera sia manifesto, non meno è vero quello che spiritualmente s'intende, cioè che ne l'uscita de l'anima dal peccato, essa sia fatta santa e libera in sua potestate.　　　(*Conv* ii.i, 2–7)

(I say that, as I stated in the first chapter, this exposition must be both literal and allegorical. And to make this clear it should be known that scriptures [writings] may be understood and must be expounded chiefly according to four senses. The first is called literal, and this is the one that does not extend beyond the letter of the fictional words, as in the fables of the poets. The second is called allegorical, and this is the one that conceals itself under the cloak of these fables, and is a truth hidden under a beautiful fiction: as when Ovid says that Orpheus with his lyre made wild beasts tame and made trees and rocks move towards him; which means that the wise man with the instrument of his voice could tame and humble cruel hearts, and could move according to his will those whose life has no science and art: and those who have no rational life whatsoever are almost like stones . . . In fact the theologians take this sense otherwise than do the poets; but since it is my intention here to follow the method of the poets, I shall take the allegorical sense as it is used by the poets.

The third sense is called moral, and this is the one that teachers must note intently throughout the scriptures, for their own profit and that of their disciples: as we can see in the Gospel that, when Christ ascended the mountain to be transfigured, of the twelve apostles he took with him but three; in which we can understand the moral meaning to be that in the most secret things we should have few companions.

The fourth sense is called anagogical, that is 'sense above'; and this is when a scripture is expounded spiritually, which, even though it is true also in the literal sense, by the very things it signifies conveys the meaning of the supernal things of the eternal glory, as may be seen in that song of the Prophet which says that when the people of Israel went out of Egypt, Judah was made holy and free. For though this is manifestly true according to the letter, what is intended spiritually is no less true, that is, that when the soul comes out of sin, it is made holy and free in its own power.)

Prudently, Dante does not go as far as explicitly equating his poems with the Biblical text, and draws a significant distinction between theologians and poets by emphasising that the literal sense is true only for the former, whereas for the latter it is a 'beautiful fiction', a charming lie or mask which envelops the truth of the allegorical meaning. Dante declares that his intention is to follow the 'modo de li poeti', and therefore he does not claim truth for the letter of his poems – indeed, he cannot do so, because the treatise is meant to provide an apology for himself and for his behaviour after the death of Beatrice, when he had written poems for another 'Donna Gentile' ('Gentle Woman'). Dante wants to prove that this 'other woman' (perhaps the same one that appears under the name of 'Donna Pietosa' in the *Vita Nuova*) is an allegory of Philosophy. To be a lover of Philosophy, and not of another real woman, would acquit Dante of unfaithfulness to the memory of Beatrice, and even enhance his worthiness insofar as Philosophy is the 'daughter of God' (*Conv* II.xii, 9; II.xv, 12). Thus, also on account of this self-defence, Dante needs to argue that the literal level of the poems must be understood as only a fiction – certainly beautiful, but strictly a fiction written in the 'manner of the poets'.

The distinction between poets and theologians was not new: as I pointed out above, the interpretation of poetry according to a twofold standard of letter and allegory was common among medieval grammarians and rhetoricians, while the fourfold interpretation – ultimately derived from John Cassian (*c.* 360–435) and summarised in the well-known thirteenth-century distich which ran, 'Littera gesta docet, quid credas allegoria, / Moralis quid agas, quo tendas anagogia'[2] – was reserved for the Holy Scripture. As Charles Singleton has put it, the basic difference between the two methods is that 'poets create, and theologians only interpret', or that the poet's words work according to a principle which can be encapsulated as 'this for that', while God's principle is 'this and that'.[3] The poet's word has only two layers, the truth which has to be conveyed and the fiction in which the truth is dressed, whereas the theologian's mode is not one of construction but only of interpretation, because the author of the Holy Scripture is God, who inspires the scribes with prophetic truth. In God's Writ both the letter and the other senses are true, because he is the only one who can signify through both words and things and is the author of two 'books': the Bible, written in words, and the world, 'written' in things. St Thomas Aquinas, for instance, stated that God is the unique *auctor* of things and can use them to signify, whereas men can be *auctores* of words only, and have to use them to convey meanings.[4]

Dante's assertion that he wants to follow the 'modo de li poeti' would thus seem to disclaim any attempt to identify his poems with Scriptural writing; indeed he mentions the distinction between poet and theologian only when he writes about allegory and points out that, while the literal level is either true or untrue, the allegorical is always true. But he does not mention the opposition again when he writes about the other two levels of poetic interpretation, the moral and the anagogical, which traditionally belonged only to Biblical exegesis and for which therefore Dante cannot find examples in the fictional 'manner of the poets'. Juxtaposing the two methods without any further distinction thus gives rise to several problems, and the issue in *Convivio* remains rather confusing. To sum up, what Dante explicitly says is that he wants to follow the manner of the poets, but he does not actually deny the possibility of a fourfold interpretation of poetry. However, when he has to provide an example for each level, he is able to offer poetic ones (from Ovid's *Metamorphoses*) only for the first two, whereas for the moral and the anagogical senses he can only find examples in the Scriptures. Later on in the treatise, Dante repeats that the exegesis of the *canzoni* is carried out through the literal and allegorical meanings, while the moral and the anagogical have only incidental interest; but, also in this case, he does not rule out the possibility that they may also be resorted to:

> Io adunque, per queste ragioni, tuttavia sopra ciascuna canzone ragionerò prima la litterale sentenza, e appresso di quella ragionerò la sua allegoria, cioè la nascosa veritade; e talvolta de li altri sensi toccherò incidentemente, come a luogo e a tempo si converrà. (*Conv* II.i, 15)

(Therefore, for these reasons, I shall for each *canzone* first of all discuss the literal sense, and after that I shall discuss its allegory, that is its hidden truth; and at times I shall touch incidentally upon the other senses, as will suit place and time.)

As many of Dante's critics have pointed out,[5] Dante is missing (or even intentionally disregarding in a strategic move that can enable him to reduce an otherwise unbridgeable gap, as Joseph Mazzeo has suggested[6]) the fundamental difference between the 'modo de li poeti' and that of the 'teologi', and this is what gives rise to the confusion and the wavering between the two. Whatever (wilful?) misunderstanding there may be (in fact, thanks to the ambiguity thus created), Dante reduces the distance between 'poeti' and 'teologi' and succeeds in introducing the four exegetical levels of holy texts into literary criticism. If Dante was aware of the problems left open by the *Convivio* – and this, it has been suggested, may be one of the reasons why he abandoned the composition of the treatise – the *Epistle to Can Grande della Scala* may be seen as an attempt to solve some of those contradictions, and some preliminary remarks upon this text are therefore also due before we can discuss it in detail in relation to the *Wake*. It is also worth pointing out here that the authorship of the *Epistle* has long been a matter for debate, and the attribution to Dante is still by no means certain. The parties for and against count many illustrious scholars among their number, and I have no wish to take sides in this context. What matters for our purposes is that the theory of the fourfold meaning, first proposed in Dante's *Convivio*, was later applied to the *Commedia* in a letter of dedication of the *Paradiso* to Dante's patron Can Grande, and that although the first recorded attribution of the *Epistle* to Dante, by

Filippo Villani, was not made until the end of the fourteenth century,[7] the epistle was accepted as authoritative on the subject (although not necessarily, or explicitly, as Dante's own) by Dante's early commentators, including Guido da Pisa, Dante's son Pietro, Iacopo della Lana, and Giovanni Boccaccio. Joyce's critics, contemporaries and friends have generally assumed the *Epistle* to be Dante's,[8] and for simplicity's sake I shall generally treat it as such, though I would invite my readers to bear the doubtful attribution in mind throughout the following discussion.

The *Epistle* dedicates the third *cantica* of the *Commedia* to Can Grande della Scala, Dante's patron at Verona. Written in Latin, it gives indications as to how the poem should be read and interprets the 'prologue' of the *Paradiso* on the basis of the four levels of meaning:

Ad evidentiam itaque dicendorum, sciendum est quod istius operis non est simplex sensus, immo dici potest *polysemos*, hoc est plurium sensuum; nam primus sensus est qui habetur per literam, alius est qui habetur per significata per literam. Et primus dicitur literalis, secundus vero allegoricus, sive mysticus. Qui modus tractandi, ut melius pateat, potest considerari in his versibus: 'In exitu Israel de Aegypto, domus Iacob de populo barbaro, facta est Iudaea sanctificatio eius, Israel potestas eius.' Nam si ad literam solam inspiciamus, significatur nobis exitus filiorum Israel de Aegypto, tempore Moysis; si ad allegoriam, nobis significatur nostra redemptio facta per Christum; si ad moralem sensum, significatur nobis conversio animae de luctu et miseria peccati ad statum gratiae; si ad anagogicum, significatur exitus animae sanctae ab huius corruptionis servitute ad aeternae gloriae libertatem. Et quamvis isti sensus mystici variis appellentur nominibus, generaliter omnes dici possunt allegorici, quum sint a literali sive historiali diversi. Nam allegoria dicitur ab *alleon* graece, quod in latinum dicitur alienum, sive diversum.   (*Epistle to Can Grande*, §7)[9]

(For the elucidation, therefore, of what we have to say, it must be understood that the meaning of this work is not of one kind only; rather the work may be described as 'polysemous', that is, having several meanings; for the first meaning is that which is conveyed by the letter, and the next is that which is conveyed by what the letter signifies; the former of which is called literal, while the latter is called allegorical, or mystical. And for the better illustration of this method of exposition we may apply it to the following verses: 'When Israel went out of Egypt, the house of Jacob from a people of strange language; Judah was his sanctuary, and Israel his dominion.' For if we consider the letter alone, the thing signified to us is the going out of the children of Israel from Egypt in the time of Moses; if the allegory, our redemption through Christ is signified; if the moral sense, the conversion of the soul from the sorrow and misery of sin to a state of grace is signified; if the anagogical, the passing of the sanctified soul from the bondage of the corruption of this world to the liberty of everlasting glory is signified. And although these mystical meanings are called by various names, they may one and all in a general sense be termed allegorical, inasmuch as they are different (*diversi*) from the literal or historical; for the word 'allegory' is so called from the Greek *alleon*, which in Latin is *alienum* (strange) or *diversum* (different).)

In the *Epistle*, Dante glibly 'resolves' the contradictions deriving from the *Convivio*'s juxtaposition of the two 'modi' by doing away with the distinction between poet and theologian itself, and thus making the duality between the truth and the fiction of the literal level disappear. Now allegory is not only restricted to words (*in verbis*) but is also *in facto*, and the letter both corresponds truthfully and faithfully to the facts it describes ('literam') and also signifies other meanings ('significata per literam'). The twofold method of the poet and the fourfold method of the theologian are integrated, and the remaining distinction is made in two stages: the primary opposition is between the 'litera' and the 'significata per literam' (allegory in the broader sense of meaning 'other'); but the allegory can also be further divided into three layers: allegory proper, tropology or moral sense and anagogy or spiritual sense. Thus, the four levels of meaning are preserved, and their application to poetry can be rescued and reassessed. (Another way in which the truthfulness of the literal level is made possible is through the adoption of the figural relationship: according to this manner of interpretation, characters and events contained in the Old Testament, in classical authors, in pre-Christian history or in myth are seen as prefigurations of characters and events which represent their fulfilment in the New Testament and Christian history. The figural pattern confirms the literal truth of both foreshadowing and fulfilment while preserving their spiritual meaning, as it is that kind of relationship whereby God signifies *in facto* what he wishes to make known; it would be, in other words, what Dante calls in the *Convivio* the 'allegory of the theologians'.[10]) Still the poet refrains from explicitly presenting his work as part of Scriptural writing: he does say that his conceptual inspiration comes from God (Dante calls himself a 'scribe' of God-inspired words in *Paradiso* x, 27, and the *Commedia* is called 'poema sacro', 'sacred poem' in *Paradiso* xxv, 1); but he is a poet, and as such he takes upon himself the full responsibility, and therefore also the full merit, of what he has written and how he has written it ('Agens

igitur totius et partis est ille qui dictus est, et totaliter esse videtur',
Epistle to Can Grande, §14; 'The author, then, of the whole and of the
part is the person mentioned above, who is seen to be such
throughout.' By contrast, the human *auctores* of the Bible were not
held responsible for what they had said, insofar as they were chosen
as 'voices' for the Holy Spirit, to which they only played the role of
scribes. The exegetes could thus justify why the prophets could also
be sinners: they sinned as men, but spoke prophetically when
inspired by God).

Whereas a fourfold mechanism of interpretation of the poem's
meaning is still deemed necessary, the twofold distinction between
the manner of the poets and that of the theologians no longer applies
to the allegory but shifts, more coherently perhaps, to the formal
aspect of writing, the 'forma sive *modus* tractandi' ('the form or
manner of treatment', *Epistle to Can Grande*, §9, my emphasis),
described in the *Epistle* (as it was in the *Convivio*, although less clearly
expressed) as 'poeticus, fictivus'. The 'way of dealing with the
subject-matter' contains forms typical of philosophical discussions
('definitivus, divisivus, probativus, improbativus') as well as the
forms of sacred and secular literary discourse ('poeticus, fictivus,
descriptivus, digressivus, transumptivus' and the 'exemplorum posi-
tivus' (§9), which, like the *modus parabolicum*, is especially found in the
Scripture). In this, Dante seems to have moved nearer to St.
Thomas's discussion of figurative language and of poetic techniques,
which the Aquinate justified by accepting that metaphorical and
symbolical meanings, parables, similes and all figures of speech
could be used by the poet in the construction of the literal meaning
without impairing its value or truth:

Although spiritual things are set forth under the figures of corporeal things,
yet those things which are intended by sensible figures to concern spiritual
things do not pertain to the mystical sense, but to the literal; because the
literal sense is that which is first intended by the words, either speaking
properly or figuratively.[11]

Taken to its logical consequences, if the letter consists in what the
author *intends* to convey, the letter could in fact turn out to be the
allegory, i.e. the truth that the author wants to communicate.[12] But
for Dante (or the hypothetical forger of the *Epistle*) this possible
contradiction is brushed aside: if the distinction between the poet
and the theologian is that poets construct and theologians interpret,
now that the opposition has been relocated in the manner of dealing

with the subject-matter, the implication need not be that the poet's word must be false but only that the poet does not create the historical facts he writes about; these are instead integrated in a complex poetical structure which shows that they convey 'other' meanings too, according to the same mechanism of signification characteristic of the Scripture. So, it does not really matter whether the *Commedia* tells of an actual vision or whether the journey is a poetic framework for the expression of truths: the *Epistle* makes it clear that the letter of the poem is also true, and not a 'beautiful fiction', whether one understands this to be a real vision in which the journey into the world beyond would have happened as a real *elevatio ad coelum*,[13] or whether one reads it with such scholars as Joseph Mazzeo, who writes that the *Commedia* 'is on the one hand fiction because the journey never happened; it is on the other hand truth because the elements of the poem, cosmological, ethical, and personal are true'.[14]

Dante's repeated assertions in the *Commedia* of his inability to remember what he has experienced and to convey it through the imperfect means of language – an aspect which will be discussed in detail in chapter 4 – also contribute to prop up the (fiction of the) 'truthfulness' of the vision. If the 'letter' of the poem were meant to be taken only as a 'bella menzogna' ('beautiful fiction' or, literally, 'lie'), Dante's difficulty in reproducing the vision would then have to be read as his artistic inability to compose an adequate fiction; but if the literal level is also taken to be true, then the insufficiency of the poet and of the language become a further proof of the exceptionality of the other-worldly experience.

THE TERMINOLOGY OF THE MIDDLE AGES[15]

One of the received notions of Joycean criticism is that Dante's theory of the four levels of meaning is important for all of Joyce's works, and especially for *Finnegans Wake*, the 'polysemous' (*Epistle to Can Grande*, §7) text *par excellence*. Everything in the book, from its complex structure down to the single word, must be interpreted on several levels of meaning. As my first epigraph for this chapter shows, the *Wake* encourages its readers to spell out not only these many confused readings (seventy, like the alleged number of post-babelian languages), but also *how* every word is bound to carry such excess of polysemy (*FW* 20.14–15). Therefore, one may suppose that Joyce would include in *Finnegans Wake* references to the author who –

the first to do so in European vernacular writing – vindicated a fourfold polysemic status for literature, and, in particular, that he would include references to the works in which the method had been elaborated. Even if the *Wake*'s allusions to any author or text are generally parodic, this inclusion would imply that the theory of layered interpretation should also be taken to be applicable in some form to the *Wake* itself: the problem for the reader would then be to discover in what (presumably comic and subversive) form. Richard Ellmann writes that when Joyce was planning the novel, he

set out upon this radical technique, of making many of the words in his book multilingual puns, with his usual conviction. He called it 'working in layers.' After all, he said to Frank Budgen, 'The Holy Roman Catholic Apostolic Church was built on a pun. It ought to be good enough for me.' To the objection of triviality, he replied, 'Yes. Some of the means I use are trivial – and some are quadrivial.'   (*JJ*II 546)

Joyce may have been jocularly hinting through the pun that he was going one step beyond triviality into the more advanced use of the *quadrivium*, but the word also suggests his use of 'quadrivial', or fourfold, patterns: the Vichian cycle of the three ages transformed by the *ricorso* into a four-part model of historical development, the four attributes of the Italian vernacular (which I shall discuss in chapter 3), or the four levels of meaning. All these patterns may then be alluded to in such words as 'quadriliberal' (*FW* 477.19), as Mary Reynolds has suggested,[16] and 'quadrifoil' (124.21, primarily evoking a four-leafed shamrock, 'quadrifoglio' in Italian) together with all the four-part structures that interact in a web of intricate cross-references.

The relevance of the four levels of meaning for the interpretation of Joyce's works, *Finnegans Wake* in particular, was pointed out very early by his readers and critics. As I indicated in the Prelude, Samuel Beckett does not explicitly refer to the theory of polysemy in 'Dante. . . Bruno. Vico. . Joyce' (1929), but he quotes excerpts from the *Convivio* and places them side by side with two key passages from *Work in Progress* in which Joyce may allude, as I shall suggest later, to Dante's text:

Yet to concentrate solely on the literal sense or even the psychological content of any document to the sore neglect of the enveloping facts themselves circumstantiating it is just as harmful; etc.   ('DBVJ' 13)

Who in his hearts doubts either that the facts of feminine clothiering are there all the time or that the feminine fiction, stranger than the facts, is there also at the same time, only a little to the rere? Or that one may be

separated from the orther? Or that both may be contemplated simultaneously? Or that each may be taken up in turn and considered apart from the
other? ('DBVJ' 13–14)

The fact that Beckett draws together the *Convivio* and these
excerpts from *Work in Progress* suggests the existence of a close link
between the works of the medieval poet and those of the modern
writer, although Beckett, in a typically oblique (and Joycean)
manner, does not explicitly connect them. Despite the many radical
revisions that *Work in Progress* had undergone by the time it was
published, the passages quoted by Beckett in 1929 and composed by
Joyce in 1924[17] were hardly touched up at all, and they appear
almost verbatim at *FW* 109.12–16 and 109.30–6, which suggests that
Joyce's idea of how to employ Dante's texts, and in particular the
theory of the stratified polysemy of the literary work, was devised at
an early stage in the composition of *Finnegans Wake* and did not
greatly change afterwards.

One of the first critics to acknowledge explicitly Joyce's debt to
Dante was Louis Gillet in the article 'James Joyce and His New
Novel', originally published in 1931, eight years before *Finnegans
Wake*: 'The text has to be read like Dante's, according to several
superimposed meanings. There is a literal meaning, an allegorical
meaning, and perhaps several others – almost as many as the skins of
an onion. As in writing of music, each sentence should be given on
several parallel lines.'[18] But it was Harry Levin who, in 1941, for the
first time tried to distribute the 'meanings' of the *Wake* according to
Dante's fourfold pattern when he pointed out, in his now classic
James Joyce: A Critical Introduction, that the four levels of meaning may
be seen as a 'useful' tool to tackle the *Wake*:

We have so little critical equipment for divining a complex piece of
symbolism that we may be excused for borrowing the terminology of the
Middle Ages. That 'divine comic,' Dante Alighieri, explained to Can
Grande della Scala that his own work could be interpreted at four different
levels, and it may throw some light on *Finnegans Wake* to consider Joyce's
'monomyth' in those terms. Anagogically, it envisages nothing less than the
development of civilization, according to Vico's conceptions. Allegorically,
it celebrates the topography and the atmosphere of the city of Dublin and
its environs. Literally, it records the misadventures – or rather the
nightmares – of H. C. Earwicker, as he and his wife and three children lie
in their beds above his pub, and broken slumber reiterates the events of the
day before. Morally, it fuses all these symbols into a central theme, which is
incidentally Milton's – the problem of evil, of original sin.[19]

After Levin, it has become usual for other critics to recognise a fourfold pattern in Joyce's works, and not only the *Wake*.[20] But Levin did not need to apologise for borrowing a 'terminology of the Middle Ages': this is not a case of simple borrowing of a useful tool on the part of the befuddled reader, and the method, I would argue, is consciously used by Joyce, who weaves into the *Wake* several allusions both to the *Convivio* and to the *Epistle*; the reader, then, is justified in using it – indeed, s/he is expected to refer to it to gain a better understanding of how Joyce's book functions with regard to the distribution and creation of meaning, but also, and perhaps above all, with regard to Joyce's treatment of literary sources.

I would then like to reconsider this literary/interpretative relationship, using Harry Levin's reading as my starting point but also going back to Dante's texts in order to see whether the theory of polysemy can indeed be taken as a straightforward, uncontroversial tool, applicable to another text without any further specifications; the theory will then be tested again on the *Wake* in order to find out how far it can be followed as a hermeneutic model. Thus, the attempt to answer the first, basic question – is Dante's theory of the four levels of meaning helpful for reading *Finnegans Wake*? – will inevitably raise others: is it just a reading strategy, in Levin's words a piece of external 'critical equipment', that the critic applies to Joyce's book in order to find his or her way around an otherwise nearly illegible text (thereby showing the need for the reader to make use of the earlier work in order to understand the later one, rather than studying what operations the later text has performed on the earlier one), or is it, on the contrary, an instrument whose interpretative function is already *inscribed in*, rather than having to be *applied to*, the *Wake* and whose traces in the text can therefore be confirmed by internal evidence? And, should this second hypothesis be proved tenable, how is the theory integrated into the *Wake*'s self-referential interpretative system? What kind of (hermeneutic) relationship is established between the medieval exegetical model and the modern literary polysemic work?

THE EPIEPISTLE AND THE ENVELOPING FACTS

If the premises of Levin's interpretation are revised, the meanings that he attributes to each level will also have to be reconsidered. Levin's starting point is that the literal level consists in the characters dreaming, or having nightmares, while sleeping in their beds, and in their reliving the day's events. This is only partially correct: as Beckett's notorious slogan goes, '[Joyce's] writing is not *about* something; *it is that something itself*' ('DBVJ' 14): Joyce, then, did not write a book *about* a dream (that is, about a character dreaming something): he wanted to write the dream in 'night language', to plunge the reader directly into the dreamer's mind at work, regardless of the identity of the dreamer.[21] If the literal level of Dante's *Divine Comedy* is the 'status animarum post mortem' (*Epistle to Can Grande*, §8), that of *Finnegans Wake* is the 'status animarum', as it were, *per somnium* – i.e., already inside the dream, in the sleeper's mind, or the 'semitary of Somnionia' (*FW* 594.08) where the sleeping lie dead to the world. Interpreting the literal level as the fact that the characters are dreaming or having nightmares while sleeping in their beds (in other words, as the context of the dream instead of the dream itself) would mean shifting from the picture to the frame, but the literal meaning can only be the immediate surface of the dream, told in the peculiar 'Wakean' language that creates a multiplicity of 'other' meanings. Moreover, Levin's interpretation is based on the assumption that it is HCE who is having the dream represented in the *Wake*, whereas the identity of the dreamer is by no means certain: to put it baldly, is it a 'modern' man – such as a publican – dreaming that he is Finn MacCool, and many more, or is it Finn lying under the city of Dublin and dreaming that he is one – or more – of its inhabitants? Or is it none of these?

Let us suggest, as a first tentative, and probably simplistic interpretation, that the literal meaning of the *Wake* as a whole is the dreamt story of H. C. Earwicker, publican, and his family: his wife Anna Livia Plurabelle, their twin sons Shem and Shaun, and their daughter Issy. HCE's 'misdemeanour' in Phoenix Park, his encounter with the cad, the rumours about him, the row in the pub, the children's games and homework, the parents' love-making in the bedroom, and so on to include all the episodes that happen to the 'charictures in the drame' (*FW* 302.31–2 – characters in the dream, caricatures in the drama – and, if caricatures, the drama will probably turn out to be a comedy), should be regarded as the story narrated in the book, the literal or 'historical' sense. (What I have just proposed, in fact, is very much like a boiled-down version of the plot summary first divulged by Joseph Campbell and Henry M. Robinson in their classic *A Skeleton Key to Finnegans Wake*,[22] and not everyone would nowadays agree this is the best account, although 'best accounts' are not what is really at stake here. Derek Attridge proposes a useful reconsideration of the function of narration and 'narrativity' in the *Wake*;[23] as will become clear in the rest of this chapter, Attridge's central point – that *Finnegans Wake* foregrounds 'narrativity' over actual narratives, 'metaphoricity' over metaphors, and so on – also applies to the *Wake*'s treatment of polysemy, whose importance as a principle and a system far outweighs the actual meanings that can be identified in the text.)

If the literal level of Levin's interpretation is thus rephrased, the description of the other senses must also be revised. Levin's reading of the allegorical level as the topography of the city may be generally correct but probably too reductive: while the topographical elements may be seen, *at one level*, as the allegorical ('other') meaning of HCE and his family, they also constitute, *at another level*, the physical context for HCE's story, and they must therefore be seen as elements of the literal level 'hiding' or 'containing' other allegorical meanings. Our starting working hypothesis may then be that the events presented at the literal level can be read allegorically as the vicissitudes of Everyman and of all mankind through history. The male character-role HCE is present every time his initials appear in the text; consequently, all the characters he stands for are evoked every time his presence is manifest. He is thus Here Comes Every-body (*FW* 32.18–19); Haveth Childers Everywhere (*FW* 535.34–5), i.e. the father of mankind, be he Adam or God (or, indeed, both); but he is also 'Heinz cans everywhere' (*FW* 581.05), the by-product of capitalism; his initials, which appear also in the order 'hec', may stand for 'hic est corpus meum', the words pronounced by the priest at the Eucharist in remembrance of Christ's sacrifice – and there-fore, through transubstantiation, he is also Christ himself; and so on, to embody practically all characters in history, legend, literature – literally 'every man'.

This is one of the ways in which a polysemy that literally rests on the 'letter' can function in *Finnegans Wake*: the 'character''s presence is marked by the appearance of his or her initials, but the initials may stand for anything else beginning with the same letters. Thus, an identification of all things, no matter how heterogeneous, is grounded in the sharing of the same initials – the sharing, that is, of an apparently outward, superficial and *literal* feature. This is the case of course also for all the other character-roles: the wife ALP, the twins Shem and Shaun who embody all opposites, and the daughter Issy, Isolde or Iseult, whose personality splits in her mirror image, or divides into seven parts when she forms, with the other girls, the colours of the rainbow, or in 28 + 1 in association with her school friends the 'Maggies', when they form the leap year month of twenty-nine days. (A slight problem emerges from all this: in talking about HCE, ALP, Shem, Shaun and Issy, we are leaving out of the equation the typical Dubliner family of Mr and Mrs Porter and their children Kevin, Jerry and Isobel; and if we do consider the Porters as the book's protagonists, then we have two alternative sets of names for the same 'literal' family. But let us put this problem on hold for the moment and proceed.)

As Harry Levin rightly points out, the story of the family is also 'the topography and the atmosphere of the city of Dublin and its environs': HCE is 'Howth Castle and Environs' (*FW* 3.03; Howth Head is the promontory on Dublin Bay, to the north of the city); ALP is the river Liffey, whose springs are in the Wicklow mountains and which flows through the city of Dublin before reaching the Bay; Issy is the riverside village of Chapelizod, or the 'Chapel of Iseult', the legendary Irish princess of the Tristan story; and Shem and Shaun, finally, are the two banks of the river. Other more detailed identifications follow from the first: HCE, for instance, is also the giant Finn MacCool of Irish tradition, lying dormant, or calmly slumbering, under the territory of the city and the surrounding landscape (*FW* 6.33–5, 7.20–1) with the Head of Howth as his head (*FW* 7.29), the two hillocks in Phoenix Park as his feet (*FW* 3.22, 7.30–2) and, in Joyce's typically irreverent humour, the obelisk of Wellington's Memorial, also in Phoenix Park, as his erected penis (9.09). As the left and right banks of the river, the brothers Shem and Shaun also identify with the people that live on them; in the 'Anna Livia Plurabelle' chapter (*FW* 1.8), for instance, they are the two washerwomen washing the dirty linen of HCE's family in the river and chatting across the opposite banks until nightfall, when they are transformed into a tree and a stone.

But in this very basic attempt to identify and distinguish the letter and the allegory, we are already coming up against significant problems. To start with, if the letters HCE and ALP signal the presence of – i.e. *stand for* – the archetypal man and woman, it would seem that the letters are, appropriately, the literal level, while each actual embodiment of the 'characters' – which would include the 'alternative' Porter family – should already be displaced to the allegorical one. Or perhaps each character exists at the literal level when s/he is named, while the other characters, embodiments or avatars evoked by the same letters are located on the allegorical ('other') level. For instance, chapter 1.8 ostensibly tells of the washerwomen on the Liffey, their gossiping and metamorphosis; how can one say, then, that this is an allegorical reading and not the literal surface of the text? In either case, the reader seems to be asked to separate the letters (or explicit names) from the 'actual' characters, and, in the first option proposed, identify the letters with the literal level and the 'embodiments' with the allegorical, while in the second, we would have to do just the reverse. We seem to be getting entangled in a double reversal where the literal becomes allegory and the allegory becomes literal – where each element moves fluidly between levels of signification. We must then reconsider what I earlier provisionally identified as the literal level, the story of HCE and his family. This story is not linear; it does not have any apparent coherent development. It is made up of many different plots, sketches, scenes of dialogue, confrontations of characters, short interludes. Only after several readings does this multilingual ('polygluttural', *FW* 117.13), polymorphic, metamorphosing and multidimensional surface ('The proteiform graph itself is a polyhedron of scripture', *FW* 107.08) reveal some form of coherence, which the reader is able to identify thanks to the return of character roles and, especially, the return of types of relationship between them (antagonism and conflict between male roles, desire of male characters towards the female ones, the temptation and titillation of young female figures or protectiveness of the older ones towards the male figures). Speaking of the 'return of character roles', of course, already suggests an analogy between these roles and the recurring initials; the 'literal' level (or was it allegorical? Like ALP in the final chapter of the *Wake*, 'I'm getting mixed', *FW* 626.36) is further split, or doubles up, in yet another distinction. The different 'stories' thus appear to be different versions of the same basic ones, with similar underlying significance. They are one by one – or, more often, many of them simultaneously – brought to the surface and cast into a role that we could perhaps call the 'literal meaning', but they are then plunged back again into the volcanic magma of the text, to surface again, at other moments and usually in particles, through linguistic hints, suggestions, overtones, *letters*. The 'literal level' is therefore extremely complex, made up, in turn, of several levels which cross and interfere with one another, not exactly like the orderly layers of the 'skins of an onion' of Gillet's definition, but rather like several threads of different lengths and thickness woven together to form a multicoloured and irregular fabric. Let us consider the fundamental and ever-recurring motif of the 'fall' in the *Wake* – perhaps a banal example in itself, but one which, by its very obviousness, will serve our purposes better than more complex examples, where the problems encountered may be due to the difficulty of the passage rather than be inherent in the method of analysis under observation.

The primary association of 'fall' is to Adam and Eve's original sin, which is, in a way, the fall *par excellence*: it is the first in the chronological and causal order of sins and the efficient cause of the whole of human history after that original lapse. While this anteriority gives it a primary place in the *Wake*, there are many other instances of 'fall' in the book that could rise to the same higher status. Tim Finnegan's fall from the ladder in the comic ballad 'Finnegan's Wake', for instance, can also claim a sort of paradigmatic priority in the book, since it is the one which is alluded to in the title; the same can be said of HCE's 'sin' of sexual exposure in Phoenix Park, since it is the one that sets the plot in motion. In fact, all instances are linked to one another, fused together, so as to make each recall all the others whenever they appear; the apparent preeminence of one or another instance of the 'fall' over the rest (as is true of all other recurrent elements and motifs) depends each time on which one is selected in the text as the carrier of the 'main' narrative structure of the particular episode – which one, that is, appears as the immediate literal sense while the others are more or less explicitly alluded to and made present in the text through a figurative use of language. HCE's sin in the park repeats Adam and Eve's sin in Eden and it is related also to Tim Finnegan's fall, since 'HCE' and 'Tim Finnegan' are different names which denote different aspects of the same character-role. As the reader tries to unravel 'main narratives' and 'subsidiary plots', 'characters' and their roles, s/he inevitably has to find shelter in the use of inverted commas: nothing is free from doubt, and even when one level of the polymorphic meaning of a word or concept may be expected to carry the main narrative and emerge over other aspects, fragments of these diverse layers (i.e. sub-layers of the literal level of meaning, as in the Thomist interpretation) keep coming up to the surface at the same time, obscuring the main thread.

(Let me open a parenthesis here, and explain that by talking about 'main narratives' I am not taking issue with what some critics would argue – that in fact in *Finnegans Wake* there is no 'main' narrative, or meaning, insofar as it is a non-hierarchical text in which nothing can be said to be more true or more important than anything else. While I agree in principle that different interpretations can be held as equally valid, as I shall myself argue later, I also want to point out the rather obvious fact that distinctions and divisions must be made within the text – indeed, that they are inherent in the text. This means both that there exist, in the text itself, principles – formal, structural, conceptual, linguistic, etc. – by which the subject-matter is ordered and organised and which make it possible for a plurality of meanings to be conveyed; and that, in following these principles, the critic finds an order in the text – an order that, ultimately, arranges the text according to the hierarchy implied in the herme-neutical model assumed or the principle privileged in each reading. As the debate on the creative allegory of the poets and the interpretative allegory of the theologians shows, the medieval concept of polysemy is also as much a theory of structured writing as one of structured reading.)

The motif of the 'fall' occurs for the first time on the first page of *Finnegans Wake*:

The fall (bababadalgharaghtakamminarronnkonnbronntonnerronntuonn-thunntrovarrhounawnskawntoohoohoordenenthurnuk!) of a once wallstrait oldparr is retaled early in bed and later on life down through all christian minstrelsy. The great fall of the offwall entailed at such short notice the pftjschute of Finnegan, erse solid man, that the humptyhillhead of humself promptly sends an unquiring one well to the west in quest of his tumptytumtoes . . .   (*FW* 3.15–21)

The fall is accompanied by the onomatopoeic effect of thunder in the first hundred-letter word of the *Wake*, which is also a multilingual synonymic – and to some extent apparently tautological – emphasis of the concept. The episode is 'retaled . . . down through all christian minstrelsy', which leads the reader to assume that the text may refer to the original sin, the very important 'Fall' which is so fundamental to Christian religion as to be told again and again ('retaled' = 'retold') and reinvented ('re-taled') both orally as in the minstrel tradition, and in writing in Christian literature (Adam and

Eve's names, in inverted order, have already been mentioned on the first line of the *Wake*). However, the spiritual meaning takes on economic overtones with the echo of the dramatic fall of the Wall Street stock-exchange in 1929 ('a once wallstrait oldparr') which had such dire consequences for world economy and for many people – that the (story of the) fall can also be 'retailed' in bed adds an interesting twist to the concept. There is also the evocation of a 'great' (and literal) fall of(f) a (straight) wall, which may perhaps suggest a literal crashing down of the wall of the tower of Babel, struck by God's thunderous wrath as it was being built, since the beginning of the hundred-letter-word contains a 'stuttering' refer- ence to Babel ('bababadal'), confirmed by an enactment of the confusion in the use of many different languages to express the idea and convey the sound of thunder. But, at the literal level, 'the great fall of the offwall' must also include Humpty Dumpty (and therefore a reference to Lewis Carroll), who did actually fall off a wall ('*humpty*hillhead . . . *tumpy*tumtoes', emphases added), and the people that were building the tower of Babel, whose 'fall', in the sense of sin, is turned into a literal fall from the walls they were building. And, to complicate matters, one learns that these events also entailed the 'pftjschute of Finnegan', rendered through another word uniting onomatopoeia to semantics ('pftjsch' + French *chute*, 'fall') and in which we can hear the sibilant swish of Finnegan coming flying down. All the layers here isolated (religion: Adam and Eve; socio- economy: Wall Street; nursery rhyme: Humpty Dumpty; Bible: the tower of Babel; folklore: Tim Finnegan), no doubt among the many others that could be identified, are woven together and share a portion of the surface of the text, or 'literal level'. One cannot help noticing that in the literalisation of the Babelian fall-as-sin into a fall from the wall, the text – or the diligent explicator – may already be voiding the possibility of metaphorical or figurative language, dis- allowing the depth that Aquinas attributes to the 'literal level', running the risk of flattening it, as it were, into an imageless, ultimately unimaginative, language. Fortunately, despite the anxiety of polysemic interpretation, the final effect is that of a multiplication of images: the sin + the literal falling off (as well as all the others), which could be summed up in Singleton's catchphrase for the 'mode of the theologians': 'this and that'.

However, we are now faced with a further problem: how do we distinguish a figurative use of language at the literal level from an allegorical (= 'other') level of meaning? The linguistic indices that actually appear on the narrative surface make it difficult to separate what is intrinsically implied (allegorical meaning) from what is on the contrary a figurative use of language and could therefore be ascribed, as in the Thomistic interpretation, to the 'letter' of the text. Given the enormous number of legendary, historical, mythological, anecdotal, Biblical and literary references, if one considers that allusions of this kind are to be taken as a figurative use of language and therefore as pertaining to the literal level, it would seem that nothing is left for the allegorical level, unless the allegory is understood as an abstraction, a pattern of 'common denominators' (with regard to sequences of events, 'characters' and their relationships) that underlie the basic structure of all episodes in the *Wake* and can therefore be defined as the universal characteristics of mankind and the historical development of civilisation – which is, incidentally, what Levin ascribes to the anagogical level.

These matters are indeed dizzying and hard to disentangle, just as it is hard to disentangle and keep separate all the threads of allusions which can be found in *Finnegans Wake*. The logical conclusion would be that while the assumption of the theory of the fourfold meaning could be a useful tool, but one which is external to the *Wake*, any rigorous distinction between the actual meanings is virtually impossible and any attempt at a strict application of the model is bound to be unsuccessful, being even more confusing than the text which it proposes to explain. One would indeed end up where Levin had started, accepting the theory of the fourfold meaning as an interpretative grid to map on to the *Wake* but not as a structure which the *Wake* appropriates and incorporates as part of its semiotic system, as, on the contrary, I am arguing. If my assumption is founded and the *Wake* does offer some keys to its riddles, the solution must then be sought in *Finnegans Wake* itself, in particular in its allusions to the theory as Dante expressed it in the *Convivio* and the *Epistle to Can Grande della Scala* and in the way these explicit references are treated and transformed. We shall see that Joyce himself confuses the terms of Dante's formulation of the theory, subverting his source-model and therefore showing it to be inadequate if it is applied too rigidly to the *Wake*. This does not mean, however, that the model should be discarded: it is in fact only by understanding exactly where it fails and how it is transformed that the reader can discover something about the intertextual relationship that the *Wake* establishes with the sources from which it borrows (or thieves) and the transformation (or metamorphosis) which it works upon them. Most of the *Wake*'s references to the theory of the fourfold meaning can be found in chapter 1.5, entirely devoted to the discussion and interpretation of the 'letter', or Anna Livia's 'untitled mamafesta' (*FW* 104.04); in this episode both the *Convivio* and the *Epistle to Can Grande* are drawn upon and fused together.

The 'letter' is one of the ever-returning motifs in *Finnegans Wake*; different versions are given in various parts of the text, and ultimately the invitation to 'Leave the letter that never begins to go find the latter that ever comes to end, written in smoke and blurred by mist and signed of solitude, sealed at night' (*FW* 337.11–14) identifies the letter with the *Wake* itself, this obscure and circular book of the night which never quite begins and never quite ends, whose meanings are as difficult to grasp as mist or smoke. The longest, most complete occurrence appears in book IV (*FW* 615.12–619.19);[24] it starts with a 'Dear' and ends with a 'P.S.' that clearly define its spatial limits and its nature as epistle. The word 'Reverend' at its beginning (615.12) associates the letter with the whole of the *Wake*, whose first word, 'riverrun' (3.01) is a near-homophone in Anglo-Irish. Most of the main themes and motifs of *Finnegans Wake* appear in this last version. It is signed 'Alma Luvia, Pollabella' (619.16), which suggests that Anna Livia is its author and thus justifies the title of '*mama*festa', although in other parts of the book the writer seems to be Shem the Penman, the artist-type in the *Wake*. But if this is the 'Letter, carried of Shaun, son of Hek, written of Shem, brother of Shaun, uttered for Alp, mother of Shem, for Hek, father of Shaun. Initialled' (*FW* 420.17–19), then Shem could also be simply the 'scribe' who writes down what his mother dictates and addresses to HCE (and signs it with the initials, or letters, or characters that, as we know by now, can pertain to either the literal or the allegorical levels). Shem was indeed 'Formelly confounded with amother' (125.11–12), as the reader is told at the end of the 'mamafesta' chapter; but we know that, in the last analysis, the entire family has had a part in writing/scribing/delivering the letter:

But resuming inquiries. Will it ever be next morning the postal unionist's . . . strange fate . . . to hand in a huge chain envelope, written in seven divers stages of ink, from blanchessance to lavandaiette, every pothook and pancrook bespaking the wisherwife, superscribed and subpencilled by yours A Laughable Party, with afterwite, S.A.G., to Hyde and Cheek, Edenberry,

Dubblenn, WC? Will whatever will be written in lappish language with inbursts of Maggyer always seem semposed, black looking white and white guarding black, in that siamixed twoatalk used twist stern swift and jolly roger?   (*FW* 66.10–21)

(I shall come back in chapter 4 to the role of the mother as giver of the word, and the embroiled relations between writing, creating meaning, and family relations in the context of the quest for self-authorisation and for a language that can both transcend the 'letter' and ground it in the physical.)

HCE appears consistently as the letter itself ('huge chain en-velope') and its addressee ('to Hyde and Cheek, Edenberry') throughout the *Wake*, while Shaun the Post(man), predictably, is the deliverer; but the entire Earwicker family, except perhaps the father himself, participate in the writing itself: 'blanchessance' suggests Issy (as Iseult of the White Hands in the Tristan myth), while 'lavandai-ette' seems to indicate ALP, in whose waters the washerwomen wash the family's dirty linen (one of the functions of the letter is to excuse HCE's sin and clear his reputation); the details of the text, 'bespaking the wisherwife', would confirm it. However, this may also point to the washerwomen – that is, Shem and Shaun – as the writers; the letter clearly resounds with ALP's tones ('written in lappish language'), but Issy may 'burst' in a few words ('with inbursts of Maggyer', perhaps through Shem and Shaun if 'semposed' combines Shem and Post), together with the twins ('black looking white and white guarding black, in that siamixed twoatalk'). The letter was lost, and later found again under a heap of dung by a hen, Belinda or Biddy Doran (*FW* 112.26–7); it was saved by Shem, stolen by Shaun and passed on by him as his own discovery. At the end of 1.5, it is Shem who is qualified as a stealer of notes ('that odious and still today insufficiently malestimated notesnatcher . . . Shem the Penman', FW 125.21–3), but the tone and wording of this remark suggest that this is the voice of Shaun denigrating his antagonist twin-brother. Earlier in the chapter it is in fact suggested that it was 'keepy little Kevin' (Shaun) who obtained for himself a reputation of 'future saintity' by outwitting his brother and taking from him ('euchring') what Shem – 'another heily innocent' – had found (FW 110.32–6).

An exegesis of the letter is offered in chapter 1.5. It is here that the 'mamafesta', a text that has been known under many names and therefore cannot honestly be defined as 'untitled' (cf. the three-page-long list of titles, *FW* 104.05–107.07) and has appeared in a constantly changing, protean multitude of forms ('The proteiform graph itself is a polyhedron of scripture',[25] *FW* 107.08), is now examined. The reader is informed about the 'enveloping facts . . . circumstantiating it' (*FW* 109.14) – that is, presumably, the context and circumstances of writing and of discovery. A reiterative analysis of the letter is carried out in different critical styles (textual, Marxist, psychoanalytic, etc.); then it is identified with the 'Tunc' page of the Book of Kells, through a parody of the style and language of its most famous interpreter, Sir Edward Sullivan. Like the letter, the Book of Kells had been buried for years by the monks at Kells to protect it from the Danish invaders, until it was rediscovered and dug out of its 'mound'. Joyce considered the weirdness of its fine illuminations, the intricacies and suggestiveness of its design, a powerful analogy for the peculiar style and language that he created for *Finnegans Wake* and for the essential quality that he tried to achieve in all his works. Since he was particularly fond of its illuminated 'letters',[26] it would not be by chance that it is especially in the chapter where the Letter or 'mamafesta' is analysed that the Book of Kells and its beautiful 'Tunc' page become a major subtext. Even more significant is that not so much the Book but Sullivan's interpretation becomes the basis for the parodic analysis of the 'letter': in this chapter, as in the second book of the *Convivio*, the text becomes secondary, almost accessory, to the act and system of interpretation. There are hints even that the 'Tunc' page of the Book of Kells may have been inspired by *Finnegans Wake*: 'the cruciform postscript from which three *basia* or shorter and smaller *oscula* have been overcarefully scraped away, plainly inspiring the tenebrous *Tunc* page of the Book of Kells' (*FW* 122.20–3). The logical inversion of precedence – the ancient book deriving from the one which is being written and which claims an archetypal primacy over the whole of literature – is also reflected in the transformation of the illuminated page of the manuscript into a 'tenebrous' one, in the obscure revisionism that allows reality to signify only through its reinterpretations in the language of the night; but it also recalls the paradoxical circularity of the modernist topos of the book announcing its own writing (*Ulysses* by Stephen, *A la Recherche* by Marcel – the *Divine Comedy*, if I am allowed an anachronism that places Dante among the modernists, by the pilgrim Dante).

'But to return' (*FW* 295.15; constantly returning to the text as well as to one's critical readings is a move that the *Wake*, as much as Dante, encourages and indeed shows to be necessary for the exegete; I shall come back to this point later): as I have engaged, in the last pages, in a descriptive account of the role of the 'letter' in *Finnegans Wake*, I have been repeatedly slipping into precisely the type of exegetical question that the theory of polysemy also raises, and I have used 'letter' in at least three meanings (and so has the *Wake*): as alphabetical units, letters can be combined together in infinite ways to produce different meanings, can acquire symbolic meanings of their own (e.g., alpha and omega as symbols of absolute beginning and end), or signal the presence of 'characters', reminding us perhaps of the cabbala's detection of God through the appearance of the letters of his name. As epistle, the letter enables messages to be communicated, whether in daily life or in the literary transmission of texts and documents – maybe by having to dig it out of the midden heap of the past. A letter of course may also accompany a present, dedicate a book. As 'literal meaning', the letter implies a stratified conception of writing, exactly the message that Dante was transmitting through his *Epistle*, the letter that accompanied the *Paradiso* and dedicated it to Can Grande della Scala (who may be overheard in the *Wake*'s 'scaliger', 491.28, together with the fifteenth-century Italian scholar by that name and the ladder-carrier [Latin *scaliger*] Tim Finnegan).[27] Dante's *Epistle* also contained instruction as to how the poem must be read at its several levels, qualifying in a way as a manifesto of poetics: notations of literary criticism and poetic intent that the *Wake*'s 'mamafesta', though more obscurely, also offers.

It may be worth recalling that Dante claims in the *Convivio*, when he explains the reasons that made him write his treatise, that he must explain his own poems, as only their author knows what their true meaning is: 'movemi desiderio di dottrina dare la quale altri veramente dare non può' ('I am moved by the desire to give instruction which no one else can truly give', *Conv* I.ii, 15). Even more significantly in our context, the first reason he gives is that he is moved by the desire to clear his name and avoid 'infamy' (*Conv* I.ii, 15), a motivation that brings him very close indeed to HCE and his wife's campaign to clear his name.

The first scholarly step for any researcher must be to establish the origins of the text; thus, after the statement of the polymorphic nature of the letter, a quest for its 'true' author begins: 'who in hallhagal wrote the durn thing anyhow?' (*FW* 107.36–108.01) is the question to be asked, and the researcher must equip him/herself with patience: 'Now, patience; and remember patience is the great thing, and above all things else we must avoid anything like being or becoming out of patience' (*FW* 108.08–10). After all, the Dantean scholars who have embarked on the same quest – who the hell wrote the damned *Epistle* anyway? – have had to be patient for over six centuries, and still do not know the answer, though they cannot afford to lose their patience, their greatest critical asset. Philologists know that they must turn to the text, but as soon as we go back to the letter, the search for clues as to the authorship turns in frustration into a search for another, and brighter, interpreter who can help find out what it is all about:

> then as to this radiooscillating epiepistle to which . . . we must ceaselessly return, whereabouts exactly . . . is that bright soandsuch to slip us the dinkum oil?[28] (*FW* 108.24–8)

However, 'radiooscillating' points to the nature of the letter as polymorphous text oscillating between different forms and different possible interpretations and re-interpretations, in this case also oscillating between the written form inherent in the letter and the oral or 'radiophonic' aspect of a text relying on 'sound sense' (*FW* 109.15) as much as on its visual or graphic aspect; and the repetition of the first syllables betrays the presence of HCE, who has a 'doubling stutter' (*FW* 197.05). Unfortunately, the quest leads the researcher nowhere: ten pages later we are told that 'we must vaunt no idle dubiosity as to its genuine authorship and holusbolus authoritativeness' (*FW* 118.03–4), but all we know is that 'somebody . . . wrote it, wrote it all, wrote it all down, and there you are, full stop' (*FW* 118.12–14) – that's all we can be sure of.

In fact, by turning and returning to the text, not only have we missed its author, but we may have already lost sight of the text itself: depending on the interpretation we give to the prefix 'epi-', the 'epiepistle' may be a meta-commentary upon the epistle (a letter about or around the letter; perhaps a Dantean, or maybe apocryphal, *Epistle* about the epistle; and the *Epistle*, as we know, is already a commentary upon a text, an epi-text as it were, brightly trying 'to slip us the dinkum oil'); or it may be the outer (additional?) layer over the epistle – is it a *sovrasenso* (literally 'over-sense', *Conv* ii.i, 6)? Or is it perhaps the envelope? Perhaps it is, because attention is now devoted to the envelope: 'Has any fellow . . . ever looked sufficiently longly at a quite everydaylooking stamped addressed envelope?' (*FW* 109.01–8). Have we paid enough attention to it? Though 'Admittedly it is an outer husk' (*FW* 109.08), just a surface, an outward and therefore apparently discardable feature, yet the one thing that will strike us first is just as important as its content ('its face . . . is its fortune,' *FW* 109.08–9), and as Beckett had already pointed out in 'Dante. . . Bruno. Vico. . Joyce',

> to concentrate solely on the literal sense or even on the psychological content of any document to the sore neglect of the enveloping facts themselves circumstantiating it is just as hurtful to sound sense (and let it be added to the truest taste) . . .   (*FW* 109.12–16)

The text goes on to develop a strong concern with appearance, face, clothing and what is underneath the surface; the final version of the second passage that Beckett had already quoted from *Work in Progress* is:

> Who in his heart doubts either that the facts of feminine clothiering are there all the time or that the feminine fiction, stranger than the facts, is there also at the same time, only a little to the rere? Or that one may be separated from the other? Or that both may then be contemplated simultaneously? Or that each may be taken up and considered in turn apart from the other?   (*FW* 109.30–6)

In the *Convivio*, after the illustration of the four senses, Dante had gone on to say:

> E in dimostrar questo, sempre lo litterale dee andare innanzi, sì come quello ne la cui sentenza li altri sono inchiusi, e sanza lo quale sarebbe impossibile ed inrazionale intendere a li altri, e massimamente a lo allegorico.   (*Conv* ii.i, 8)

(And in demonstrating this, the literal sense must always come first as the one in whose meaning the others are contained, and without which it would be impossible and irrational to attend to the others, and especially to the allegorical.)

The literal meaning 'always come[s] first' and encloses the others, so that they follow in the interpretation: they are 'there also at the same time, only a little to the rere'. Of course, one should not concentrate only on the literal sense, neglecting the 'enveloping facts': the circumstances of writing and of the transmission of the text, or the envelope into which the letter is sealed. However, if we keep Dante's words in mind, the 'enveloping facts' should be the letter itself: 'lo litterale . . . ne la cui sentenza li altri sono inchiusi' ('the literal . . . in whose meaning the others are contained').

The confusion is based on the ambiguity of 'letter', whether it is interpreted as 'epistle' or as 'literal sense'. The second passage too (*FW* 109.30–6) deliberately confuses Dante's terms. If the letter is the sense which enfolds the other three, one could say that it 'clothes' or 'cloaks' them. Now, allegory, as 'alien' or 'different' meaning, may be qualified as 'stranger' ('stranger than the facts', where the facts would have to be the literal or historical sense; but see also Dante's apostrophe to the reader in *Inferno* IX, 62–3, which invites him to look at the 'dottrina che s'asconde / sotto 'l velame de li versi strani', 'the doctrine that conceals itself under the veil of the strange verses'). What in *Finnegans Wake* is 'stranger', however, is the 'fiction', which in the words of the *Convivio* is in fact again the literal sense, the 'beautiful fiction' that veils or 'cloaks' allegory. This 'fiction' is 'only a little to the rere', this time like the allegorical meaning in Dante: 'sempre lo litterale dee andare innanzi' ('the literal sense must always come first').

By deliberately blurring the issue and by drawing attention to the envelope as well as to the letter proper, Joyce is moreover pointing out that layers of meaning do not stop at the literal sense but, on the contrary, go on proliferating in all directions. The emphasis on the envelope makes the point that the form is just as important as its content – form and content are in fact one and the same thing. Similarly, the letter could not be delivered and reach its target (the addressee and the goal of communication) without the envelope. In other words, the envelope also bears a message, the 'instructions for use' directed to the postman and to the receiver, specifying where and to whom the letter should go and where it comes from. In a way, Dante's letter to Can Grande, with its directions and 'instructions for use', is to the text of the *Paradiso* what the envelope is to the letter.

In the passage from *FW* 109.30–6 quoted above, both the 'clothiering' and the 'fiction' are feminine. In a book where all identities are elusive, feminine ones seem to be even more immaterial. Issy, who is often associated with her mirror image, certainly has a misleading side to her personality. But in this context of letter and added meanings, outer and hidden senses, one may also be reminded of the passage of the *Convivio* where Dante states that the true value of a poem lies in its content and not in its form, often charming but misleading, and compares it with a woman whose beauty can be judged only when all exterior ornaments are laid aside:

sì come non si può bene manifestare la bellezza d'una donna, quando li adornamenti de l'azzimare e de le vestimenta la fanno più ammirare che essa medesima. Onde chi vuole ben giudicare d'una donna, guardi quella quando solo sua naturale bellezza si sta con lei, da tutto accidentale adornamento discompagnata . . .   (*Conv* I.x, 12–13)

('just as the beauty of a woman is not in good evidence when the adornment of her make up and clothes bring her more admiration than she brings herself. Thus whoever wants to judge a woman justly should look at her when only her natural beauty is with her, unaccompanied by any incidental adornment . . .)

In the *Convivio*, where Dante still professes to be following the 'manner of the poets' for whom the letter is a charming lie and only the hidden allegorical meaning is true, form and content are separate. Joyce, for whom form and content coincide because they are one and the same thing, may be bringing into the *Wake* an allusion to the text of Dante's *Convivio* by associating 'letter' and 'other' meanings with appearance and reality and the theme of clothes and feminine ornaments, 'fictional' insofar as they may be misleading; but in the same way as he blurs the distinction between Dante's two main levels, the traditional opposition between external appearance and hidden truth, on which any theory of allegory needs to rely, also loses any sharpness.

'To concentrate solely on the literal sense' is 'hurtful to sound sense'; 'sound sense' surely means 'rightful judgement', but the *Wake* goes on to add, 'to the truest taste', which on the one hand points to aesthetic taste, but on the other also makes the reader reinterpret 'sense' as 'sensorial perception' rather than 'understanding', and 'sound' as 'hearing'. It is another ironic touch which draws attention to the importance of the sound in *Finnegans Wake*. Sound, or the external form, may be no more than 'incidental adornments' for the *Convivio*, but it is an essential part of the sense (meaning) of the *Wake*, where the phonological level produces its own significance, alone or by comparison and contrast with the printed form of words. The content, or 'hidden truth' of the *Convivio*, is ironically transformed in the *Wake* into the sense of taste – a sense which is of course pertinent to an essay whose title means 'banquet', as well as to the *Wake*, whose title song celebrates in true Irish style the wake or banquet for Tim Finnegan's death and resurrection (and suddenly Beckett's 'carefully folded ham-sandwich' seems to acquires a more 'soothing' dimension).

As I pointed out earlier, Aquinas held that the figurative use of language must not be interpreted as the allegorical meaning of a text, but that it is part of the literal level and that the literal sense is what the author wants to say (*intentio auctoris*); now, if the intention of the author is to communicate the significance which is hidden, the hidden sense must be considered as the true literal sense. Taking this one step further, we would have to say that the true literal sense turns out to be the allegorical one, because it represents the true intention of the author. If we look at it in a Wakean perspective, we also see that during a dream the *intentio* of the unconscious is to release meanings once they have been censored and processed by the dream work, liberating them and letting them come to the surface through linguistic indices which can still be obscure but possess some qualities that can enable the analyst – or the literary critic, or the exegete, as the case may be – to discover beneath them the truth (*a* truth, perhaps), the 'true intention' of the author/mind. Whether it is by a conscious contamination of Dante with St Thomas or not, it looks as though Joyce, starting from Dante, goes beyond him, to fall back again on Aquinas, the mentor of Stephen Dedalus's youthful aesthetic elaborations.[29]

TROPOLOGIES

Since Joyce's treatment of Dante's exposition of the function of letter and allegory is subverted throughout, it remains to be seen what happens to the other two levels that are contained in the sense 'other', the moral and the anagogical levels, and it may now be predicted that they will also be transformed in/by the *Wake*. Let us first of all look at the moral sense. Harry Levin reads it as the fusion of all the symbols of the other levels into the central theme of evil and original sin. It seems to me that Levin is proceeding by successive stages of abstraction, in that he is drawing a central theme from what is already an abstraction – the 'common denominator' which underlies all basic plot patterns and recurrent relationships between the character-roles. In the mythology of the *Wake*, evil and original sin are part of the historical development of mankind, of the nature of man (Everyman) and of the pattern of life, death and rebirth which Joyce fuses so well with the Vichian cycle. They would seem to belong, therefore, to the allegorical rather than to the moral level. Moreover, interpreting the moral sense (defined by Dante as the teaching that can be drawn from the literary work) in Levin's terms poses another problem insofar as it presupposes a didactic conception of literature which is difficult to attribute to James Joyce: already in *Stephen Hero* and in *A Portrait*, as well as in the early reviews and articles, there emerges an a-moral (which of course does not mean unethical) conception of the artist's role, proceeding especially from *fin de siècle* aestheticism – particularly D'Annunzio – and from Nietzsche's philosophy, and compounded by the Flaubertian concept of the impersonality of the work of art and its artistic independence from the author's ideas and ethical beliefs.[30] If anything, here in *Finnegans Wake* the study of the letter's sloping handwriting shows 'a sure sign of imperfectible moral blindness' (*FW* 122.35–6), reiterated several times by allusions to the characters' moral turpitude (e.g. *FW* 522.14 and 523.28) or moral absence, for instance when a personage named 'Slippery Sam' is described as 'physically present howsomedever morally absent' (*FW* 341.35–342.01). There is also another character named 'Sordid Sam', and later we are warned that 'There are sordidly tales within tales' (*FW* 522.05); is this the same 'skeezy Sammy' of the 'Dave the Dancekerl' episode (in *FW* III.2) – or perhaps his opposite half (cf. 'skeezy' as 'schizo-') – that is being corrupted by scruples, that is threatened with burning at the stake (like Giordano Bruno), who is (religiously, or heretically) full of poetic tropes but is invited to act literally and not metaphorically?

I can feel you being corrupted. Recoil. I can see you sprouting scruples. Get back. And as he's boiling with water I'll light your pyre. Turn about, skeezy Sammy, out of metaphor, till we feel are you still tropeful of popetry.
(*FW* 466.07–11)

One may be even led to wonder whether this slippery, schizoid Shem-character (Shem is described as a 'mental and moral defective', *FW* 177.16, by the Shaun-oriented narrator of the 'Shem the Penman' chapter, *FW* I.7) has anything to do with Sam Beckett, one of the early interpreters of *Work in Progress*, the one responsible for the first association of Joyce's banquet with Dante's *Convivio* and its exposition of polysemic poetics, and the one who has been associated with the character who – like Dante in the darkest hour of his morally reprehensible life – finds himself 'lost in the bush' ('You is feeling like you was lost in the bush, boy? . . . Bethicket me for a stump of a beech ', *FW* 112.03–5; I shall come back to this passage again in the next chapter). One may even wonder whether the 'moral blindness' quoted above could in fact also evoke Joyce's poor vision, or Stephen's amoral and unapologetically uncompromising artistic stance, prefigured from the start by Dante (Riordan)'s rhyme 'Pull out his eyes / Apologise' in *A Portrait of the Artist* (8).

The quest for the 'moral' meaning of the story, inevitably accompanied by its denial, crops up here and there (see e.g. *FW* 306.27–8, 434.18, 550.03), but it is the nature of the polysemy of the *Wake* that makes it impossible to distinguish an explicit moral sense: for the moral to be found, there needs to be a univocal truth behind the text, and whereas this might be true of Dante's works, it is certainly not of *Finnegans Wake*; if in the *Wake* everything can evoke by implication a potentially infinite number of other meanings, always by definition more than one can see or expect – as my second epigraph suggests by adding yet another layer of exegesis to an already too unwieldy proliferation of meanings – there can be no possible single moral to be inferred, and therefore no teaching as to what is right or wrong, or as to how to behave righteously. Nevertheless, it is exactly from this lack of clear direction that readers can draw a conclusion about the *Wake*: an indication, that is, as to how to behave with regard to the text itself; or, in other words, instruction about how they are to perform their role of readers.[31]

The 'meandertale' (*FW* 18.22) of the *Wake* forces its readers to an equally meandering manner of reading; it is necessary to go back and forth in the text to establish the relevant connections; one must read the lines and between the lines to unveil the mystery hidden in the 'sibylline' (*FW* 31.36) or, in Dante's words, 'sotto 'l velame de li versi strani' (*Inf* IX, 63); divide and recompose words, go beneath their difficult surface, find the connections between words, themes, portions of text, extricate meanings, construct coherent readings, confront them, draw conclusions, however provisional these may have to be; and, finally, give up the possibility of reaching a single final and comprehensive interpretation of a text which 'is, was and will be writing its own wrunes forever' (*FW* 19.35–6) – a text, that is, which 'tropes' its own meanings and therefore does not just *stand for* an 'other' level of signification; and perhaps, finally, which compels us to interpret this hermeneutic relativity, this inability to give any single or univocal answer to the many questions raised, as the 'moral' message inscribed in the text. But this is by no means a nihilistic or sceptical message: the answers are not denied, they are given in great quantities; all the keys are hidden in the text: 'The keys to. Given!' (*FW* 628.15) is the last hint that Anna Livia gives us on the last page of the book, in her final monologue, before flowing into the sea. We are given all the clues: the artist, like Dante in *Purgatorio*, has no time to explain in detail the meanings of his poetry:

> A descriver lor forme più non spargo
> rime, lettor; ch'altra spesa mi strigne,
> tanto ch'a questa non posso esser largo;
> ma leggi Ezechiel . . .   (*Purg* xxix, 97–100)

(To describe their forms, I do not spread any more rhymes, reader, for other spending constrains me so that I cannot be large in this one; but read Ezekiel . . .)

Dante indicates the sources, has already given (or merely suggested) to us a method of interpretation and shown how it can(not) be applied; now it is up to us to find our own way in the text.

The 'moral teaching' of the *Wake* – the way the reader is expected to behave towards the text – is therefore closely connected with the 'reading instructions' therein inscribed, the ever-present self-referentiality of the text, and also, of course, the nature of the 'letter' as 'epiepistle'. Yet again, and unlike what Dante says, once applied to the *Wake* the levels of meaning turn out to be impossible to distinguish, collapsing into one or fragmenting into too many, thus collapsing and fragmenting the theory they are drawn from. The original sense is turned around, turned about, 'troped' as it were (from the Greek *tropos*, 'turn', and the Vulgar Latin *tropare*, 'to invent, find' in the sense of compose poetry, analogous to the Classical Latin *invenio* and also found in such forms as *trouvère, trobar, troubadour*). After all, this is just another *literalisation* of the moral sense, also called 'tropological', and it is related to the self-referentiality that the works of both writers share. Dante constantly critically re-examines his earlier works in a new light, and scatters through his texts more or less explicit instructions as to how the text must be understood, read, completed. We know about the *Convivio* and the *Epistle*; the *Vita Nuova* is made up of both poetry and prose, part of the prose being an explanation of the poems, and the poems being a transposition in the poetic medium of events or feelings narrated in the prose. The *De vulgari eloquentia*, besides being a theoretical treatise on language, is a rhetoric, or *poetria*, of the *canzone* and an ordering of Dante's ideas on that poetic form, with many examples drawn from his own production. The *Divine Comedy* is full of indications to the reader about how the poem should be read; many of its metaphors turn around the image of the student and the teacher: Virgil and Brunetto Latini, for instance, are or have been Dante's 'maestri'; the reader sitting at his desk is the poet's disciple, Dante throughout his journey 'notes' what he has learned.

Mary Reynolds suggests that, in the case of *Ulysses*, Joyce was inviting a fourfold Dantean reading through the *schema* that he distributed to his friends, and that this was his 'equivalent of Dante's *Letter to Can Grande*'.[32] The same can be said for the numerous *letters* that Joyce sent to Harriet Weaver and other friends listing words and explaining, or just making suggestions about, difficult points in *Work in Progress* (*Letters* I 246; 295). A similar concern drove him to have his 'twelve apostles' write the essays of the *Exagmination* about his work in order to encourage, to use Dante's metaphors, the 'common herd' that do not 'sit at the table where the bread of angels is consumed' (*Conv* I.i) to read Joyce's puzzling work.

Finnegans Wake too, of course, is a highly self-referential text that constantly refers to and redefines its own nature: it is the 'nighty-novel' (*FW* 54.21), the book of the night, made up of 'once current puns, quashed quotatoes, messes of mottage' (*FW* 183.22–3), like the *Convivio* allegorising words as food, or the 'usylessly unreadable Blue Book of Eccles, *édition de ténèbres*' (*FW* 179.26–7), the new night edition of Joyce's earlier epic of the inhabitants of 7 Eccles Street, *Ulysses*, originally published with a blue cover. It is the 'book of Doublends Jined' (*FW* 20.15–16), the book of Dublin's Giant and also 'of the two ends joined', with a clear allusion to its circular structure which joins the last sentence to the first (see also *Letters* I 251). Another aspect of the self-referentiality are the marginal notes of *FW* II.2, where the text is printed like medieval manuscripts with glosses on three sides: the twins' on the right and left margins, and Issy's at the bottom of the page. This cyclic or tropic pattern is in fact already implied in the first word of the title, 'Finnegans', which has been interpreted also as 'fin-negans', i.e., the book that denies the end by continuing its 'last' sentence into its 'beginning'; but one should also take note of the way each of Joyce's works takes up and further elaborates on questions of poetics more or less explicitly proposed by the earlier ones (I shall follow some of these threads in chapter 4).

Implicit in this structure is the need to read the text several times, with broader and deeper insight at each new start.[33] Such a method is inherent in the stratified structure of the text, which requires that the reader go through it at least once for each meaning that s/he can discern, and build coherent readings that can then be compared and drawn together. Dante also emphasised the need for a repeated confrontation with the polysemic text. After the illustration of the literal sense of the *canzone* 'Voi che 'ntendendo' in the second book of the *Convivio*, he goes on to explain the allegorical meaning and introduces the passage from the former to the latter sense with the following words:

Poi che la litterale sentenza è sufficientemente dimostrata, è da procedere a la esposizione allegorica e vera. E però, principiando ancora da capo . . .

(*Conv* II.xii, 1)

(As the literal meaning has been adequately explained, we need to proceed to the allegorical and true exposition. And therefore, beginning again from the beginning . . .)

The interpretation of each level of meaning requires a new reading of the entire text from a different perspective. As a matter of fact, the *Wake* too suggests that the new reading (the new beginning which must follow the last sentence in the book) has to be carried out from a different point of view: the end of *Finnegans Wake*, on page 628, is 'spoken' by Anna Livia, while the beginning, on page 3, is 'spoken' by a different narratorial voice – not clearly identified but stylistically more matter-of-fact and emotionally less involving than Anna Livia's at the end of her monologue and her death-like flow into the sea. Indeed, if not emotionally, 'we' readers are grammatically included in the narration at the beginning of *Finnegans Wake* ('brings us . . . back,' *FW* 3.02), a change prepared by Anna Livia's shift from the 'I' to the 'we' as she is about to flow into the sea, when the end and the new beginning are announced: 'End here. Us then. Finn, again!' (*FW* 628.13–14).

Finnegans Wake is then a tropology, a 'tropos-logos', a turning and returning discourse in which the image of the circle and of cyclic patterns (Vichian, Dantean or otherwise) plays a powerful role. As any part of text, word or part of word in the *Wake* may be made to signify different meanings through rhetorical artifice, it may also be said to be a 'tropos-logos' based on the 'logic of the trope' (the trope is defined in classical rhetoric as a swerve of the semantic direction of a word that shifts from its original content to a new one). The pattern of semantic renovation implicit in the structure of the trope may be taken as symbolic also of the literary interrelationship – it is in fact very similar to the description that Harold Bloom gives of his first principle of poetic influence, the *Clinamen* (originally Lucretius's word for the swerve of the atom in the universe).[34] But Bloom's theory implies a wish on the part of the later poet to 'correct' the precursor,[35] whereas the relationship between Joyce and Dante – Joyce and any other writer, indeed any two great writers – is more one of exploiting the earlier one in order to create a new, original and (in the specific case of *Finnegans Wake*) accretional work; of distortion, of conscious thieving and metamorphosing, as I have described it in the introduction; of eating as it were at the 'banquet' (*Convivio*) of the earlier text (but not necessarily of feeding off the earlier text: eating at somebody's table is not always parasitism), and of turning about and upside down its contents in order to expose its untenability for the interpretation of the modern work. Not an anxiety-laden text but a 'morally' ('tropologically') a-moral one which, like Stephen in 'Scylla and Charybdis', refuses to pay its debts at the same moments as it acknowledges them.[36]

BASER MEANINGS

The anagogical meaning remains finally to be considered. Harry Levin interprets it as the 'development of civilization, according to Vico's conceptions', but there are at least two problems with this reading. One is that Vico's cyclical view of history, although structurally the main one, is not in fact the only theory that contributes to the complex view of the evolution of human civilisation in *Finnegans Wake*. Joyce includes at least two other important theories, those of Giordano Bruno and Edgar Quinet, Vico's French translator; these allow us to place the development of society and man into the larger perspective of a cosmic theory of the universe and the transformation of all things (Bruno) and to relate its incessant flux to the existence of constant natural forces that are ultimately more powerful and more resistant than human structures (Quinet).[37] The interconnection of these theories underlies the whole book as well as each of the single episodes that replay variations of the recurrent themes, and, insofar as it concerns the (hi)story of (Every)man, it should perhaps be ascribed to the allegorical level rather than to the anagogical, or spiritual, sense.

The second, more fundamental problem with Levin's identification of the anagogical meaning is that anagogy should in fact project the text outside and above history. Dante defines the anagogy as the spiritual *sovrasenso*, when the literal sense in the Scriptures is interpreted as signifying 'de le superne cose de l'etternal gloria' ('[the meaning] of the supernal things of the eternal glory', *Conv* ii.i, 6); and the concept of *sovrasenso* confers therefore a transcendental, emphatically ahistorical meaning to this fourth level. In *Finnegans Wake*, however, divinities (and religion in general) are immanent in history, they are in fact (wo)man her/himself, fragile, mortal, sinful and guilty. The anagogical sense coincides thus with the everyday spiritual aspects of human existence rather than, as in Dante, the spiritual dimension of Christian religion. It is spiritual, as opposed to material, in that it refers to mental events, to the unconscious, to memory, to feelings and impulses: all facets of a whole of which religions are also a part, but just one among many others, and one which exists not on an independent, higher (or 'outer') level of reality but as an interior, psychological human need and as a cultural fact. In this sense, the whole of *Finnegans Wake* is 'anagogical' insofar as it is a dream-like (i.e. a non-bodily, therefore 'spiritual') construction abstracting its subject-matter from actual (literal, historical) things, which must however be interpreted in order that this 'historical' level may be reconstructed. Once again, the *Wake* completely inverts the meaning of Dante's theory of interpretation: for the medieval writer the letter 'dee andare innanzi' (*Conv* ii.i, 8; 'must always come first') and includes 'superior' things; in *Finnegans Wake* the 'spiritual' sense appears together with the literal sense and contains it in itself at the same time as it is contained in it. The *sovrasenso* is not something which is superimposed and points above to a higher morality or spirituality; on the contrary, it emerges from the depths of consciousness, as in the *lapsus linguae* or in dream, and it can pave the way to base, obscene readings that no one with any sense of decency would even dare to hint at: 'A baser meaning has been read into these characters the literal sense of which decency can safely scarcely hint' (*FW* 33.14–15).

The sordid tales within tales of *Finnegans Wake* (522.05) thus constitute yet again an inversion of Dante's ideas as well as a literalisation of them. Dante explains the theory of the four levels of meaning in the *Convivio* in order to confer higher nobility and worthiness on the vulgar – i.e., vernacular – tongue, making it capable of treating subjects until then excluded from its range. Dante's defence of the *vulgare* is now taken literally, and vulgar (in the current sense of 'low') meanings and expressions are introduced into the idiom of the *Wake* and justified through various references to the Father of the Italian language. Thanks to this distortion of Dante's polysemic method, Joyce vulgarises language and literature and makes his new-founded language a medium capable of treating practically any and every subject at once, both high and low, thus incidentally and ungratefully showing that Dante's method does not quite work according to plan – though it can work in unforeseen ways, opening unexpected doors.

'THIS', 'THAT' AND THE 'OTHER'

There is at least an analogy between Dante and Joyce's use of polysemy that ought be pointed out. For both writers the polysemic method becomes one of construction as well as one of interpretation. The allegory (in its comprehensive meaning of 'sense other') can be synthesised in the formula 'this and that', and no longer 'this for that', as was the case with the allegory of the poets in the *Convivio*. However, the analogy ends here, and the nature of the polysemy of Dante's and Joyce's works is different. For Dante the various levels of meaning are built upon one another, each can be singled out and distinguished from the others, and they all work together towards the evocation of a single truth; for him the various layers of meaning cannot contrast with one another and point to different explanations, as that would require two or more different truths, which is finally inconceivable for the orthodox Christian medieval mind, even when as daring and anti-ecclesiastical as Dante's. In Joyce's text, on the contrary, several meanings are compounded together, intersect one another, are rarely univocal, more often point towards different directions thus allowing for opposite interpretations that exist simultaneously and are never exclusive of one another.

Joseph Mazzeo makes an interesting point about Dante's definition of allegory in the *Epistle*, where it can also be taken as a general term subsuming the three senses allegorical proper, moral and anagogical; one of Dante's aims in his discussion of allegory, Mazzeo writes, 'is not so much to advance a theory of explication as to describe a theory of the selection and ordering of significant experience', thus enabling him to compress into one single week – the length of time it takes the pilgrim to complete the journey described in the *Commedia* – the intellectual and personal experiences of a lifetime.[38]

Thus Dante's theory of the four levels of meaning is a means of selection and ordering of significant experience: not so in Joyce, where it is, rather, a means of inclusion – and probably of disordering – of all experience, equally significant. Whereas in Dante the *alleon* is conveyed (hidden) by the letter, in *Finnegans Wake* it is simultaneously present together with the letter, and, as we have seen, it may be the letter itself which is in fact hidden. The reference to what is 'other', moreover, is not only an allusion: it is perhaps better described as an extreme form of *figura*, or even a relationship of identity. Humpty Dumpty's fall from the wall *is*, and does not just stand for, Adam and Eve's fall into mortal sin, and HCE's fall *is* the figural fulfilment of the original fault of our protoparents; HCE's arrival into Dublin Bay *is* the arrival of all invaders that have conquered the island at different times of history, and so on for every event, 'character' or detail of the book.

As the *alienum* is everything that is 'other' from what is printed on the page, and the printed word has both a literal and an allegorical meaning, taking this to extreme consequences, the words of the book mean both what is there and what is not – that is to say, *potentially* everything; one of Joyce's favourite and best-known word-plays is the pun on word/world: the word on the page is a microcosm containing in itself the entire macrocosm. The road from Dante's selective polysemy to the *Wake*'s all-inclusiveness passes through Giordano Bruno's theory of the coincidence of the opposites in the one and his conception of the infinity of the universe and its simultaneous presence in all things. But it also goes through the adoption and adaptation (in fact, as can be expected, distorting and 'troping', thieving and metamorphosing) of the theories of the 'vulgar' language of the *De vulgari eloquentia*, and in the next two chapters I shall explore what aspects of Dante's theory of the evolution of language and what characteristics of the noble *vulgare* are appropriated by the *Wake*, how they help in making the idiom of *Finnegans Wake* an all-inclusive medium and how they contribute to the shaping of its thematic structure and of its radical narrative technique.

CHAPTER 2

The confusioning of human races

confusionary overinsured everlapsing

(*FW* 333.06–7)

In alldconfusalem

(*FW* 355.11)

If the *Convivio* sets forth a defence of the vernacular language 'in practice' by employing it in ways which had not yet been attempted before and by applying the exegetical theory of the four levels of meaning to vernacular poetry, the *De vulgari eloquentia*, written in Latin during the first years of Dante's exile, develops a related aspect of Dante's life-long speculation about language by providing a historical and philosophical justification of the existence of many different languages and dialects (*Dve* i.i–viii), by searching for and attempting to define a *vulgare illustre*, or noble vernacular, that can rise above the multifarious variety of the post-Babelian idioms (i.ix–xix), and, finally, in the second book, through the elaboration of a formal vernacular poetics (ii.i–xiv). Book ii, however, was left unfinished in the middle of a sentence, and the rest of the treatise never written.[1] That is why the first book, the only complete history of language and quest for a 'perfect idiom' ever written until then, has always received greater critical attention;[2] I too shall concentrate on this part, because it is the one which offers the greatest 'circumstantial similarity' ('DBVJ', 17) with Joyce's *Finnegans Wake*. After a brief outline of the contents of the *De vulgari eloquentia*, I shall look in this chapter at how Joyce uses Dante's history of the creation of language and of Babelic confusion; then, in chapter 3, I shall turn to how *Finnegans Wake* exploits Dante's conception of the 'redemptive' illustrious vernacular.

The subject of Dante's enquiry and its originality are stated from the outset: 'Cum neminem ante nos de vulgaris eloquentie doctrina

quicquam inveniamus tractasse' ('Since we do not find that anyone
has dealt with the theory of the vulgar tongue [vernacular language,
or eloquence in the vernacular] before us', *Dve* i.i, 1); the vernacular
under investigation is thus defined:

vulgarem locutionem appellamus eam qua infantes assuefiunt ab assisten-
tibus, cum primitus distinguere voces incipiunt; vel, quod brevius dici
potest, vulgarem locutionem asserimus, quam sine omni regula nutricem
imitantes accipimus.   (*Dve* i.i, 2)

(We call the vulgar tongue that to which children become accustomed
through those who are about them when they first begin to distinguish
sounds; or, to put it more shortly, we assert that the vulgar tongue is that
which we acquire without any rule by imitating our nurses.)

This 'natural' idiom learned from birth is then distinguished from
Latin ('gramatica'), a language that Dante considers to be 'artificial'
and therefore less noble than the vernacular (*Dve* i.i, 4). Dante traces
the history of the vernacular back to its origins – indeed, to the
origins of language itself: language was given to man at creation,
and God endowed man alone with its faculty because neither angels
(pure intellects who communicate directly through God) nor animals
(who lack rationality) need it (i.ii).

The next questions are, who the first speaker was (Adam), and
what he said; according to Dante, the first word uttered by the first
man must have been God's name, 'El' (*Dve* i.iv). After Babel, Adam's
sacred language remained only with the sons of Heber, who had not
taken part in the construction of the tower, so that Jesus Christ, born
among the Jews, descendants of Heber, would speak not in the
language of confusion but in the language of grace. This implies that
the original language must have been Hebrew: 'Fuit ergo hebraicum
ydioma illud quod primi loquentis labia fabricarunt' ('Therefore
Hebrew was the language formed by the lips of the first speaker', *Dve*
i.vi, 7). As we shall see later, Dante adopts a different point of view in
Paradiso XXVI.

Dante then gives a vivid account of the building of the tower of
Babel and its outcome (*Dve* i.vii; I shall look at it in more detail
later). After Babel the people scattered and languages began to
decay and change. The people who came to Europe brought with
them a threefold idiom (*ydioma tripharium, Dve* i.viii, 2) and settled,
some in the south of Europe, others in the north, and a third body,
now called Greek, partly in Europe and partly in Asia. The idiom
spoken in the south of Europe split into three further languages: the

language of 'sì' ('yes' in Italian), the language of 'oc' (in Provençal) and the language of 'oïl' (in French). Why do languages continue to diversify? According to Dante's interpretation, God's punishment of the sin of Babel made men forget the original sacred language, so that new idioms had to be invented; but since man is a 'most unstable and changeable animal' (*Dve* i.ix, 6), these newly invented languages must also be unstable and changeable. To make up for the impossibility of communicating across time and space, men later also devised an artificial, conventional and unchanging language called 'grammar', or Latin (*Dve* i.ix, 11).

The rest of the enquiry concerns the language of 'sì', according to Dante the best because, in his reversal of chronological and genetic precedence, it was the one on which the artificial 'grammar' was founded. There are fourteen main dialects in Italy but, Dante explains, sub-differences amount to over a thousand (*Dve* i.x): is there one among them that can be called *the* Italian language? A quest now begins, for which Dante uses different metaphors: it is first a 'hunt' in the 'wood' of the dialects, then a 'sifting' of them. The main Italian dialects are examined methodically one by one, offering many examples and demonstrating Dante's ability to perceive different inflections. However, all the dialects are found to be inadequate and rejected, including Florentine (*Dve* i.xi), and at the end of this first phase of the quest the metaphor of the hunt is taken up again to compare this sought-for Italian language to a 'beautiful panther' (*Dve* i.xvi) that leaves its scent everywhere but cannot be seen anywhere; in the same way, the Italian language cannot be found anywhere but all dialects carry some scent of it. If this noble idiom cannot be found empirically, then its nature must be inferred rationally; Dante defines it as 'illustre, cardinale, aulicum et curiale' ('illustrious, cardinal, courtly and curial') and claims that it is the one by which all other Italian dialects are measured, weighed and compared (*Dve* i.xvi, 6). The meaning of the attributes of the Italian vernacular will be discussed in detail in the next chapter; first, we need to turn back to the moment when disaster struck – but was it really disaster?

RETEMPTER

Dante's account of the building of the tower of Babel and of its consequences is especially interesting for a reading of *Finnegans Wake*, a text in which the issue of Babelic confusion and linguistic difference acquires a central narrative and thematic position. While the *Wake* generally refers directly to the Biblical narrative of the episode (or indeed to no text in particular: the shared oral tradition is often enough), at times it also seems to filter references to the episode through Dante's medieval version.

The story of Babel is 'retaled' (*FW* 3.17) in the *De vulgari eloquentia* with great originality, and Dante adds many lively details to the Biblical version. This is how the episode is introduced:

O semper nostra natura prona peccatis, o ab initio et nunquam desinens nequitatrix! Num fuerat satis ad tui correptionem, quod per primam prevaricationem eluminata, delitiarum exulabas a patria? Num satis, quod per universalem familie tue luxuriem et trucitatem, unica reservata domo, quicquid tui iuris erat cataclismo perierat, et que commiseras tu, animalia celique terreque iam luerant? Quippe satis extiterat. Sed sicut proverbia-liter dici solet, 'Non ante tertium equitabis', misera miserum venire maluisti ad equum. Ecce, lector, quod vel oblitus homo vel vilipendens disciplinas priores et avertens oculos a vibicibus que remanserant, tertio insurrexit ad verbera, per superbam stultitiam presumendo.   (*Dve* i.vii, 2–3)

(O human nature, ever prone to sin, wicked from the start and forever afterwards! Was it not sufficient for your correction that, deprived of light for your first transgression, you were exiled from your delightful homeland? Was it not sufficient that because of the universal lust and cruelty of your kind, excepting one single household, all that was under your dominion perished in the flood, and that the animals of the earth and the sky had already been punished for the evil deeds which you had committed? Indeed this should have been enough. But, as the proverb says, 'You shall not ride till the third attempt', you, wretched, chose to ride a wretched horse. See, reader, how man, either forgetting or despising his former discipline, and turning his eyes from the marks of the whiplashes that still remained, for the third time rose up to be whipped, presuming in his foolish pride!)

Dante's passionate apostrophe to man's sinful nature closely relates the episode of Babel to the two main former sins: the original fall of Adam and Eve and the wickedness of the entire race punished by the flood and the consequent death of all living beings with the exception of one single household ('unica reservata domo'). The construction of the tower of Babel was the third great sin of humankind, and, for the third time, humankind was punished as a whole. The symbolic value of number three is well known: it is the number of completion or fulfilment, a magical number and the number of the Trinity, and numeric symbolism in all of Dante's works is very important.[3] Human perfection is in fact often associated with number four, and three is reserved for the spiritual or the divine; but in the passage quoted, Dante sarcastically insists upon the 'spiritual' significance and perfection of human number three and illustrates the recurrence of sin through a popular proverb: at last, after two attempts, men succeeded in 'riding the wretched horse', achieving the ultimate iniquity which won them the harshest punishment, the loss of the sacred tongue of Adam. Thus Babel acquires the aura of the worst sin, as it were the 'most perfect' in its wickedness.

In the previous chapters, Dante had explained that language is the faculty that distinguishes men from both animals and angels: it was created in Eden together with Adam's soul, in an indissoluble link: 'certam formam locutionis a Deo cum anima prima concreatam fuisse' ('a certain form of speech was created by God together with the first soul', *Dve* i.vi, 4). What Adam was granted, then, was more than just the faculty of speech: 'Dico autem "formam" et quantum ad rerum vocabula et quantum ad vocabulorum constructionem et quantum ad constructionis prolationem' ('And I say "a form" with reference to the words for things, to the grammatical construction of these words, and to the inflexions of this grammatical construction', *Dve* i.vi, 4). Critics disagree about the right interpretation of Dante's words: is it a complete language or, as Umberto Eco interprets it, a set of principles for a universal grammar, something more than a faculty but less than a natural language?[4] Because it was God-given, this 'forma locutionis' was perfect and could not change unless by divine intervention, as indeed happened at Babel: 'Hac forma locutionis locutus est Adam; hac forma locutionis locuti sunt omnes posteri eius usque ad edificationem turris Babel, que turris confusionis interpretatur.' ('In this form of speech spoke Adam, and in this form of speech spoke his descendants until the building of the tower of Babel, which is interpreted [translated] as the tower of confusion', *Dve* i.vi, 5). In the *Divine Comedy*, however, Dante puts forward a different view regarding two issues: whether man is granted a complete language or the faculty of speech, and whether the language spoken by Adam was the same that men spoke until Babel. In *Purgatorio* xxv Dante learns from Statius that each soul is endowed with the faculty of speech – not a formed language – at the moment of its creation. In his explanation about the generation of man, Statius first tells of the progression of the foetus from the vegetative and sensitive phase, and then comes to the development of rationality:

> Ma come d'animal divegna fante,
> non vedi tu ancor . . .   (*Purg* xxv, 61–2)

Charles Singleton translates this line as, 'But how from animal it becomes a human being you do not see yet',[5] and indeed Dante had explained in the *De vulgari eloquentia* that what distinguishes men from animals is rationality, and that men, unlike animals (who do not speak), need a rational and sensitive means of communication (*Dve* I.iii, 1). But the word that Dante now uses to define the 'human being' is 'fante', from the Latin *fari* ('I speak'), and a literal translation would therefore have to read, 'but how from animal it becomes a speaker, you do not see yet': rationality and faculty of speech are thus closely related. Only at this point does God infuse the living breath into the foetus, so that it may become a single, unified soul ('fassi un'alma sola', *Purg* xxv, 74), uniting its three faculties. One of the implications that can be drawn from this bond of reason, language and soul is that the loss of the integrity of the soul (with the original sin) must have inevitably entailed the loss of the integrity of language – which brings us to the second point of Dante's revision of his theory of language in the *Divine Comedy*. In canto xxvi of the *Paradiso*, Adam replies to Dante's questions about the original language and explains:

> La lingua ch'io parlai fu tutta spenta
> innanzi che a l'ovra inconsummabile
> fosse la gente di Nembròt attenta . . .   (*Par* xxvi, 124–6)

(The tongue that I spoke was all extinguished before the people of Nimrod were engaged in their unaccomplishable work . . .)

Whereas in the *De vulgari eloquentia* Babel engenders both linguistic mutability (corruption of the original) and linguistic plurality (multiplication of tongues), in the *Commedia* it marks the beginning only of plurality, and the introduction of changeability and decay is, perhaps more coherently, already attributed to the first fall also as far as the language is concerned (significantly, in the *Divine Comedy* it is Adam's task to explain both the original sin and the loss of the original language);[6] what still remains is the very close connection between soul and language. In the *De vulgari eloquentia* the parallel between first and third sins is also emphasised by the fact that whereas we can say that the flood punished a generalised evil rather than a particular sin, in the cases of both the Fall and Babel men's fault was a very specific *praesumptio*, the desire to reach a divine condition and be as great as, if not greater than, God.

The question of the original language and its relationship with the Fall and with Babelic confusion plays an important role also in the thematic and linguistic texture of *Finnegans Wake*, in which the first three sins are foregrounded from the first three paragraphs: the first hundred-letter word, in a context where various 'falls' are recalled, starts with a 'stuttering' evocation of Babel ('bababadal', *FW* 3.15), also a polyglot onomatopoetic (as well as semantic) rendering of the thunder symbolising the voice of God which can be read either as a Vichian announcement of the end of one age and the coming of the next, or, Biblically, as God's wrath for the sins of men (or, on a more 'realistic' level, one could suppose that the thunder may announce heavy rains and thus hint at the flood which, in the previous paragraph is evoked but has 'not yet' happened: 'passencore [*pas encore*, French 'not yet'] . . . not yet . . . not yet . . . Rot [also 'not'] a peck of pa's malt had Jhem or Shen brewed [hinting at Noah's distilling of the first wine] by arclight and rory end to the regginbrow [rainbow, cf. German *regenbogen*] was to be seen ringsome on the aquaface', *FW* 3.04–14).

The original sin is hinted at from the very first words of the *Wake* through the names of the sinners: 'riverrun, past Eve and Adam's' (*FW* 3.01); the direct reference is to the Franciscan church known as 'Adam and Eve', on the right bank of the river Liffey, but what is particularly interesting, especially after Beckett's comments on Dante's 'curious mistake', is the inversion of the names, 'Eve and Adam's'. We may recall that the 'mistake' imputed to Dante is the notion expressed in the *De vulgari eloquentia* that the Bible records that the first speaker was Eve when she addressed the serpent, whereas, Dante emphasises, we must rationally infer that it can only have been a man, therefore Adam. Of course, Beckett points out, nowhere does the Bible say that Eve was the first to speak and that animals had already been given names by Adam ('DBVJ' 20). As I pointed out in the Prelude, the bracketed passage in which Beckett engages in this argument with Dante, following a mocking reference to readers unable to understand the *Wake* and the nature of its language, is apparently disjointed from its context, but I would surmise that the connection may rest in the parallel that Beckett has been drawing between Dante's and Joyce's innovative languages and their quest for the antecedents of such innovation and simultaneous rejection of such authority: Dante finds them in the Bible (in the story of Adam which, in his 'curious mistake', he criticises and inverts), Joyce (among other sources) in Dante and Dante's 'curious' reading of the Bible, which he turns over through the vulgarisation, in a literal way, of Dante's noble vernacular. There may be another circumstantial reason for quoting the words from the *De vulgari eloquentia* that signal what Beckett calls Dante's amusing incredulity: Eve's act of speaking is described in the treatise as 'foemina profluisse', and the evocation of the 'flowing forth' (*pro* + *fluere*) of a woman's speech may reflect back on to the curious inversions, textual recirculations and flowing parallels of the *Wake* and recall the flux of Anna Livia's language, especially in her final flowing monologue which 'recirculates' to the 'riverrun' and the 'curious' inversion of the first line. This vocal flux also involves a shift from the female voice of the last pages to the apparently male one of the beginning, although this 'male' voice may still retain something of Anna Livia's vocal presence (and of Dante's opposite male-oriented 'mistake'?) in the anteposition of Eve's name to Adam's. Significantly, the title chosen for the Italian translation of the 'ALP' chapter (1.8), which Joyce wrote with the help of Nino Frank and, later, of Ettore Settanni, was 'I fiumi scorrono', literally 'the rivers run' or 'flow', which links the opening of the *Wake* with the flowing of ALP's voice. I shall come back to the (feminine) river of words later in the book, but, in this context, another intriguing detail that deserves to be mentioned is Boccaccio's definition of the *Divine Comedy* as 'a great river, shallow enough for lambs to paddle in, and yet deep enough for an elephant to swim'.[7]

   Adam and Eve's fault was declared a *felix culpa* by St Augustine, insofar as it enabled God to demonstrate his infinite mercy, and men to achieve a deeper awareness of the significance of sin and of salvation. There are several allusions to the 'happy fault' in *Finnegans Wake*, and the connection that it establishes between fall and rebirth – indeed, the stress on the necessity of redemption being already implicit in the sin – makes it one of the major structural notions underlying the novel.[8] The motif appears for the first time just after the episode of the Prankquean (*FW* 21.05–23.15) as 'O foenix culprit!' (*FW* 23.16). Following the 'skirtmisshes' (*FW* 21.19) between the Prankquean and Jarl van Hoother – skirmishes that involve female clothing and thus anticipate both the 'clothiering' of feminine fictions and textual polysemy analysed in the previous chapter and the skirt that the twins will lift in *FW* ii.3 to discover the mystery of the mother's sex, to which I shall come back in chapter 4 – the story ends on a note of restoration of peace and of general welfare for the whole town, summed up in the rewriting of the motto of Dublin city (*Obedientia civium urbis felicitas*) as 'Thus the hearsomeness of the burger felicitates the whole of the polis' (*FW* 23.14–15). On a similar note, the following paragraph expresses relief and admiration for the way good follows from evil: 'O foenix culprit! Ex nickylow malo comes mickelmassed bonum' (*FW* 23.16–17). On the protean page of the *Wake*, the Augustinian formula has however much larger and ambiguous implications, evoking for instance both the legendary phoenix that rises from its own ashes after its death as well as Dublin's largest park, on the banks of the river Liffey, the Phoenix Park where H. C. Earwicker allegedly commits his sin. This sin, the 'culpa', is transformed by metonymy into the 'culprit', and Phoenix Park is assimilated to the garden of Eden where the first, original fault was committed; the 'culprit', that is, is both Adam and HCE, and the following sentence puns on the double meaning of 'malo' (Latin *malum*, both 'evil' and 'apple') and can be read either as a sort of general rule (good follows from evil) or as a more precise reference to Adam and Eve's eating of the apple and its 'happy' consequence.

Now, whereas the original sin and the flood have already found a solution – the former through God's sacrifice of himself through the Son Jesus Christ and his death on the cross, the latter in the covenant symbolised by the rainbow – the sin of Babel is still unredeemed and languages are still confused. However, in the *De vulgari eloquentia*, Dante implies that this redemption is possible. God is the loving father who punishes – or rather, mercifully corrects ('pia correctione') – out of love and for the good of his sons ('non hostili scutica, sed paterna'). In his encompassing design, every episode moves towards a final good:

O sine mensura clementia celestis imperii! Quis patrum tot sustineret insultus a filio? Sed exurgens non hostili scutica, sed paterna et alias verberibus assueta, rebellantem filium pia correctione necnon memorabili castigavit.

(*Dve* i.vii, 5)

(O boundless clemency of the heavenly power! What father would tolerate such insults from a son? But, rising up not with the scourge of an enemy but that of a father, already accustomed to dealing blows, he chastised his rebellious son with a correction at once charitable and memorable.)

The sin committed at Babel is another *felix culpa*, this time a linguistic one, and one which still has to produce its 'happy' outcome: Dante, implicitly, steps forth to accomplish this task. I need to point out here that this reading of Dante as self-fashioned redeemer is not common among his critics. A well-established line of criticism regards the *De vulgari eloquentia* as the work in which Dante seeks to overcome the impasse of the corruption of language and of the multilingualism originated at Babel by means of a noble illustrious vernacular,[9] but none of these critics interprets Dante's view of the sin of Babel as a linguistic *felix culpa*, or Dante as a self-appointed 'redeemer'; the *vulgare illustre* is, rather, a patch, a piece of remedial work to limit the damage done. Robert Hollander, on the contrary, links Dante's views of Babel and of the primal sin when he states that one of Dante's goals is 'to return to the vernacular its God-given properties as the language of Grace', which he would achieve, at least metaphorically, in the *Divine Comedy* by relating childish speech, his own vernacular and the primal speech of Adam. 'In short', Hollander writes, 'one might argue that Dante's amazingly ambitious linguistic program involves the theoretical justification of the vernacular in the realms of nature and theology, and the practical justification of the vernacular in the realm of art, where it will be shown to be as capable of *regular* use as Latin.'[10] Hollander explicitly describes Dante's theories in terms of 'linguistic fall', but for him Dante's position is that it is 'gramatica', and not the vernacular, that can provide 'a sort of redemption of the linguistic "Fall"'.[11] However, Dante has explained that after the confusion of languages which made it impossible for men to communicate through time and space, 'grammar' (Latin) was *invented* in order to restore the possibility of communication, and it is therefore an artificial language, unchangeable and incorruptible, rationally constructed on fixed rules but not natural to men ('Hinc moti sunt inventores gramatice facultatis; que quidem gramatica nichil aliud est quam quedam inalterabilis locutionis idemptitas diversis temporibus atque locis'; 'This is what moved the inventors of the art of grammar, which is nothing else but an inalterable identity of speech in different times and places', *Dve*, I.ix, 11). Of the two varieties, it is the vernacular tongue that is presented in the *De vulgari eloquentia* as the nobler ('nobilior', *Dve* I.i, 4), and although this interpretation is reversed in the *Convivio*, there is no hint, in either treatise, that it is Latin that can provide a redemption of the linguistic fall. The possibility of redemption, it seems clear to me, is not in Latin but in a language that still needs to be fashioned and formalised by the poet, what Dante defines as the 'vulgare illustre, cardinale, aulicum et curiale'. In this project Dante figures as the 'redeemer' of a linguistic fault that can thus turn out to be 'happy'; through this planned 'redemption', the vernacular will be shown to be not just as capable of regular use as Latin, but superior to Latin, in that it is natural and coextensive with man's rational nature.

The interpretation of the *De vulgari eloquentia* as an attempt to 'redeem' Babel has been altogether rejected by other critics; Ileana Pagani, for instance, opposes what she calls the 'religious–philosophical–metaphysical' reading, and argues that Dante does not aspire to recuperate an idealistic Edenic condition, and therefore does not reject concrete dialectal and linguistic differences; on the contrary, these differences constitute his necessary starting point and he fully accepts them.[12] While most of Pagani's conclusions are convincing and I agree with her interpretation of the *De vulgari eloquentia* as not seeking to return to pre-Babelic conditions, I find it difficult to accept her hostility to any interpretation of Babel as a sinful and negative moment in the linguistic history of mankind. The point is not to recuperate an inevitably lost condition, which would indeed be impossible, but rather to redeem men – insofar as they are users of language – from a sin which has caused the loss of the pre-Babelic condition, in the same way as Christ's Redemption does not establish again the Edenic prelapsarian condition (nor does it make the original sin a lesser fault, 'happy' though it may have been) but offers to man the opportunity to achieve purity again through the knowledge and the experience of sin. In fact, I would say that Babel needs to be a sin in order for Dante to cast himself in the role of redeemer.

Umberto Eco has recently proposed an interpretation similar to the one I am sketching here:

an illustrious vernacular . . . was, to Dante, the only way in which a modern poet might heal the wound of Babel . . . Out of this bold conception for the restoration of a perfect language, and of his own role within it, comes a celebration of the quasi-biological force displayed by language's capacity to change and renew itself over time instead of a lament over the multiplicity of tongues. The assertion of language's creativity, after all, stands at the base of Dante's own project to create a perfect, modern, natural language, without recourse to a dead language as a model . . . Thus Dante puts forth his own candidacy as a new (and more perfect) Adam.[13]

There are some problems in Eco's view of Dante casting himself in the role of Adam, and other problems generally in Dante's position that remain unsolved: Adam named things, but Dante finds them already named – what he is implicitly aspiring to is to become not a new Adam but a new Christ. What he can 'invent' is the universality of the natural tongue through the formulation of a set of rules that everyone would have to respect, but given the 'most unstable and changeable' (*Dve* i.ix, 6) nature of man, surely he could not hope for his universalising rules to last. In fact, while Dante has to emphasise, as Eco points out, the quasi-biological nature of language that will in theory allow him to achieve a modern universal idiom, at the same time he is in practice caught in the paradox that this very linguistic organicism will quickly 'age' and thus make his model obsolete. It is this impasse that probably led Dante to abandon the project; but again – somewhat similarly to his brushing aside the problems implicit in his application of the four levels of exegesis to his poetry in the *Convivio* (and later in the *Epistle to Can Grande*, if indeed he wrote it) in order to make a point about the near-sacredness of (his own) non-Scriptural poetry and establish an exegetical model for it – it is not the feasibility of the project or its logicality that matters, but the assertion of a principle: that the poet has the solution, that poetry is the solution (albeit permanently 'in progress'), that the struggle goes on and the poet – despite all his disclaimers – will not bend his head before God's judgement and will take upon himself the messianic role. Blake was right: the poet is satanic, and, as we shall see, in his pride and Ulyssean deviousness (Ulyssean 'poly-tropy'?) Dante comes perilously close, like Shem to Lucifer, like HCE to Nimrod and to the fallen Adam; if he is a *redemptor*, he is also a 'retempter' (*FW* 154.06), successfully saving the language fallen through pride by successfully tempting himself into the sin of pride (as we know, Stephen himself is not immune from donning the roles of both Christ and Lucifer).

Thus, despite the linguistic and ideological discrepancies between the *De vulgari eloquentia* and the *Convivio*, where it is Latin that is declared nobler than the vernacular,[14] the whole conception and structure of the latter (the choice to write it in Italian and to apply the theory of the four levels of meaning to vernacular poetry) is part of the same project of 'redemption' as the rules of vernacular poetic composition of the former. The language thus refined would not and could not be the same as the perfect language spoken before Babel, but it can be just as good in harmony, nobility and expressiveness. If this project were realised, then the sin of Babel would be expiated, the language redeemed, and the fault would truly have been happy – and, as suggested by my second epigraph, Babel could even be called a 'confusalem', the site of the death and redemption of language as Jerusalem was of the soul of man. The closing lines of the first book of the *Convivio* also show the sense of the religious task of the poet and of the sacredness of (*his*) language:

Questo sarà luce nuova, sole nuovo, lo quale surgerà là dove l'usato tramonterà, e darà lume a coloro che sono in tenebre e in oscuritade per lo usato sole che a loro non luce. (*Conv* i.xiii, 12)

(This shall be the new light, the new sun, which shall rise where the old shall set, and shall give light to those who are in darkness and in obscurity for the old sun that does not shine for them.)

The very ambitious task of the poet/theorist in the *De vulgari eloquentia* is to make 'the new light, the new sun' of the language rise and shine: the poet is the light-giver, light-bringer – a Lucifer who models his words on the language of the Scriptures[15] and translates the light of Christ's coming into the light of the advent of the new language, and the Saviour's miracle of the multiplication of bread into the poet's bestowing of knowledge: 'Questo sarà quello pane orzato del quale si satolleranno migliaia, e a me ne soperchieranno le sporte piene' ('This shall be that barley bread that will satiate the multitudes, and my baskets will be full and overflowing with it', *Conv* i.xiii, 12).

As we have seen, Beckett quotes Dante's words on the language as 'new light' in 'Dante. . . Bruno. Vico. . Joyce' as an appropriate description of Joyce's renewal of the formal characteristic of literary language ('DBVJ' 19–20); Dante is thus by implication given the role of inspiring light for Joyce's new language, but there we find the usual ironic counterpoint: 'the new light, the new sun' is turned into the obscure language of the 'nightynovel' (*FW* 54.21), thereby circularly placing again this self-fashioned, presumptuous light-bringer at the centre of darkness (like the 'real' Lucifer in Dante's *Inferno*).

In another typical instance of circumstantial similarity, like Dante's works, *Finnegans Wake* also links echoes of the tower of Babel or its consequences with references to the original sin as *felix culpa*. After all, for both Dante and Joyce, Babel may be said to be the happy event which justifies their work: without the confusion of the tongues, neither the *De vulgari eloquentia* nor the *Wake* would have been written. Thus it is not by coincidence, I think, that the 'Nightlesson' of *Finnegans Wake* (chapter II.2) echoes and parodies the concrete example of (already pre-Babelian) linguistic change that Adam gives Dante in *Paradiso* XXVI, the evolution of the word used for God's name from 'I' into 'El': in the *Wake*, the identification of God's name as 'El' (*FW* 246.06)[16] is queried (it appears in the form of a question) and is followed shortly by references to Babel (*FW* 246.11) and to the *felix culpa* motif ('felixed is who culpas does', *FW* 246.31), in an indirect confirmation both of Dante's link between original language, original sin and Babelic confusion, and of the possibility of reading Babel as another *felix culpa*. Indeed this last quotation actively encourages sin on the grounds that it will make the sinner happy, insisting on the simultaneous presence of redemption and confusion that this chapter's second epigraph also evokes.

If the tower of Babel is an equivalent of the original sin, a re-enactment of the Fall, then the various characters or actors or caricatures that take part in the 'drame' (*FW* 302.31–2) must be involved in some form of role-playing, of being themselves and embodying someone else (or something else) at the same time; and we need therefore to start looking at the Nimrodic roles of Dante's works and of Joyce's, at the *culpa* and the culprits, and at the tower itself. This analysis will continue in the next chapter with the saviours and the remedies; for the moment I shall still concentrate on the *pars destruens* of Dante's treatise and the blurring of roles that both texts suggest.

AWFUL TORS AND VISIONBUILDERS

During the trial of Festy King in chapter I.4 (a situation in which the identities of the accused and of the witness are confused and keep shifting as the two structural oppositions of the book, warring brothers and father/son, are superimposed on to the trial), the theme of Babel and the 'happy fault' motif are drawn together when the witness 'W.P.' is cross-examined and is asked whether the initials of the names of HCE add up to HERE COMES EVERY-BODY. The witness's reply – 'Holy Saint Eiffel, the very phoenix!' (*FW* 88.23–4) – can be read in more than one way: it could be an exclamation followed by the requested identification (such as could be, 'Holy Jesus, yes, that's the very man!'), but the entire sentence could also identify HCE with both the tower and the phoenix. HCE is a sort of towering giant who recalls Dante's Nimrod, described in the *Inferno* as a gigantic tower forming, among the other giants, what looks like the betowered, fortified wall around the town of Monteriggioni:

> me parve veder molte alte torri;
>
>   . . .
>
> 'sappi che non son torri, ma giganti'
>
>   . . .
>
> però che, come su la cerchia tonda
> Monteriggion di torri si corona,
> così la proda che 'l pozzo circonda
>   torreggiavan di mezza la persona
> li orribili giganti . . .   (*Inf* XXXI, 20–44)

(I thought I saw many tall towers . . . 'know that these are not towers, but giants' . . . for, as on its round circle [wall] Monteriggioni crowns itself with towers, so did the horrible giants . . . tower with half their bodies over the bank that encircles the pit . . .)

As 'Eiffel Tower', HCE is a modern giant perpetrating a modern sin, and both the giant and the fault are 'holy' and 'felix' ('phoenix' has acquired this overtone since 'O foenix culprit', *FW* 23.16), like the phoenix foreshadowing rebirth. In 'O foenix culprit' fault and culprit dovetail through a metonymy that transforms the action into the agent; now, following Dante's suggestion in *Inf* XXXI, the trope conflates the agent and his attributes (Nimrod and his tallness) with the material product of the action (the tower).

A more complex compounding of motifs and themes occurs in chapter III.3, yet another trial, when Yawn is examined by the four old men. During the questioning HCE intervenes (or is summoned), his version of the story is broadcast, and his words alternate at times with those of a TV speaker. HCE begs ALP to pity him ('Pity poor Haveth Childers Everywhere with Mudder!' 535.34–5), but the speaker interrupts him in a patronising and scornful voice, and explains, drawing Babelic confusion and *felix culpa* together again:[17]

He has had some indiejestings, poor thing, for quite a little while, confused
by his tonguer of baubble. A way with him! Poor Felix Culapert!

$$(FW\,536.07-9)$$

If 'Haveth Childers Everywhere' is Adam, the father of all, 'indiejestings' may also refer to the eating of the apple which caused a very
severe spiritual 'indigestion' to Adam and Eve and their descendants.
The indigestion seems however to have been taken as a sort of joke –
'in the jesting' – combining mirth and the ensuing sorrow or pain in
yet another reverberation of the motto from Giordano Bruno's
Candelaio, 'In tristitia hilaris, in hilaritate tristis'. Another layer of
meaning is brought to bear on the passage by the echo of Oliver
Cromwell's retort 'Away with these baubles'.[18] The obscene pun on
culpa or 'culprit' in 'Poor Felix Culapert' probably comes from the
Italian *culo aperto* (literally, 'open arse'), a vulgar expression alluding
to sodomy, also used when somebody is reproached, punished or
subjected in a harsh, humiliating manner. This of course applies to
Adam and Eve and to the men after Babel, but in context it takes a
political colouring: HCE is the representative of the Irish race,
conquered and humiliated by Cromwell, yet *felix* in its subjected
state, self-pitying and acquiescent, incapable of 'manly' reaction.
Obedience, after all, is the motto of Dublin city ('obedientia civium
urbis felicitas'), and the motifs of the *felix culpa* and Dublin's motto
often appear together, favoured by the cognate words *felix* and *felicitas*
(the connection is further enriched through Milton's *Paradise Lost*,
whose first line, 'Of man's first disobedience, and the fruit', is
parodied in the *Wake*, for instance at *FW* 343.36).

After HCE's appeal for pity and the speaker's interposition, the
'Communicator' (HCE himself) advocates order and peacefulness in
a long speech in which he mentions a version of Dublin's motto:
'Obeyance from the townsmen spills felixity by the toun' (*FW*
540.25–6) that suggests plentiful, overspilling happiness on condition
that the citiziens practise acquiescent obeyance – presumably to his
law. He goes on praising his own achievements in the city and, in
particular, the building of a cathedral with high spires and towers:

by awful tors my wellworth building sprang sky spearing spires, cloud
cupoled campaniles: further this. By fineounce and imposts I got and grew
and by grossscruple gat I grown outreachesly: murage and lestage were my
mains for Ouerlord's tithing . . .   (*FW* 541.05–9)

The repeated allusions to the building of the tower of Babel are
masked under the building of a cathedral, an achievement made

possible by raising money through unscrupulous taxation, financial speculation, cheating ('fineounce and imposts'). The tone betrays the material intent of money-making beneath the hypocritical boasting of a pious purpose, remindful among other things of medieval lords building churches to 'expiate' their sins, and erecting palaces with high towers that would top those of their neighbours in order to manifest their greatness, a practice evoked by several passages in the *Comedy*, not least in the canto of Nimrod. The Eiffel Tower returns also in this passage ('awful tors'), turning the building into a proud attempt to outrageously outreach ('outreachesly') anything previously built – what the men who built the tower of Babel also wanted to do – and to pierce the sky with its spires, rather than build monuments to heaven's praise. The sexual allusions ('I got and grew and by grossscruple gat I grown out-reachesly') liken the building of the tower to a sexual erection. In the geography of *Finnegans Wake*, the Wellington memorial in Phoenix Park is Finn MacCool's penis; it may be worth recalling that Wellington was a son of Ireland who had led the British empire to many victories – the most famous was of course that over Napoleon at Waterloo – and it is therefore ironic that HCE should see the memorial as a sign of 'ruru redemption' (*FW* 36.24–5). The sexual allusions together with the possible reference to the Wellington memorial connect this passage to HCE's 'fall' in Phoenix Park, although the violence of the language ('sprang', 'sky spearing spires', 'outreachesly') suggest rape rather than the milder sin of voyeurism and exposure of himself with which he is more often associated in the contexts of the episode that is supposed to have taken place in the Park, and hint instead at a much more serious offence, linked in turn to other roles that HCE can also acquire, such as that of the invaders penetrating into Ireland through the river Liffey.

The excerpt from *FW* 541.05–9 that I have quoted above echoes an earlier passage from *Finnegans Wake*, the first description of the building of the tower of Babel that we encounter in the novel, dovetailing with the story of Tim Finnegan:

Bygmester Finnegan, of the Stuttering Hand, freemen's maurer, lived in the broadest way immarginable . . . and during mighty odd years this man of hod, cement and edifices in Toper's Thorp piled buildung supra buildung pon the banks for the livers by the Soangso. He addle liddle phifie Annie ugged the little craythur. Wither hayre in honds tuck up your part inher.

Oftwhile balbulous, mithre ahead, with goodly trowel in grasp and ivoroiled overalls which he habitacularly fondseed, like Haroun Childeric Eggeberth he would caligulate by multiplicables the alltitude and malltitude until he seesaw by neatlight of the liquor wheretwin 'twas born, his roundhead staple of other days to rise in undress maisonry upstanded (joygrantit!), a waalworth of a skyerscape of most eyeful hoyth entowerly, erigenating from next to nothing and celescalating the himals and all, hierarchitectitiptitoploftical, with a burning bush abob off its baubletop and with larrons o'toolers clittering up and tombles a'buckets clottering down.   (*FW* 4.18–5.04)

The Eiffel Tower returns ('eyeful hoyth entowerly'), as well as the Woolworth Building in New York, skyscrapers in general and references to the activity of building. The sexual allusion is present too, together with the pattern of growing and expanding ('tuck up your part inher'; 'he would caligulate by multiplicables the alltitude and malltitude . . . to rise in undress maisonry upstanded (joy-grantit!) . . . with a burning bush abob off its baubletop'). The same web of associations can be found in several other passages in the *Wake*. In chapter II.3, for instance, drunkenness (e.g. 'liquid courage'), building (see for instance 'scaffolding'), finance and commerce ('bullyon', 'fight great finnence'), tower of Babel ('ba-beling'), Eiffel Tower ('towerds', 'deiffel'), Fall and foul sin ('foully fallen'), creation ('leaden be light') are once again intertwined in a single sentence (*FW* 313.29–314.06), followed by the thump of a fall ('Bump!', *FW* 314.07) and another thunderword (*FW* 314.08–9). Similar, very synthetic, conflation of themes can also be found for example in 'this habby cyclic erdor be outraciously enviolated' (*FW* 285.01–2), where an echo of the motto of Dublin city can be heard together with the references to the sexual violence and to the outrageous attempt to reach heaven.

If HCE can be a tower like Dante's Nimrod (in the passage quoted above his intials identify him with the construction itself: 'this man of hod, cement and edifices'), other traits also identify the two: like Nimrod, HCE is a giant and a hunter, speaks a confused language, and is described in ways that explicitly recall the biblical builder of the Tower:

Ever read of that greatgrand landfather of our visionbuilders, Baaboo, the bourgeoismeister, who thought to touch both himmels at the punt of his risen stiffstaff and how wishywashy sank the waters of his thought?

(*FW* 191.34–192.01)

The project, or vision, whose construction he inspired, was an attempt to reach heaven – likened once again to a sexual erection ('his risen stiffstaff') – inevitably followed, as in the rule of *contrapasso*, by a fall ('sank'). Of course Dante himself could be described as the (greatgrand)father of all visions, the town 'master' (he was a *priore* of Florence before the exile) whose inspiration to reach heaven came from Love (God, Beatrice). (More on Dante as Nimrod in the next chapter.)

In chapter II.3, Butt also links together tower, ascending/descending movement, vulgarity and building activity in the story of the Russian General (see *FW* 344.13–17; I shall discuss this episode in detail in the next chapter). But in this role, HCE must be seen as the protagonist of yet another fall, preceding that of Nimrod, preceding even that of Adam: the fall of the rebel angels led by Lucifer. It is another sin of pride, an outrageous attempt to reach higher followed by the inevitable contrapuntal fall. The episodes follow the same pattern, and the *Wake* weaves them together:

This wastohavebeen underground heaven, or mole's paradise which was probably also an inversion of a phallopharos, intended to foster wheat crops and to ginger up tourist trade (its architect, Mgr Peurelachasse, having been obcaecated lest he should petrifake suchanevver while the contractors Messrs T. A. Birkett and L. O. Tuohalls were made invulnerably venerable), first in the west, our misterbilder, Castlevillainous, openly damned . . . (*FW* 76.33–77.04)

Buried in his (temporary) grave before his disappearance and 'rebirth' (first down, then up), HCE is in his inverted and not quite successful ('wastohavebeen') paradise, in turn presented as an inversion of Lucifer ('phallopharos' can be read as variations on the Italian *faro*, 'lighthouse', and the suffix *-ferous*, from the Latin *-fer*, 'bearer'; of course, as we know by now, HCE has a phallic relationship with heaven); and Lucifer, in Dante's cosmology, is at the centre of the earth, positioned upside down for those who are on their way 'up', out of Hell (cf. *Inf* xxxiv).[19] And it is clearly significant that the architect of this undergound heaven should be named after a cemetery, Père-Lachaise (and what is the world envisioned by Dante if not an immense cemetery?), where Ireland's most notorious sodomite, Oscar Wilde (in some ways, Joyce's equivalent of Dante's Brunetto), is buried.

At times, Joyce seems to be referring to the details of the building of the tower of Babel through Dante's version. In the excerpt from

FW 4.18–5.04 quoted above, one can hear echoes of Dante's account of the episode:

Siquidem pene totum humanum genus ad opus iniquitatis coierat, pars imperabant, pars architectabantur, pars muros moliebantur, pars amussibus regulabant, pars trullis linebant, pars scindere rupes, pars mari, pars terra vehere intendebant, partesque diverse diversis aliis operibus indulgebant, cum celitus tanta confusione percussi sunt, ut qui omnes una eademque loquela deserviebant ad opus, ab opere multis diversificati loquelis desinerent et nunquam ad idem commertium convenirent. Solis etenim in uno convenientibus actu eadem loquela remansit: puta cunctis architectoribus una, cunctis saxa volventibus una, cunctis ea parantibus una, et sic de singulis operantibus accidit. Quot quot autem exercitii varietates tendebant ad opus, tot tot ydiomatibus tunc genus humanum disiungitur; et quanto excellentius exercebant, tanto rudius nunc barbariusque locuntur.

(Dve I.vii, 6–7)

(For almost all of the human race had come together in this iniquitous work: some gave orders; some were the architects; some built the walls; some levelled them straight; some laid on the mortar with trowels; some cut stones; some carried it by sea, some by land; and different groups were engaged in different other jobs, when they were struck by such confusion from heaven, that all those who had been using one and the same language to attend to the same job, were estranged from their work by many different languages, and never again came together in the same activity. For the same language remained only to those who were engaged together in the same job: for instance, one for the architects; one for those that rolled the stones, one for those that prepared them; and so for each group of workers. And as many varieties of jobs as there were in the work, so the human race was accordingly divided into as many different languages; and the more excellent the job, the ruder and more barbarous the language they now spoke.)

Whereas the Bible describes the event in very few words ('And they said one to another, Go to, let us make brick, and burn them thoroughly. And they had brick for stone, and slime had they for mortar. And they said, Go to, let us build us a city and a tower whose top *may reach* unto heaven; and let us make us a name, lest we be scattered abroad upon the face of the whole earth', Genesis, 11.3–4), Dante embroiders the story with plenty of original, vivid and realistic details. The frantic activity of the builders is rendered by the accumulation of phrases beginning with the anaphora 'pars'; suddenly the parallel series is interrupted by the time clause 'cum celitus tanta confusione percussi sunt', which introduces divine intervention. The account of the consequences follows, and repetitions and parallelism return – this time, however, their function is to emphasise the differences. Epiphoric repetition now accompanies the anaphora: 'cunctis . . . una'. The stress thus laid on the word 'una' is quite ironical in its contrast with the *true* 'one' language that existed before: then everyone shared one language and one common goal; now their activity is fragmented, their language confused. The only link that remains is the common fate that condemns men to dispersion and misunderstanding. The groups are no longer parts of a larger unit ('pars') but different, separate units ('cunctis . . . una') that add to a multiplicity.

Joyce's 'description' of the building quoted above (4.18–5.04) seems to owe as much to Dante's expanded version as to the Bible. Compare, for instance, Dante's 'architectabantur . . . architectoribus' with Joyce's 'hierarchitectitiptitoploftical'; Dante's 'pars trullis linebant' ('some laid on the mortar with trowels') with Joyce's 'with goodly trowel'. The several jobs of the workers co-operating in the building of the tower are summed up in the figure of Tim Finnegan/ HCE, mason, architect, engineer and surveyor ('he would caligulate by multiplicables the alltitude and malltitude'), joiner ('seesaw'), who carries and piles materials and buildings on the bank of the river(s) (cf. Dante's 'pars mari, pars terra vehere intendebant'). The word 'hierachitectitiptitoploftical' seems to hint at the higher rank in the hierarchy, that of architect, as being the loftiest and the most likely to fall, or tip off, probably as a consequence of being tipsy. Dante's specification that the builders of Babel would never be able again to come together ('coierat') in such commerce or intercourse ('commertium') may suggest to the reader some – probably unintended on Dante's part – joke on a sexual overtone of the sin (like the Fall) and of building as commercial activity – like HCE's building of towers and fake cathedrals. We can finally hear an echo of the situation described by Dante's words 'et quanto excellentius exercebant, tanto rudius nunc barbariusque locuntur' (those who were highest in the hierarchy of tasks fall lowest in the attribution of language) in 'with larrons o'toolers clittering *up* and tombles a'buckets clottering *down*' (my emphases; the names and vicissitudes of Lawrence O'Toole, archbishop of Dublin, and of his less fortunate contemporary Thomas à Becket are one of the several layers of the passage: these two historical figures crop up time and time again in the *Wake* and can be linked with Shaun and Shem respectively). A close echo of these words can be heard again at *FW* 114.17–18: 'and with lines of litters slittering up and louds of latters slettering down', in a context (that of the analysis of the 'letter' in 1.5), which has been shown in the previous chapter to be densely woven with references to Dante's *Convivio*, and, as we shall see in the next pages, may also contain several allusions to the *De vulgari eloquentia*.

The pattern of going up and coming down of letters and of people – a sort of counterweight systematisation of the *coincidentia oppositorum* – is taken up time and again in the *Wake*, often with echoes of this first occurrence; see for instance 'the topes that tippled on him, the types that toppled off him' (*FW* 136.18–19), possibly alluding yet again to tropes and letters ('types'), and followed shortly after by 'he crashed in the hollow of the park, trees down, as he soared in the vaguum of the phoenix, stones up' (*FW* 136.33–5), conflating the up and down motif with that of the phoenix and of the *felix culpa*. Another allusion to Dante may indeed be discovered here if 'sounds like a rude word' (*FW* 136.36) is taken to suggest the 'vulgar' words of the *De vulgari eloquentia* and 'you might find him at the Florence' (*FW* 137.04–5) evokes Dante's home town masked as the name of a pub.

'Bygmester Finnegan, of the Stuttering Hand' refers both to Tim Finnegan and to the main character of Ibsen's *Masterbuilder*, Bygmester Solness. The 'Stuttering Hand' describes one of HCE's characteristics, the stutter (at *FW* 4.30 he is described as 'Oftwhile balbulous'); Tim Finnegan's hand is 'stuttering', i.e., shaking, because he is drunk; at the same time, as Mary Reynolds has pointed out,[20] in attaching the attribute to 'Hand', Joyce may also have introduced in this context a reference to Dante's *Paradiso*: 'l'artista / ch'a l'abito de l'arte ha man che trema' ('the artist who in the custom of his art has a hand that trembles', *Par* XIII, 77–8). In this canto, Thomas Aquinas explains to Dante that Adam's and Christ's wisdom cannot be equalled in anyone else, because only they were created directly by God. All other men, on the contrary, are God's creatures through nature: as nature is imperfect, so they must also be imperfect, and Aquinas illustrates the imperfection of nature's shaping of things by comparing it to the work of the artist whose hand trembles.

If this is indeed an allusion to Dante's line as Reynolds suggests, it constitutes an apt illustration of Joyce's method of intertextual reference, often based on conflating and deflating different sources. The paragraph starts with an allusion to the *Paradiso* and the inadequacy of the artist, and then goes on to illustrate the episode of Babel by echoing a different text, the *De vulgari eloquentia*, where Dante claims that the artist can make up for the disastrous consequences of the Babelic confusion by raising the vernacular language to a newly founded nobility and worthiness. The initial allusion thus acquires multiple implications. It identifies Tim Finnegan, hod carrier and masterbuilder, with the artist whose shaking hand makes it impossible for him to realise a perfect work of art, and certainly neither Tim nor the builders of Babel had any hope of achieving perfection, always already condemned to a fall by the texts that inscribe them. But if Babel is a *felix culpa*, it makes sense to draw part of the allusion from the canto of *Paradiso* in which Aquinas speaks of the perfect wisdom of Adam, the first man and sinner who was in Eden and then fell down to earth, and of Christ, the Saviour who came down to earth, was buried underground in his 'mole's paradise', and rose again after three days, taking Adam with him. At the same time, Dante, who (implicitly) puts himself forward as the 'saviour' of the vulgar tongue, is, ironically, like Tim, the drunken sinner whose hand trembles and who falls, the artist whose work can only be imperfect. The varieties of idioms from which he sought to distil a unique, worthy 'illustrious vernacular' still exist, confused and dispersed, and the Italian vernacular from which Dante hoped to get his triumph, has not triumphed: it did not last – in fact it was never even approached – and Dante's attempt has failed – but it has 'happily' failed, leaving languages scattered, not foreclosing the possibility of existence for another synthetic (but also analytic) work like the *Wake*, which also needs linguistic differences in order to exist – to exist not (like Dante's 'ungrateful' treatise) to suppress the differences it feeds on, but to achieve through them the highest and widest possible polysemy. For Dante, plurality maintains a positive value only when it implies the possibility of several significant layers within the word and within the text, when the differences can be related to a common mould and do not contrast with one another. On the contrary, it acquires a negative meaning when it reveals difference without complementarity and is due to the evolution (or, in Dante's terms, corruption and decay) of the individual languages in diverse directions. But this is only the surface, the 'beautiful fiction' that envelops Dante's real implications: on the one hand, the possibility of polysemy is only a remedial strategy for a language that has lost the capacity of deixis, the capacity, that is, to point exactly to what it says and signify it unequivocally, and it springs from the same fundamental corruption of human nature as post-Babelian linguistic difference. Men need polysemy because the Fall has projected them into history. On the other hand, at the same time as Dante condemns the corrupt variety of languages, he needs it in order to play the highest role a poet can hope for, that of Christ-like saviour of the word. In this sense, the unlimited polysemy of *Finnegans Wake*, unashamedly founded on the gift of linguistic plurality and rejecting the didacticism of the moral sense in favour of a less univocal tropology, may finally be more honest, more innocent, like Tim's drunkenness, and a great deal simpler than Dante's. (Of course, Dante's failure to establish the *vulgare illustre* is offset by the historically more interesting, and extremely successful, establishment of *his* language as the Italian vernacular language.)

CONFUSIONING

According to the *De vulgari eloquentia*, after God's chastisement, the men who shared the same tasks remained united in one language but could no longer communicate with those who had been engaged in different activities (*Dve* i.vii, 7), and from this moment they started to disperse on the face of the earth. It is relevant in this context that in *Finnegans Wake* the encounters between opponents (HCE and the cad, and the subsequent re-enactments of their first meeting in Phoenix Park) are carried out through languages described by different adjectives or expressions, and often defined with an emphasis on their vulgarity, obscenity or on their derivative nature. HCE's encounter with the cad with a pipe (*FW* 1.2)[21] takes place on the anniversary of the 'confusioning of human races' (*FW* 35.05), a phrase that brings together the confusion of languages with the division of men into different peoples and their scattering on earth. HCE and the cad make use of different varieties of language: 'my British to my backbone tongue' (*FW* 36.31–2); 'repeated in his secondmouth language' (*FW* 37.14–15). In a later re-enactment, the 'attackler' (*FW* 81.18) and the 'Adversary' (*FW* 81.19–20) are described as 'making use of sacrilegious languages' (i.e. post-Babelic, *FW* 81.24), while the same man asks questions in the 'vermicular' (*FW* 82.10–12). After some 'collidabanter' (*FW* 82.15) and exchange of money, calm intervenes and 'the starving gunman' (*FW* 83.06) makes a remark 'in languidoily' (*FW* 83.15). Different, decayed languages ('fornicular', *FW* 319.28; 'raw lenguage', *FW* 323.05) are also used by Kersse the Tailor and the Norwegian Captain in chapter II.3. In the same chapter, Butt and Taff highlight individual linguistic differences when they recount the story of Buckley and the Russian General in 'paramilintary' (parliamentary, paramilitary) language (*FW* 338.20), 'Stranaslang' or strange, foreign languages or slangs (*FW* 338.22), '*lipponease*' or Japanese language (*FW* 339.01), 'lewdbrogue' (*FW* 343.31), and even a '*scimmianised twinge*' (*FW* 344.08) that reverts Butt's tongue to an animal, apish conditions thus paralleling Biblical and Dantean linguistic history with Darwinian evolution. These linguistic clashes that emphasise vernacular, derivative, unholy, post-Babelian tongues, also recall the paradigmatic skirmishes set up in the Prankquean episode together with the first appearance of the *felix culpa* motif.

The use of various idioms, registers, jargons due to different jobs (as in Dante's theory of the origin of the diverse languages), social class or group is reflected in chapter 1.2 in the spreading rumours about HCE and in the composition of the ballad which decrees his public fall after the 'private' fall in Phoenix Park – this seems to replay the 'private' Fall of Adam and Eve in Eden, which left a perpetual stain on men's souls and the 'public' fall of men at Babel, affected ever after in their social life by the confusion of tongues. A similar pattern can be found in chapter 1.3, in the attempt to track down the confused destinies of the authors of the ballad, all of them gone to different parts of the globe and now dead (a link is also established here between on the one hand the history of Ireland and the 'exile' of the 'wild geese' and on the other the biblical falls and exile from Eden and from the common language[22]). We do not know anything about the first character (Hosty, now appearing as 'Osti-Fosti', *FW* 48.19), except that he is dead: '*Ei fù*' (*FW* 49.02).[23] Of the others we learn that before dying they scattered all around the world: A'Hara was in the Crimean war (*FW* 49.02–15); Paul Horan went into a mental hospital in the northern counties (*FW* 49.15–21) while Langley disappeared from the austral (southern) plain (*FW* 50.06–18); Sordid Sam passed away 'propelled from Behind into the great Beyond' (i.e. kicked into Hell? *FW* 49.21–50.05), and Father San Browne, a.k.a. Padre Don Bruno, simply died. The words through which their deaths are announced are 'he was', each time in a different language: '*Ei fù*' (Italian), '*Booil*' (Russian 'Byl'), 'He was', '*Han var*' (Danish), '*Bhi she*' (Irish 'bhì sé') and '*Fuitfuit*' (Latin 'Fuit'). There is method in this plurality, recalling Dante's method of apportioning linguistic difference: the death of Osti-Fosti (Italian *fosti* = 'you were', second person singular), the main author and singer of the ballad, is announced in Italian, by many considered the language of music *par excellence*; A'Hara's, who fought in the Crimean war, in Russian; Father San Browne's, a clergyman, in Latin.

After describing the fate of the authors of the ballad, chapter 1.3 goes on to tell about the different versions of HCE's fall, and what happened to him. At a certain point, for instance, the words 'Favour with your tongues! *Intendite!*' (*FW* 54.05–6, confusing tongues and ears, speaking and listening), introduce a passage in which different languages, peoples, political groups or parliamentary institutions, forms of greeting or of polite conversation, offers of drinks and food, exchange of money in different currencies, different items of clothing – all of them representatives of different cultures – are juxtaposed, but do not actually harmonise: even if the word 'Casaconcordia' appears in this context (*FW* 54.10) and there are expressions that appear to reproduce rhythms of polite conversation (e.g. *FW* 54.12–14), in fact the sentences do not allow any pattern of coherent, meaningful conversation to emerge, and they remain unconnected, pointing to a lack of 'concordia' and to the difficulty of communicating after the confusion of tongues at Babel determined the independent and unrelated development of the peoples and their cultures. Similarly, before the end of chapter II.1, or the 'Mime of Mick, Nick and the Maggies', the following passage:

He does not know how his grandson's grandson's grandson's grandson will stammer up in Peruvian for in the ersebest idiom I have done it equals I so shall do. He dares not think why the grandmother of the grandmother of his grandmother's grandmother coughed Russky with suchky husky accent since in the mouthart of the slove look at me now means I once was otherwise. Nor that the mappamund has been changing pattern as youth plays moves from street to street since times and races were . . .

(*FW* 252.35–253.07)

establishes a relationship of interdependence between the sequence of generations, expressed in both male and female terms, linguistic change in time, the variety of languages in space, the spreading of peoples over the map of the city and of the earth, and racial, or even individual, variations. In the *De vulgari eloquentia* Dante applies to the sinners of Babel the same law of analogy and *contrapasso* that regulates the distribution of penalties in the *Divine Comedy*: those who held the highest functions are punished with the harshest tongues ('et quanto excellentius exercebant, tanto rudius nunc barbariusque locuntur'). In the *Inferno* the giant Nimrod, instigator of the construction of the tower, is punished with an incomprehensible language known only to himself:

> '*Raphèl maì amècche zabì almi,*'
> cominciò a gridar la fiera bocca,
> cui non si convenia più dolci salmi.   (*Inf* xxxi, 67–9)

('*Raphèl maì amècche zabì almi,*' the fierce mouth began to cry, to which sweeter psalms were not suited.)

> questi è Nembrotto per lo cui mal coto
> pur un linguaggio nel mondo non s'usa.
>   Lasciànlo stare e non parliamo a vòto;
> ché così è a lui ciascun linguaggio
> come 'l suo ad altrui, ch'a nullo è noto.   (*Inf* xxxi, 77–81)

(This is Nimrod, for whose ill deed one single language is not used in the world. Let us leave him be and not speak in vain, for every language is to him as his is to others, which is known to no one.)

The early commentators of the *Divine Comedy* thought that Nimrod's words had been invented by Dante in order to give a concrete example of the effects of the Babelic confusion of tongues, and that it was therefore useless to try and interpret their meaning. Modern readers have argued that Dante probably formed the giant's words by distorting Hebrew words which he could find in the Bible or in medieval lexicons; what matters is that Dante clearly meant these words to be perceived as incomprehensible sounds ('così è a lui ciascun linguaggio / come 'l suo ad altrui, ch'a nullo è noto'): listening to him is just a waste of time ('non parliamo a vòto'). A similar procedure of deformation can be found in the *Inferno* when Pluto, the monster guardian of the fourth circle of Hell, cries:

> 'Pape Satàn, pape Satàn aleppe!'   (*Inf* vii, 1)

In this case too, scholars, from the early commentators to the moderns, have advanced a number of interpretations to explain the meaning of the cry, referring to Hebrew, Latin, Arabic words, but, again, no definitive reading has prevailed.[24] A conclusion can however be drawn from the comparison of these two lines of distorted language – their value must be different: in the former instance only Nimrod knows what his words mean, in the latter, although neither Dante nor the readers know the exact significance of Pluto's utterance, Virgil understands the meaning it wants to convey:

> e quel savio gentil, che tutto seppe,
>   disse per confortarmi: 'Non ti noccia
> la tua paura, ché, poder ch'elli abbia,
> non ci torrà lo scender questa roccia.'
>   Poi si rivolse a quella 'nfiata labbia,
> e disse: 'Taci, maladetto lupo!
> consuma dentro te con la tua rabbia.'   (*Inf* VII, 3–9)

(and that gentle sage who knew all, said, to comfort me, 'Do not let your fear harm you; because whatever power he may have, he shall not prevent us from descending this rock.' Then he turned back to that bloated face and said, 'Be silent, accursed wolf! Consume yourself within with your own rage.')

Virgil knows that Pluto's words are an expression of his rage, intended to scare off Dante and his guide; he also knows that they need not be scared and can continue their descent, willed by Heaven.

Ettore Settanni, who briefly collaborated with Joyce and Nino Frank on the translation of 'Anna Livia Plurabelle', remembers Joyce's reaction to his puzzlement at the chapter:

Joyce sorrise, si avvicinò alla biblioteca, poi venne verso di me e mi indicò il gioco dantesco di 'Pape Satan Pape satan aleppe'. 'Padre Dante mi perdoni, ma io sono partito da questa tecnica della deformazione per raggiungere un'armonia che vince la nostra intelligenza, come la musica.'[25]

(Joyce smiled, approached the library, then came toward me and pointed out to me the Dantean play of 'Pape Satan Pape satan aleppe'. 'May father Dante forgive me, but I started from this technique of deformation to achieve a harmony that defeats our intelligence, as music does.)

Joyce was aware of the importance of Dante's 'technique of deformation' as a means to obtain effects that go beyond the conventional relationship between sound and meaning, beyond reason, in order to appeal to the senses and imagination.[26] Talking to Settanni, he chose to quote the example of deformed language from *Inferno* VII, 1. He could have selected the other instance of Dante's 'technique of deformation', Nimrod's cry, which would also have offered an explicit link with the central episode of Babel. Joyce's choice may have been just a coincidence, of course, the first instance that came to mind, and one with clear 'demonic' overtones; however, readers of the *Inferno* realise that whereas Nimrod's utterance is incomprehensible to anyone else but the giant himself, Pluto's words escape Dante's comprehension but are understood by Virgil, at least as far as their general meaning and intended effect are concerned. One can surmise that Joyce selected the line from *Inferno* VII as his starting point because it allowed for the possibility of meaningful interpretation despite the difficult, apparently obscure surface: *Finnegans Wake* is not intended as a book written in perfectly solipsistic language, like Nimrod's impossible to understand – quite the contrary: the language of the *Wake* is difficult, obscure, but it is such insofar as it incorporates many other languages while deforming them, like the line spoken by Pluto, still allowing for the interpretation of its meanings.

OBLIVIO

The different languages that followed Babel had to be 'reinvented' by the men who were scattered all over the earth. The means of God's punishment, Dante declares in his original interpretation, was the forgetting of the previous common language; the 'Confusion' 'nil fuit aliud quam prioris oblivio' ('was nothing else but forgetfulness of the former language', *Dve* I.ix, 6). Men had to reinvent their languages, and they did so according to their own changeable and unstable nature ('homo sit instabilissimum atque variabilissimum animal'; 'man is a most unstable and changeable animal', *Dve* I.ix, 6). By introducing the notion of forgetfulness, Dante can account for both the initial fall and the progressive decay of the new idioms that causes them to differentiate more and more in the course of time ('nec durabilis nec continua esse potest'; '[human language] can be neither lasting nor continuous', *Dve* I.ix, 6). Each new act of speech is, in a way, an attempt to remember, to 'balbly call to memory' (*FW* 37.16) the original and lost language; since the linguistic fall, each language is foreign, barbarous, a 'stuttering', 'balbulous' idiom. So is the 'nat' language in which *Finnegans Wake* is written. When we fall asleep at night, we 'forget' the day world and its language with its conventions. What we remember are 'bits and pieces', fragments woven together in new relations, according to laws and a logic different from those that govern waking life. When we wake up we try to remember the dream, but we can recall only the bits and pieces and try to join them together according to rules that are different from those of the night. A dialectic of forgetting and remembering governs the whole of the *Wake*, from its stuttering beginnings to the final monologue when ALP tries to remember but can only forget, or perhaps tries to forget but is forced to remember: 'Impossible to remember persons in improbable to forget position places' (*FW* 617.08–9); 'Forget, remember!' (*FW* 614.22). Like in Dante's version of Babel, where the memorable punishment was the forgetting, memory and oblivion are inextricably bound together in reciprocal implication.

Man is forever exiled from the original language, scattered on the earth, yet again in exile from the original land (*Dve* i.viii, 1) after having been exiled from Eden. This post-Edenic, post-Babelian condition is also that of the artist who, exiled, encounters languages different from his own. The *De vulgari eloquentia*, written in the first years of Dante's exile, would have been inspired and prompted by a direct contact with dialectal differences and by the reflection that must have ensued on the origin of languages, the cause of their differences, their formal and phonic values. Away from Florence, Dante had to reconsider his role as a poet, the composition of his readership, his relationship with it, the language in which he should address it. Both the *De vulgari eloquentia* and the *Convivio* reflect Dante's awareness of the link between exile and language, and indeed suggest that Dante needed exile just as he needed the sin of Babel to become a 'saviour'. Beckett refers to Dante's anti-municipalism as an example of heroic superiority ('DBVJ' 18), yet the complacence of the poet for his role of great man without a home can be read between the lines of Dante's scorn of municipalism and of his self-pity:

né io sofferto avria pena ingiustamente, pena, dico, d'essilio e di povertate. Poi che fu piacere de li cittadini de la bellissima e famosissima figlia di Roma, Fiorenza, di gittarmi fuori del suo dolce seno – nel quale nato e nutrito fui in fino al colmo de la vita mia, e nel quale, con buona pace di quella, desidero con tutto lo cuore di riposare l'animo stancato e terminare lo tempo che m'è dato –, per le parti quasi tutte a le quali questa lingua si stende, peregrino, quasi mendicando, sono andato . . .   (*Conv* i.iii, 3–4)

(nor would I have unjustly suffered punishment, the punishment I mean of exile and of poverty. Since it was the pleasure of the citizens of the most beautiful and famous daughter of Rome, Florence, to cast me from her sweet bosom – in which I was born and nurtured until the culmination of my life, and in which, may it please her, I desire with all my heart to rest my wearied mind and end the time which is granted me – to almost all the regions over which this tongue extends, a wanderer, almost a beggar, I have been . . .)

Nam, quicunque tam obscene rationis est ut locum sue nationis delitiosissimum credat esse sub sole, hic etiam pre cunctis proprium vulgare licetur, idest maternam locutionem, et per consequens credit ipsum fuisse illud quod fuit Ade. Nos autem, cui mundus est patria velut piscibus equor, quanquam Sarnum biberimus ante dentes et Florentiam adeo diligamus ut, quia dileximus, exilium patiamur iniuste, rationi magis quam sensui spatulas nostri iudicii podiamus. (*Dve* I.vi, 2–3)

(For whoever has such offensive reasoning as to believe that his birthplace is the most delightful under the sun, such a one will place his own vernacular, that is, his mother-tongue, above all others, and consequently believe that it actually was that of Adam. But we, for whom the world is our homeland, just as the sea is to the fish, though we drank of the Arno before we cut our teeth, and though we love Florence so dearly that for this love we are unjustly suffering exile, we rest the shoulders of our judgement on reason rather than on feeling.)

Joyce's case is similar to Dante's: exile, although chosen and not imposed, brought him into contact with different cultures, traditions, idioms. From his school years Joyce had manifested his interest in foreign languages: he learned French, Italian, Dano-Norwegian, German, took lessons in Irish, Spanish, Dutch, Russian. For Stephen, in *A Portrait of the Artist as a Young Man*, the language spoken by the English dean of studies is an 'acquired speech':

The language in which we are speaking is his before it is mine. How different are the words *home*, *Christ*, *ale*, *master*, on his lips and on mine! I cannot speak or write these words without unrest of spirit. His language, so familiar and so foreign, will always be for me an acquired speech. I have not made or accepted its words. My voice holds them at bay. My soul frets in the shadow of his language. (*P* 189)

The artist's awareness of linguistic difference is that of the exile, whose original language is not, nor can ever be, 'his' any longer, whose present language is a foreign one, one that has had to be learned because the old one had to be forgotten. Stephen's fretting in the shadow of a language not his crystallises, as in Dante, a condition which is as much psychological and artistic as it is political and national. For Joyce, as for Dante, the solution is not in going back to the irrecoverable pre-Babelian (Celtic) language, nor in quietly accepting the present one, but in taking advantage of differences and making the most of them. As in Dante's case, Joyce's spontaneous awareness of multilingualism was naturally enhanced by life on the Continent and by the conditions that he found in the cities where he resided, all of them the recipients of polyglot communities: Trieste was an active port town where Italian (in the distinctive local accent), Slavonic, German, Turkish, Albanian and other languages could be heard in the streets. Joyce found a similar situation in Zurich and Paris; the former was a shelter for refugees, exiles, expatriates of many nationalities; the latter the centre of European culture, the mythical city of transgression and novelty where artists congregated from all over the world. In all three cities could languages be observed in action, listened to in their peculiar accents, inflections, intonations, and offer an inexhaustible quarry for interlinguistic puns, becoming Joyce's ideal habitat.

And again, as in Dante's case, Joyce relished his condition of exile; indeed, exile was one of the key factors which released for Joyce the spring of identification (with Dante in this instance, but also with other exiles, such as Giordano Bruno). In December 1918, when he was almost thirty-seven, Joyce wrote in a letter to Martha Fleischmann that he felt old and that he was thirty-five years of age, the same age that Shakespeare was when he conceived his passion for the Dark Lady, the same age that Dante was when he entered his dark night (*Letters* II 432). Biographical data are altered and made to conform to the 'spiritual' biography modelled on the lives of his predecessors.

Several passages in the *Wake* refer to the exile of the artist, often in connection with the vicissitudes of language after Babel. The 'letter' or 'mamafesta' chapter, which I have discussed above in relation to the theory of the four levels of meaning, also correlates Babelic confusion and dispersion of people and echoes the *De vulgari eloquentia*:

Because, Soferim Bebel, if it goes to that . . . every person, place and thing in the chaosmos of Alle anyway connected with the gobblydumped turkery was moving and changing every part of the time: the travelling inkhorn (possibly pot), the hare and turtle pen and paper, the continually more and less intermisunderstanding minds of the anticollaborators, the as time went on as it will variously inflected, differently pronounced, otherwise spelled, changeably meaning vocable scriptsigns.   (*FW* 118.18–28)

'Soferim Bebel', 'suffering Babel'; suffering, that is, the dire consequences of the construction of the tower of Babel described in the lines that follow: a world dominated by chaos ('chaosmos') where everything and everyone continually moves, changes, emigrates. Language is also moving and changing: 'every person, place and thing' is part of a riddle whose answer is 'the noun'.[27] The list of all the things that move and change culminates in a description that fits the state of practically every natural language ('variously inflected, differently pronounced, otherwise spelled, changeably meaning vocable scriptsigns'), but may also echo passages of the *De vulgari eloquentia* such as the one that follows the tirade on exile quoted above and which I have already reported earlier: 'Dico autem "formam" et quantum ad rerum vocabula et quantum ad vocabulorum constructionem et quantum ad constructionis prolationem' (*Dve* I.vi, 4). Compare also this passage on the mutability of man and language:

omnis nostra loquela . . . per locorum temporumque distantias variari oportet . . . Si ergo per eandem gentem sermo variatur, ut dictum est, successive per tempora, nec stare ullo modo potest, necesse est ut disiunctim abmotimque morantibus varie varietur, ceu varie variantur mores et habitus, qui nec natura nec consortio confirmantur, sed humanis beneplacitis localique congruitate nascuntur.   (*Dve* I.ix, 6–10)

(every language of ours . . . must change through distance of time and place . . . If, therefore, the speech of the same people varies, as has been said, successively in the course of time, and cannot in any way stand still, necessarily will the speech of people living apart and distant from one another differently vary; just as manners and dress differently vary, since they are not made stable either by nature or by intercourse, but arise according to men's inclinations and local agreement.)

And see, finally, Dante's definition of the *vulgare* as the nobler of the two languages, vernacular and Latin: 'tum quia totus orbis ipsa perfruitur, licet in diversas prolationes et vocabula sit divisa' ('because the whole world uses it, though it has been divided into different forms of inflections and words', *Dve* I.i, 4).

Languages change, the peoples are scattered 'even to the hidmost coignings of the earth' (*FW* 118.36–119.01) and can no longer communicate with one another because of the the the continually 'intermisunderstanding' minds of the 'anticollaborators', ensuring, as suggested by my first epigraph to this chapter, a continuous lapse into a condition of increasing confusion. 'The travelling inkhorn (possibly pot)' includes writers in the list,[28] especially the exiled ones (homeless, therefore 'travelling'). The variety of languages and linguistic forms is thus described,

It is told in sounds in utter that, in signs so adds to, in universal, in polygluttural, in each auxiliary neutral idiom, sordomutics, florilingua,

sheltafocal, flayflutter, a con's cubane, a pro's tutute, strassarab, ereperse
and anythongue athall   (*FW* 117.12–16)

yet again fusing linguistics, in its broadest and loosest sense, with
variety of peoples and low – *vulgar* – life.

The determination of time specified shortly after – 'at this
deleteful hour of dungflies dawning' (*FW* 118.32) – seems to recall
the *De vulgari eloquentia* more explicitly. The hour is 'deleteful', both
'delightful' and 'oblivious' – that is, the time when everything is
'deleted', cancelled from the mind: it is evening (flies' dawn), when
we get ready to go to sleep, but also the moment in history when
languages were forgotten, 'deleted' from men's minds. Nevertheless,
'we ought really to rest thankful' for this (*FW* 118.31–2): the moment
is 'delightful' because it is the *felix culpa* that paves the way for
Dante's project of redemption and Joyce's celebration of the confusion. After all, it is a 'pardonable confusion' (*FW* 119.33) – confusion
in the text, maybe in the reader's mind, but 'pardonable' because
the result of a 'pia correctione' (*Dve* 1.vii, 5). The confusion of
languages is symbolised by the many different characters referred to:
Greek (*FW* 120.19); Ostrogothic (*FW* 120.22); Etruscan (*FW* 120.23).
The vicissitudes of language, of the artist, of the mind falling asleep,
are finally bound together:

the vocative lapse from which it begins and the accusative hole in which it
ends itself; the aphasia of that heroic agony of recalling a once loved
number leading slip by slipper to a general amnesia of misnomering one's
own . . .   (*FW* 122.03–6)

The aphasia, or loss of language (at Babel and each night as we fall
asleep) takes the form of the general amnesia which led necessarily
to reinvention of new idioms, to having to give new names (inevitably misnomers) to things, each of them a progressive slip away
from the original language and further into oblivion. It is now time
to see how Dante manages to emerge successfully from the 'accusative hole' of linguistic confusion and positively build his vision in the
synthetic phase of his treatise.

CHAPTER 3

Distilling vulgar matter

Whatever gold one might sift *ex sterco Vergilii*, excrement was still excrement[1]

encaustum sibi fecit indelibile

(*FW* 185.25)

In the last chapter we have seen how *Finnegans Wake* borrows, exploits and subverts Dante's historical account of the breakdown of the one original language into a multiplicity of different, decayed idioms. This chapter will show how the constructive part of the *De vulgari eloquentia*, the 'proposal' to overcome differences through a noble, illustrious language, represents an important force behind the *Wake*'s experimentation with narrative form, its exploration of new notions of character, its integration in such typical and pervasive themes as the father/son battle or the artist's original creation and his transcendence of the vulgar, the commonplace, the daily – even the excremental – into the eternity of art. I shall look at the story of HCE's naming, ennobling and fall in 1.2, at Shem's distillation of an indelible ink from his own excrement in 1.7, and at HCE's concoction of a new cocktail from the dregs of his custo-mers' glasses in II.3 to show how Joyce's narrative, poetic and linguistic masterpiece situates itself at the intersection between a radically modern narrative technique and a medieval poet's lin-guistic theory. According to a medieval topos, all secular literature, even the best poetry – i.e. that written in imitation of Virgil – was 'excrement'; in the words of Robert Hollander in the first epigraph to this chapter, 'Whatever gold one might sift *ex sterco Vergilii*, excrement was still excrement.' As Hollander points out, the expression probably originates in Donatus's *Vita* of Virgil, and was a widespread interpretation of the classics in the Middle Ages. Dante walked in the wake of Virgil, and it is quite appropriate that

99

Joyce's text, written in the wake of Dante, should also treat as precious excrement the theory of the *vulgare* from which it 'sifts' the 'gold' of narrative, thematic and linguistic material, thereby transcending it into an 'indelible' poetry.

The *Wake*'s direct echoes from the *De vulgari eloquentia* and its use of Dante's theory also point to a method of linguistic composition which is in many respects similar for the two writers. Although I would not claim that Joyce directly derived his theory of a multilingual, universalising idiom for the *Wake* from the *De vulgari eloquentia*, I would suggest that Dante's treatise offered an important antecedent, strikingly similar in the method although different in scope. Joyce could turn to the medieval model both as source-material for the linguistic structure of the *Wake* (similar to his turning to Vico and Bruno for narrative and thematic antecedents, although he did not need the former to 'discover' cyclicality or the latter to think of infinite worlds or of the coincidence of opposites) and as model in relation to which he could define his own multi-lingual theory and practice. This chapter will therefore also look at how Dante's definition of the *vulgare* and its qualities – 'illustre, cardinale, aulicum et curiale' (*Dve* i.xvi, 6) – can be legitimately employed as a useful descriptive metaphor for the language of *Finnegans Wake* in order to highlight both the analogies with the idiom theorised by Dante and the ways in which 'Wakese' encompasses and surpasses it, in a manner similar to what I have described for the fourfold exegetical system. As we shall see, this investigation will also lead us to interpret aspects of Joyce's earlier works in the light of Dante's theory.

As in the previous chapters, it will be useful to start by giving an outline of Dante's argument, highlighting and briefly commenting on the main issues raised by Dante's treatise in order to provide a context for the following discussion of how these elements are incorporated and dramatised in *Finnegans Wake*.

In the *De vulgari eloquentia*, after the historical account of the origin and significance of linguistic differences, Dante examines the great variety of Italian dialects and the myriad subordinate distinctions that exist even within the walls of the same town, from street to street (*Dve* i.ix-x). Dante describes it as a thorny and intricate linguistic forest; in this tangled wood, Dante hunts for the 'beautiful panther', the illustrious Italian language:

Quam multis varietatibus latio dissonante vulgari, decentiorem atque illustrem Ytalie venemur loquelam; et ut nostre venationi pervium callem habere possimus, perplexos frutices atque sentes prius eiciamus de silva.

(*Dve* I.xi, 1)

(As the vulgar Italian has so many discordant varieties, let us hunt after the most dignified and illustrious Italian language; and so that we may have a clear path for our chase, let us first cast the tangled bushes and brambles out of the wood.)

What Dante describes as the ugliest dialects[2] are 'uprooted' and 'cleared away', the rest is 'sifted' or 'winnowed' ('exaceratis') in order to find 'the most honoured and the one that confers most honour' ('Honorabilius atque honoreficentius', *Dve* I.xii, 1). The search does not lead to any satisfactory result, although some traces of the illustrious vernacular language can be 'scented' in many places:

Postquam venati saltus et pascua sumus Ytalie, nec pantheram quam sequimur adinvenimus, ut ipsam reperire possimus, rationabilius investi-gemus de illa, ut solerti studio redolentem ubique et necubi apparentem nostris penitus irretiamus tenticulis.

(*Dve* I.xvi, 1)

(After having searched the heights and pastures of Italy without having found that panther which we are pursuing, let us now track her in a more rational manner, in order that we may, through diligent study, trap in our snares she who is everywhere fragrant but nowhere seen.)

The panther which, in the *De vulgari eloquentia*, symbolises the illustrious language is one of the animals that appear in medieval bestiaries and in the works of many medieval and ancient writers. Whereas the allegorical meaning attributed to the panther may vary (for example, it can stand for Christ, or for ardent love), one of its constant characteristics is that it attracts other animals with its smell. Because the panther, and therefore the vernacular, is for Dante 'necubi apparentem', it is also connected with the phoenix, which, in one version of the myth, never appears in any place (incidentally, this confirms the link between the phoenix and the fall and rebirth of language that I have proposed in chapter 2, a link which, as we have seen, also operates in *Finnegans Wake* through the fusion of 'phoenix' and *felix culpa* and the association of the original sin in Eden with the linguistic sin of Babel).

All of the vernaculars examined carry some trace, some 'scent', of the illustrious vernacular, but none of them can be identified with it. The opposition between multiplicity and oneness which Dante set up when he discussed the story of the tower of Babel is now taken up

again and developed. Multiplicity in this treatise still represents the
negative pole, and it is contrasted with the perfection of the one.
Dante now links the opposition of one vs. multiple to the concept of
the *unum simplicissimum*,[3] and phrases this explanation in a way that is
reminiscent of the Babelian origin of linguistic multiplicity:
compare, for instance, the sentence 'sicut in numero cuncta mensurantur uno' (*Dve* I.xvi, 2) with the repetition of the form 'cunctis . . .
una' used in the description of the confusion following God's punishment, discussed in the last chapter. The similar use of such an
important linguistic construction in the two chapters of the *De vulgari
eloquentia* (the first time in the negative context of the Babelic sin and
the ensuing corruption of language, the second in the positive
context of the rational discovery of the illustrious vernacular) once
again supports the interpretation of Dante's project of founding a
vulgare illustre as the 'happy' outcome of a previous fault, and of his
own role as the opposite of Nimrod's – or, indeed, as 'double' of the
giant. The reduction of the linguistic necessity of a unified and
unifying language to the concept of the *unum* also anticipates the
terms of the description of the *vulgare illustre* and its qualities (I shall
discuss these later) and thus becomes in Dante's theory the pivotal
point which marks the passage from multiplicity to unity and turns
what is negative into a positive asset.

Through the recourse to the concept of *unum* in his quest, Dante
qualifies the illustrious vernacular as the standard in relation to
which all other linguistic manifestations must be weighed and
measured, the perfect entity (and language is the 'noblest of actions')
which does not appear anywhere in particular but is reflected,
according to different degrees of perfection, in all the particular
vernaculars and reflects them in itself (*Dve* I.xvi, 5). The *vulgare illustre*
is qualified therefore as the *optimum* of vernaculars. As it does not
exist anywhere in particular, the task of the poet is to '(re)compose'
it, starting from the multiplicity of local vernaculars and selecting
from them what best reflects the perfection of the 'one' – that is to
say, extracting the noblest elements and reconstituting them in the
vulgare illustre, a language which will then be elegant, expressive,
worthy of dealing with the highest subjects.[4]

Dante concludes this chapter by asserting that he has finally found
the Italian vernacular. As it could not be encountered empirically,
Dante has 'discovered' it through the rational method of deduction.
He defines the language:

Itaque adepti quod querebamus, dicimus illustre, cardinale, aulicum et curiale vulgare in Latio, quod omnis latie civitatis est et nullius esse videtur, et quo municipalia vulgaria omnia Latinorum mensurantur et ponderantur et comparantur. (*Dve* i.xvi, 6)

(Having then found what we were looking for, we assert that the illustrious, cardinal, courtly, and curial vulgar tongue in Italy is that which belongs to every Italian town but does not appear to belong to any one of them; and is that by which all the local dialects of all the Italians are measured, weighed and compared.)

The opposition *omnis* vs. *nullius* recalls the one between *ubique* and *necubi* earlier used for the panther. The close parallel between the fall of man in Eden and the fall of language at Babel, and Dante's implicit presentation of his illustrious vernacular as a redemptive step, comparable to Christ's redemption of man, is confirmed on the one hand by the symbol of the panther (associated in the Middle Ages with the image of Christ) and, on the other, by the use of the concept of the *unum simplicissimum*, whose highest abstraction is God; this parallel is then emphasised again through the use of the words 'mensurantur et ponderantur et comparantur', which echo the praise of divine wisdom in the Scriptures: 'omnia in mensura et numero et pondere disposuisti' ('You ordered all things by measure, number, weight', *Sapientia* xi, 21).[5]

It will be useful to report here Dante's definition of the four attributes through which he describes the Italian vernacular. The elements which appear to be relevant for an analysis of the relationship between the *De vulgari eloquentia* and *Finnegans Wake* will be examined in more detail later.

The first adjective, *illustre*, is thus defined:

Per hoc quidem quod illustre dicimus, intelligimus quid illuminans et illuminatum prefulgens . . . de tot rudibus Latinorum vocabulis, de tot perplexis constructionibus, de tot defectivis prolationibus, de tot rusticanis accentibus, tam egregium, tam extricatum, tam perfectum et tam urbanum videamus electum . . . Et quid maioris potestatis est quam quod humana corda versare potest, ita ut nolentem volentem et volentem nolentem faciat, velut ipsum et fecit et facit? (*Dve* i.xvii, 2–7)

(By what we call illustrious we mean something illuminating and which, illuminated, shines forth . . . from so many rude Italian words, from so many intricate constructions, from so many faulty inflections, from so many rustic accents, we see it purified and brought to such a degree of excellence, of clarity, of perfection, and of polish . . . And what is of greater power than that which can sway the hearts of men, so as to make an unwilling man willing, and a willing man unwilling, just as this language has done and is doing?)

The second quality of the Italian vernacular is its 'cardinality', and the language is defined *cardinale* for the following reasons:

Neque sine ratione ipsum vulgare illustre decusamus adiectione secunda, videlicet ut id cardinale vocemus. Nam sicut totum hostium cardinem sequitur, ut, quo cardo vertitur, versetur et ipsum seu introrsum seu extrorsum flectatur, sic et universus municipalium grex vulgarium vertitur et revertitur, movetur et pausat secundum quod istud, quod quidem vere pater familias esse videtur. Nonne cotidie extirpat sentosos frutices de ytala silva? Nonne cotidie vel plantas inserit vel plantaria plantat? Quid aliud agricole sui satagunt, nisi ut amoveant et admoveant, ut dictum est? Quare prorsus tanto decusari vocabulo promeretur.   (*Dve* i.xviii, 1)

(It is not without reason that we honour the illustrious vernacular with a second adjective, that is, that we call it cardinal. Because, as the whole door follows its hinge, so that where the hinge turns the door also turns, whether it swings inwards or outwards, so the whole herd of local dialects turns and returns, moves and pauses as that [the illustrious vernacular] does, which really appears to be the father of a family. Does it not daily root out thorny bushes from the Italian wood? Does it not daily implant cuttings or plant young plants? What else are its foresters engaged in if not in removing and fetching in as has been said? Thus it well deserves to adorn itself with such a great name as this.)

The third adjective, *aulicum*, is explained as follows:

Quia vero aulicum nominamus, illud causa est, quod, si aulam nos Ytali haberemus, palatinum foret. Nam si aula totius regni comunis est domus et omnium regni partium gubernatrix augusta, quicquid tale est ut omnibus sit comune nec proprium ulli, conveniens est ut in ea conversetur et habitet; nec aliquod aliud habitaculum tanto dignum est habitante: hoc nempe videtur esse id de quo loquimur vulgare. Et hinc est quod in regiis omnibus conversantes semper illustri vulgari locuntur; hinc etiam est quod nostrum illustre velut accola peregrinatur et in humilibus hospitatur asilis, cum aula vacemus.   (Dve i.xviii, 2–3)

(The reason why we call it courtly is that if we Italians had a court, it [the vernacular] would belong to the palace. For if the court is the common home of all the realm, and an august ruler of all parts of the realm, everything that is such as to belong to all without being particular to any should properly frequent this court and dwell there: nor is any other abode worthy of so great a resident: such appears to be the vulgar tongue of which we are speaking. And this is why those who frequent all royal palaces always speak the illustrious vulgar tongue; this is also why our illustrious language wanders about like a stranger, and is welcomed in humble shelters, because we have no court.)

Finally, the fourth characteristic of the illustrious vernacular is *curiale*:

Est etiam merito curiale dicendum, quia curialitas nil aliud est quam librata regula eorum que peragenda sunt; et quia statera huiusmodi librationis tantum in excellentissimis curiis esse solet, hinc est quod quicquid in actibus nostris bene libratum est, curiale dicatur. Unde cum istud in excellentissima Ytalorum curia sit libratum, dici curiale meretur . . . Nam licet curia, secundum quod unita accipitur, ut curia regis Alamanie, in Ytalia non sit, membra tamen eius non desunt; et sicut membra illius uno Principe uniuntur, sic membra huius gratioso lumine rationis unita sunt. Quare falsum esset dicere curia carere Ytalos, quanquam Principe careamus, quonia curiam habemus, licet corporaliter sit dispersa. (*Dve* I.xviii, 4–5)

(It also deserves to be called curial, because curiality is nothing else but the justly balanced rule of things that have to be done; and, because the scales required for such balancing can only be found in the most excellent courts [of justice], it follows that whatever is well balanced in our actions is called curial . . . Indeed, though we have no court of justice in Italy in the sense of one supreme court, like that of the King of Germany, nevertheless the members of such a court are not lacking; and as the members of the German court are united under one Prince, so the members of ours are united by the gracious light of reason [or, 'divine light of the intellect']. Thus it would be false to assert that the Italians have no such court of justice, though we lack a Prince, because we do have a court, though, as a body, it is scattered.)

What appears to be particularly striking in Dante's treatise is the emphatic identification between the language and the poet. The illustrious vernacular is enlightened by the poets who use it, and gives lustre to them. Dante has to seek the language through the wood of dialects and must prune and weed and extirpate bushes, and the language is likened to a gardener that weeds and cuts brambles and keeps the garden tidy. Both the poet and the illustrious language are exiled, and must wander and seek shelter in other people's houses. This connects their fates to that of humankind after Babel and of Adam's lot after the original sin. Dante's search for the 'panther' through the forest of the *vulgares*, where he has to weigh the various dialects, evaluate them, and give his 'verdict' on each, reflects the 'curiality' of the illustrious vernacular, the quality which renders it worthy of being spoken in the court of justice, in the royal court and (in another meaning of the term) in the assembly of the noble men of the kingdom who were summoned by the prince and

consulted on matters of general interest.[6] It is therefore the standard
for taking important decisions, both as criterion of evaluation and as
medium. Most of these elements acquire a relevant role in *Finnegans
Wake*, and they will be considered in turn in the rest of this chapter.

NOMINIGENTILISATION

Both the process of linguistic composition and the theme of the
linguistic quest play an important part in Joyce's novel, together with
the more general narrative/thematic recurring pattern of the
(always frustrated) search for an explanation, for an object, for the
origin of a name, and so on. Although several 'curial' situations
occur throughout the *Wake*, no satisfactory or definitive solution is
ever found. There are many trials and interrogations, such as that of
Yawn in book III or the trial of Festy King in chapter 1.4, and quests
for objects which are never found or discovered, like the colour of
the Maggies' drawers or the 'heliotrope' in the 'Mime' chapter.[7] This
happens from the very beginning: on page 5, for instance, after the
first 'introductory' paragraphs and the interweaving of the story of
Tim Finnegan's fall with that of the tower of Babel, the question is
asked, 'What then agentlike brought about that tragoady thun-
dersday this municipal sin business?' (*FW* 5.13–14), thus soliciting an
explanation and the name of the perpetrator of a tragedy signalled
by thunder (as at Babel, as in Vico's cycles), which affected the city,
and whose association of sin and business already prefigures the
interweavings of city building, Edenic fall and financial transactions
that I described in the previous chapter. The 'search' becomes
almost a prayer for an answer (*FW* 5.18–19), and then two possible
explanations for the fall of Finnegan are offered: 'It may half been a
missfired brick, as some say' (a cause half-dismissed, or not quite
satisfactory), 'or it mought have been due to a collupsus of his back
promises, as others looked at it', an account which suggests a failure
to keep promises, the collapse of a building (again, the tower of
Babel), but also casts Tim Finnegan as a colossus, a gigantic figure
like Nimrod (I shall come back to this point later); an insertion in
brackets, however – '(There extand by now one thousand and one
stories, all told, of the same)' (*FW* 5.26–9) – already multiplies the
possible interpretations of the fall and the stories that narrate/
explain (or fail to explain) it to a very large and significant number.

Chapter 1.2 attempts to reconstruct the story of HCE's acquisition of his name in terms that remind us very closely of Dante's search for the illustrious vernacular. True, the investigation into these origins looks like a doomed quest from the start, more likely to raise doubts than to dispel them:

> Comes the question are these the facts of his nominigentilisation . . . Are those their fata which we read in sibylline between the *fas* and its *nefas*? No dung on the road? . . . We shall perhaps not so soon see.   (*FW* 31.33–32.02)

The repeated question, the dubitative 'perhaps', the deferment of the possible explanation seem aimed at discouraging any hunter set on finding a quick solution to his quest.

When HCE is given the nickname 'Here Comes Everybody' (*FW* 32.18–19), he is declared 'magnificently well worthy of any and all such universalisation' (*FW* 32.20–1), thus emphasising traits that also pertain to the *vulgare illustre*. HCE, who is described in the first two pages of the chapter as a 'grand old gardener' (*FW* 30.13, like Adam in Eden, and like Dante and the Italian vernacular in the *De vulgari eloquentia*), a 'bailiwick' and a 'turnpiker' (*FW* 31.27), soon becomes a viceroy, observing from 'his viceregal booth' (*FW* 32.36) a representation of *A Royal Divorce*. Elevated to a kinship with royal figures (*aulicum*) and through the coincidence of his personal story with the performance of the comedy staged before him, HCE is the protagonist of a 'comic' plot that can be described as going 'from good start to happy finish' (*FW* 32.24–5), a formula which also describes the story of the language according to the salvational narrative of the *De vulgari eloquentia* (from the good start of Edenic language through the linguistic *felix culpa* of Babel to the happy ending of Dante's redemption of the Babelic confusion) and may parody Dante's own definition of comedy as that which 'begins with sundry adverse conditions, but ends happily'.[8]

The setting of HCE's 'nominigentilisation' supports the identification with the illustrious and courtly language assembled from the local 'vulgar' dialects: the scene takes place 'in that king's treat house of satin alustrelike', where a 'truly catholic assemblage gathered together' (*FW* 32.25–6) by 'courteous permission for pious purposes' (*FW* 32.30–1), while HCE looks on, a 'cecelticocommediant in his own wise' (*FW* 33.03–4), perhaps a Celtic embodiment of the 'divine comic Denti Alligator' (*FW* 440.06) and of his supreme work, the pious and divine *Comedy*. Many of the ingredients from the *De vulgari eloquentia* are present here: the method of assemblage from different vulgar dialects finds its correspondent in the gathering together of the populace; the illustriousness of the vernacular may appear in 'alustrelike', and its characteristic of being *aulicum* (i.e. spoken in the royal court and residing there), also conveyed by the 'courtesy' of the permission, is translated into the representation of the 'comedy' *A Royal Divorce* and into its taking place in the 'king's' house (cf. 'palatinum foret'; 'conveniens est ut in ea conversetur et habitet', *Dve* i.xviii, 2). Finally, HCE is the 'folksforefather' (*FW* 33.04), the father of the people; being an avatar of Adam, he is naturally the father of the entire human race, and being identified with Finn MacCool, he is an ancestor of the Irish people. He is 'Haveth Childers Everywhere' (*FW* 535.34–5), the '*multipopulipater*' (*FW* 81.05) and the 'folkenfather of familyans' (*FW* 382.18) who has 'the entirety of his house about him' (*FW* 33.04–5): he is in the same position as Dante's *vulgare cardinale*, the 'pater familias' and hinge around which the family of the Italian dialects turn and revolve (*Dve* i.xviii, 1).

If a parallel of the story of Tim Finnegan with the story of Babel and of the fall of language was set up since the beginning of *FW* i.1 (pp. 4–5), the analogy is now carried further: HCE's predicament and the story of his name also find an equivalent in the situation of the dialects contemporary to Dante and his attempt to transcend their multiplicity. The 'nominigentilisation' of HCE (the ennobling of his name) corresponds to an ennobling of his social position, and this elevation of his status parallels the *De vulgari eloquentia*'s elevation of the 'populace' of *vulgares* into a single, superior language representative of the whole class of Italian vernaculars as well as of the notion of 'Italianness' itself (*Dve* i. xvi, 2–5).

In the second part of chapter i.2, when the focus on the 'nominigentilisation' shifts to HCE's meeting with the cad in Phoenix Park, the narrative too seems to move from the analogy with the unifying part of Dante's treatment of the vernaculars to a parallel with the historical part of the treatise, more concerned with Babelic fragmentation and the decay of tongues. As an ironic contrapuntal note, the story of the meeting is described in a bracketed passage as '(an amalgam as absorbing as calzium chloereydes and hydrophobe sponges could make it)' (*FW* 35.01–2), which paradoxically suggests, within the context of fragmentation evoked in the story at this point, the 'synthetic' or unifying operation similar to the one presented in the first part of the chapter as well as to the one suggested by Beckett in 'Dante. . . Bruno. Vico. . Joyce'; this simultaneous and contradictory coexistence of (al)chemical and physical amalgam and antagonism also anticipates Shem's fabrication of his synthetic, alchemical ink in 1.7, while the hydrophobe sponges may on the one hand recall another artist's (Stephen Dedalus's) hydrophobia and, on the other, evoke the customers of HCE's pub and HCE's own hydrophobic amalgam of the alcoholic leftovers from their drinks in chapter II.3 (I shall discuss these aspects later in the chapter). As pointed out in chapter 2, the exchanges between the antagonists HCE and the cad and their later re-enactment in 1.4 take place in derivative, vulgar or sacrilegious languages; if HCE's 'misdemeanour' in Phoenix Park can be read as Adam's sin in the Garden of Eden, then the specification of the date (the encounter happens on the anniversary of the 'confusioning of human races', *FW* 35.05) both conflates the two episodes of Babel and of the original sin, and inverts the chronological order of the two events, making the original sin happen on the anniversary of Babel.

The wording of HCE's posture and attitude, 'now standing full erect' (*FW* 36.14), and his '*H*eidelberg mannleich *c*avern *e*thics' (*FW* 37.01–2, my italics) associate the biblical subtext with the evolution of the human species – whether as evolutionary progress (from ape to man, as in *The Origin of the Species*) or regress (as in the suggestion implicit in the title of Darwin's later essay *The Descent of Man*, also evoked by Butt's regression to a 'scimmianised twinge', *FW* 344.08); the refusal to choose between the scientific or Biblical explanation of the origin of man may indeed imply that the performance of sin amounts to an evolution of the species, as in the case of Adam and Eve when they gained knowledge through the sinful eating of the apple.

As in other allusions to the building of the tower discussed earlier, HCE's pointing to the '*duc de Fer's* overgrown milestone' (*FW* 36.18) connects Babel with an erect penis through the reference to the obelisk of the Wellington monument in Phoenix Park and, in an implicit confirmation of both the vision of Babel as a *felix culpa* and the reversal of values in the *Wake*, the monument is described by HCE as a sign of redemption (*FW* 36.24–5); but the Wellington monument should be symbolic of neither linguistic nor political redemption, if it stands for the tower of Babel and celebrates a historical figure who led Britain to reinforce the international power of its empire – that same empire which also subjugated Ireland. The ensuing act of language is an attempt to 'balbly call to memory' (*FW* 37.16) the words heard or spoken before, which, as I pointed out in the previous chapter, evoke Dante's interpretation of the punishment suffered by the builders of Babel, the forgetting of the original language. Later, as the cad ends his evening eating and drinking, the rumours of HCE's misdemeanour begin to spread, grow increasingly more imprecise, and become 'corrupt', with a fate similar to that of the post-Babelic languages, until Hosty composes and sings the ballad, inviting the listeners to '*silentium in curia!*' (*FW* 44.04). Thus, the chapter which had begun in a 'curial' situation of investigation into the origin of the name/language, follows the vicissitudes of this name (both in the sense of proper name and of good or bad reputation) until, with the spreading rumours/decay, we find ourselves once again in the (silent) *curia*, not having been able to discover anything precise about any of the matters in question, being left in doubt also about what happened exactly on 'that' (indeed, it is not clear which) (in)famous day. We are in fact still uncertain even about the name of the hero of the ballad, of whom we are told that 'Some vote him Vike, some mote him Mike, some dub him Llyn and Phin while others hail him Lug Bug Dan Lop, Lex, Lax, Gunne or Guinn. Some apt him Arth, some bapt him Barth, Coll, Noll, Soll, Will, Weel, Wall.' The only solution to this alliterative proliferation of imperfect names, each shared only by a limited group, is to invent a new, arbitrary one: 'but I parse him Persse O'Reilly else he's called no name at all' (*FW* 44.10–14), which may remind us of the post-Babelian amnesia, when new (arbitrary) names had to be invented to describe things because the original ones were irretrievably lost.

A PULING SAMPLE JUNGLE OF WOODS

The quest for the language is naturally an outstanding feature of the linguistic puzzle of the *Wake*, and the question about what the language spoken is crops up time and time again in the text. During the interrogation of Yawn in chapter III.3 we are invited to puzzle over the riddle, 'Are we speachin d'anglas landadge or are you sprakin sea Djoytsch?' (FW 485.12–13; as in the case of the post-Babelian languages organised by Dante in a perfectly logical system of ordered confusion, these questions pair off verbs and nouns that evoke the same language: speaking English, *Deutsch sprechen*). At the beginning of their dialogue in *FW* I.1, Mutt and Jute embark on a similar attempt to establish a common language: 'You tollerday donsk? N. You tolkatiff scowegian? Nn. You spigotty anglease? Nnn. You phonio saxo? Nnnn' (*FW* 16.05–7). The answer is an increasingly emphatic series of denials, and the language is never defined. On the other hand, as Colin MacCabe has pointed out, even if *Finnegans Wake* is seen as a continuous lapsus, 'One consequence of recognising the importance of the lapsus is that it implies that *Finnegans Wake* is written in *English*.' MacCabe goes on: 'The answer to the question "Are we speachin d'anglas landadge" (485.12/13) must be "yes" because if there was not some continuity within the text then the lapsus would be impossible.'[9] In other words, interpreting the *Wake* implies measuring its distance from the standard of the language, and this can be done only if we assume that a standard – everywhere present though nowhere apparent – can be recovered in the intricacies of the text. However, I would interpret MacCabe's 'lapsus' not only as a Freudian slip of the tongue but also as lapse from the original, correct language of grace; thus the answer to the question of the language will always be a simultaneous 'yes', as MacCabe says, and 'no', or 'Nnnn', as the *Wake* suggests.

Reading the *Wake* is, one could say, like being lost in the forest of a thorny and intricate multiplicity of languages and of different accents, and having to sift them, or hunt in them, in a quest certainly not for 'the' one, noble language, or for elegance, as it is in the *De vulgari eloquentia*, but for sense. The feeling most readers of *Finnegans Wake* are likely to experience is probably in consonance with the question, asked in the 'mamafesta' chapter, where the 'letter'/ *Finnegans Wake* is examined: 'You is feeling like you was lost in the bush, boy?' (*FW* 112.03). As the 'letter' is found by the hen in the dung, it is appropriate that this bewildered person to whom the question is asked should shout out, 'Bethicket me for a stump of a beech if I have the *poultriest* notions what the farest he all means' (*FW* 112.05–6, my italics) after exclaiming, 'It is a puling sample jungle of woods' (*FW* 112.04). The problem of obscurity is conveyed through references to bushes, woods, thickets, trees and forests, also remindful of Dante's sense of being lost in the *selva oscura* at the beginning of the *Inferno*. In one sense, it is a 'pure and simple jumble of words'. At the same time, however, 'puling' may remind Italian ears of the word *pula* (Italian for 'chaff'), what is thrown away to clean the wheat. Swiftly moving between metaphors in his treatise, and allegorising his task as a poet through references to both the gardener Adam and the hunter Nimrod, Dante hunts the panther/ language in the wood and sifts the dialects in order to separate the good ones from the bad ones, the wheat from the chaff. In *Finnegans Wake* Dante's sifting of the language for illustriousness is turned into the necessity for the reader to sift the Wakean idiom for meaning – and even then, the reader cannot throw away much and must keep and accept different readings as it is too often impossible to tell the chaff from the wheat or the wood from the trees: it is a polysemic 'jungle of woods' in which even contrasting layers of meaning coexist.

However, whereas the panther eludes Dante's careful chase and the *vulgare illustre* must therefore be found rationally – what Dante claims to have achieved by the end of the first book of his treatise – elusiveness is a key component in the semantic system of the *Wake* and it cannot be done away with, even by systematic and scrupulous reasoning. Much as possible meanings may be discussed and the understanding of the text increased by scholarship, there always remains a degree of non-activated possible significance which the reader cannot decipher. By means of its programmatic all-inclusiveness and through the assumption of the concept of the microcosm containing the macrocosm, each individual word refers to another, and this one to yet another, and so on, in a virtually never-ending chain, so that 'word' and 'world' potentially coincide and definitive meaning must inevitably elude the 'hunter' in/of *Finnegans Wake*. Entering the *Wake* thus arouses in the reader sensations similar to the ones that Dante experiences when he walks through the gate of Hell in *Inferno* III – a condition that the little boy in 'The Sisters' was also familiar with.[10] The first impressions Dante registers are obscurity – both a difficulty in understanding and physical darkness – and a confusion of voices and of different, distorted accents:

> Diverse lingue, orribili favelle,
> parole di dolore, accenti d'ira,
> voci alte e fioche, e suon di man con elle
>   facevano un tumulto, il qual s'aggira
> sempre in quell'aura sanza tempo tinta,
> come la rena quando turbo spira.   (*Inf* III, 25–30)

(Diverse tongues, horrible languages, words of woe, accents of wrath, voices shrill and faint, and the sound of clapping hands, made a tumult that ever swirls in that timeless darkened air, like sand when a whirlwind blows.)

These diverse tongues and horrible languages, the shouting and the anger, the woe and the wrath, the tumult and the swirling immediately remind the reader of the punishment of Babel and what the immediate consequences of God's striking the builders of the tower must have been, and they may evoke for the Joycean reader the obscure, strange and confusing context of the *Wake*. As they proceed in their journey through this post-Babelic multiplicity, Dante and Virgil are recognised by the sinners and recognise them by their accents: Lombard, Florentine, Bolognese, and so on, and this list of languages must include the instances of invented or deformed speech that I discussed in chapter 2.[11] Eventually, the pilgrims come to meet the cause of such extreme confusion, Nimrod. What Dante sees in the journey which begins in a forest, therefore, reflects, in a way, also the fate that he has described in his treatise for the forest of post-Babelian languages. In 'Dante. . . Bruno. Vico. . Joyce', Beckett writes that Dante advocated in the *De vulgari eloquentia* a 'synthetic language' assembled from 'the purest elements from each dialect', and affirms that this is 'precisely what he did. He did not write in Florentine any more than in Neapolitan' ('DBVJ' 18). However, as I pointed out in my 'Prelude', this is not true, and indeed Neapolitan elements are very hard to find in the *Commedia*. The skeleton of his language is illustrious Florentine; on this main frame, Dante inserts a large number of borrowings from vulgar (in the sense of 'low') registers (predominant in the first *cantica* and generally diminishing as Dante ascends higher through Purgatory and Paradise), and of words, expressions, sometimes entire sentences, taken from other dialects or languages (especially Bolognese, illustrious Sicilian, and some Lombard, and then Provençal, French, and, of course, Latin). Most of these are very often adapted or Italianised, and their use is justified by the fact that Dante is accompanied by Virgil, who is sometimes allowed to speak in the Lombard dialect of his native region (anachronistically of course, since Virgil would have spoken Latin and not a tongue derived from the influence of Germanic languages on Latin), and by the fact that Bolognese, Sicilian, Provençal, French, Latin had already established poetical traditions and could be considered languages of 'high culture'.

The Italian linguist Giacomo Devoto affirms categorically: 'Dante used an essentially homogeneous vocabulary, *he did not strive to achieve a lexical synthesis*, like the one that his theory required.'[12] Another expert historian of the Italian language, Bruno Migliorini, explains:

Although Dante adheres very closely to native usage, he looks around himself and accepts, beside the terms and forms of contemporary Florentine, also words and forms which are disappearing from use, some forms of western and southern Tuscan, some *rare* words from other Italian dialects, many Latin words, several French ones. Such a broad horizon, however, has a strict limitation: *whereas the poet readily admits, when he needs them, Florentine forms and words, the others must have had some sort of literary consecration.*[13]

The language of *Finnegans Wake* can be placed somewhere in between Dante's theory and practice, borrowing while at the same time distancing itself from both. It is very similar in its method of composition and conception to the principles set forth in the *De vulgari eloquentia* in that it is an idiom which has been 'invented' especially for this book, constructed by extracting lexical, morphological, phonetic elements from a very large number of different existing languages and by grafting them on to the structure of Anglo-Irish.[14] The idiom thus obtained bears traces ('redolet', in Dante's metaphor) of all those languages, but is none of them. As in the forest of dialects searched by Dante some vernaculars come closer to the *vulgare illustre*, so different languages contribute to 'Wakese' in different measures, some of them more, others less. Laurent Milesi has demonstrated, on the evidence of Joyce's notebooks and drafts, that the issues of Babel and multilingualism were linked and developed together during the early years of the composition of the *Wake*.[15] Joyce could draw all along from the languages he spoke fluently or knew well, while the use of 'decorative languages' can often be dated more accurately thanks to the lists of items that Joyce drew either from printed material or with the help of friends and private lessons. Some of the languages used have a specific function (for instance, Norwegian is mostly linked with the appearance of HCE, who is of Viking origin). Milesi argues that whereas most of the languages, whenever they appear, are usually fused with English or other idioms, Anglo-Irish is very seldom contaminated.[16] This confers on Anglo-Irish a sort of superiority or nobility which no other language achieves in the text, and supports the analogy drawn above with Dante's use of Florentine as the prevalent frame in the *Divine Comedy* over other linguistic borrowings.

Joyce's language, like that proposed by the *De vulgari eloquentia*, is both abstract – in that it does not coincide with any actual existing language and is 'abstracted'/extracted from them – and concrete, in that it is concretely realised in the *Wake* itself. But Joyce's method of assemblage and accretion goes beyond, or beneath, Dante's. The *vulgare illustre* is a language that has been sieved, purified of any base, rough-hewn element, and is therefore the result of a process of distillation which grants it the status of a noble language, suitable only for the worthiest subjects. On the contrary, the 'night' language of the *Wake* draws its materials from several tongues (contemporary or dead, natural or artificial), incorporating every element, from the basest to the highest. In this context, the hint that 'A baser meaning has been read into these characters the literal sense of which decency can safely scarcely hint' (*FW* 33.14–15) associates the need for polysemic interpretation with the requirement to use a 'vulgar' language, and shows that the Wakean idiom can deal with any subject, the most material or vulgar or the most spiritual – indeed, it very often does it simultaneously, neutralising all difference between 'low' and 'good' language, in a move that is comparable to the way Joyce had neutralised in *Ulysses* the distinction between 'low' and 'worthy' subjects, for example by presenting Bloom to the reader as he enjoys his breakfast of kidneys and the fine tanginess of their faint scent of urine (*U* 65), as he goes to the toilet and reflects on literature, or by having Stephen and Bloom's moment of 'communion' take place as they urinate together (*U* 825).

Once the reader has acknowledged and accepted that the procedure of reading *Finnegans Wake* involves recognising and interpreting all these differences in the text, the same process can be extended also to those words in *Finnegans Wake* which are apparently written in straightforward (Irish) English and whose comprehension would therefore not normally pose any problems. Thus although Anglo-Irish constitutes the skeleton of the Wakean language, it also becomes 'foreign' in the book and requires the reader to treat it as such, to regard it in a new way. To adapt Dante's metaphor, 'Wakese' becomes the 'metron' for all the other languages used in the book, which must submit to the rules not of their own individual phonological, grammatical, semantic systems, but of the new system established by the 'nat language' of *Finnegans Wake*. We may recall again Stephen's conversation with the dean in *A Portrait of the Artist as a Young Man*, when he thinks of English as an 'acquired language'. In a way, while Joyce exploits and goes beyond Dante's project, at the same time he reverses it, expanding the potentiality of the 'one' language (Anglo-Irish) to include the numberless varieties (both 'high' and 'low') offered by multilingualism so as to create a new idiom which is, simultaneously, both the synthesis of a multiplicity and an extension (a 'pluralisation') of the 'one'.

CHIMERAHUNTER

What strikes one in the *De vulgari eloquentia* is that Dante as hunter of the panther (the illustrious language) casts himself once again into the role of Nimrod, the giant and hunter who instigated the building of the tower of Babel. Of course, whereas the hunter Nimrod caused the language to break up into a multiplicity, Dante now dons a similar role in his quest but reverses its function and searches through the confused plurality in order to transcend differences and found a unified, unifying language.

HCE, both hunter and hunted, also embodies this *coincidentia oppositorum*: in chapter 1.6 'hounded become haunter, hunter become fox' (132.16–17), and in the last chapter the '*huntered* persent human' (*FW* 618.36, my emphasis) combines both roles. Sometimes disguised as 'Ramrod, the meaty hunter' (*FW* 435.13–14), HCE is Nimrod and, like Dante's 'Nembrotto' in *Inf* XXXI, he is both a giant and a tower. The panther-hunter (Dante himself) is now downgraded to a 'molehunter' (*FW* 576.25; as we have seen in the second chapter, HCE was buried and spent some time in an 'underground heaven, or mole's paradise', *FW* 76.33–4), and becomes 'the eternal chimera-hunter Oriolopos' (*FW* 107.14),[17] the hunter of the mythical monster with a composite body, a fancy which does not actually exist anywhere and which is made up from parts of different animals, as the *vulgare illustre* is made up of parts taken from many different dialects. 'Oriolopos' combines the allusion to the mythical giant hunter Orion[18] with an echo of the episode of the meeting with the cad in the Park, when HCE is asked the time and is described as the 'oriuolate' (*FW* 35.11).[19] Through the identification with such fragmented, shattered or dismembered characters as Humpty Dumpty or the Egyptian god Osiris, and the dismembering of HCE himself in 1.4, HCE can coincide both with the fragmented condition of post-Babelic idioms and with the (chimerical) recomposition of the language achieved by the illustrious vernacular. The buried HCE can also identify with the coffin and with the letter dug out of the midden heap by the hen. The damaged letter which re-emerges from the dung and is analysed in 1.5 can therefore be both the text and the remnants of the fragmented/fragmentary body of HCE. Not being whole and thus needing (re)composition, the letter/language/ HCE (or its parts) are, like the post-Babelian languages, subject to being changed, modified in 'variously inflected, differently pronounced, otherwise spelled, changeably meaning vocable scriptsigns' (*FW* 118.26–8).

As I suggested earlier, HCE, the 'grand old gardener' (*FW* 30.13), subsumes Adam's role as 'gardener' of Eden and the one described by Dante and shared by both the illustrious language and the poet: Dante must cut off branches and root out the bushes in the tangled wood of dialects, and he rhetorically asks of the activity of the *vulgare cardinale*: 'Nonne cotidie extirpat sentosos frutices de ytala silva? Nonne cotidie vel plantas inserit vel plantaria plantat? Quid aliud agricole sui satagunt, nisi ut amoveant et admoveant, ut dictum est?' ('Does it not daily root out thorny bushes from the Italian wood? Does it not daily implant cuttings or plant young plants? What else are its foresters engaged in if not in removing and fetching in as has been said?', *Dve* I.xviii, 1). Shem the Penman, the poet-figure in the *Wake*, also shares something of this function with HCE, probably having inherited it from the father (though as we shall see later in this chapter, the father's and the son's roles are essentially different despite the similarities). As a child in the 'garden nursery', just before asking 'the first riddle of the universe' (*FW* 170.04) and thus reiterating (or establishing the prototype of?) all subsequent quests and questions, Shem plays with 'thistlewords' (*FW* 169.22–3), words that may sting, that require weeding. He also has 'an artificial tongue with a natural curl' (*FW* 169.15–16), reminiscent of the *vulgare illustre*, a natural tongue (cf. *Dve* I.i) extracted by Dante from the local dialects but which, through a process of refinement, is transformed into a somewhat artificial product.

AND MADE SYNTHETIC INK

Shem, the 'low hero' described by his antagonist twin brother Shaun in 1.7, consistently prefers artificial to natural products, including food. Artificiality comes quite naturally to Shem the artist, 'Vulgariano' (*FW* 181.14), and this could be related to Dante's theories of the natural and artificial tongues, especially if one reads Shem's gathering of the crumbs of other people's table talk as a parodic allusion to the *Convivio*:

All the time he kept on treasuring with condign satisfaction each and every crumb of trektalk . . . and if ever . . . delicate tippits were thrown out to him touching his evil courses by some wellwishers, vainly pleading by scriptural arguments . . . he would . . . let a lent hit a hint and begin to tell all the intelligentsia . . . the whole lifelong swrine story of his entire low cornaille existence . . . unconsciously explaining, for inkstands, with a meticulosity bordering on the insane, the various meanings of all the different foreign parts of speech he misused . . .   (*FW* 172.29–173.36)

Compare Dante's words in the *Convivio* describing how the medieval poet would treasure with great satisfaction the crumbs falling from the table talk of the blessed: 'E io adunque, che non seggio a la beata mensa, ma, fuggito de la pastura del vulgo, a' piedi di coloro che seggiono ricolgo di quello che da loro cade' ('And I therefore, who do not sit at the blessed table, but, having fled the pasture of the common herd, at the feet of those who are seated I gather some of what they let fall', *Conv* i.i, 10). In the treatise, from his assumed lowly position at the feet of 'the intelligentsia' that sit at the table, Dante explains, by making recourse to 'scriptural arguments' and with extreme – though not quite 'bordering on the insane' – 'meticulosity', the 'various meanings' (in theory, at least four) of his own poems. These are layered texts, similar to the 'palimpsests' which Shem 'piously' forges (*FW* 182.02), and containing abundant references to the 'whole lifelong . . . story of his entire . . . existence' – an existence whose possible 'evil courses' he also wishes to justify through his 'pleading' writing.

Dante's *vulgare illustre* is, in a way, the result of a process of distillation of the existing imperfect dialects. Somewhat similarly, Shem the Penman fabricates a 'synthetic', 'indelible ink' out of his own excrement, after having produced speech as if through culinary-alchemical processes often reminiscent of sorcery.[20] As we have seen, Samuel Beckett defines the idiom constructed by Dante as a 'synthetic language' ('DBVJ' 18), similar in method of composition and scope to that of the *Wake*, and points out that between Dante and Shem the Penman 'there exists considerable circumstantial similarity' ('DBVJ' 17). Shem playfully cooks, or concocts, a recipe which requires the use of various strange components, from egg whites and yolks (*FW* 184.18), to cinnamon, locusts, beeswax and liquorice (*FW* 184.20–1). All these ingredients must be differently cooked and go through various food-processing activities (*FW* 184.17–19), while Shem, who chants 'his cantraps of *fermented* words'

(*FW* 184.25–6, my emphasis – another suggestion of distillation) and pronounces magic formulae, is boycotted, so that

he winged away on a wildgoup's chase across the kathartic ocean and made synthetic ink and sensitive paper for his own end out of his wit's waste. You ask, in Sam Hill, how? Let manner and matter of this for these our sporting times be cloaked up in the language of blushfed porporates that an Anglican ordinal, not reading his own rude dunsky tunga . . .

(*FW* 185.05–11)

This passage carries biographical references to the linguistic and literary training that enabled Joyce to achieve the artistic maturity and independence which, in turn, made it possible for him to fly by the nets that kept Ireland in cultural, political and social subjugation and which he escaped through the choice of voluntary exile (cf. the 'wildgoup's chase'). Intersecting with this autobiographical strand, references to Dante's project of synthetic linguistic composition accumulate after the significant mention of the 'synthetic ink' and in response to yet another question for an explanation: 'ordinal', in opposition to 'cardinal' and through the association with 'Anglican'[21] and 'blushfed porporates' (the colour of the cardinal's robe), suggests both *cardinale* and *curiale*, insofar as it refers to ecclesiastical matters; purple, on the other hand, is also the colour that symbolises royalty, and may therefore also hint at *aulicum*, while the 'rude . . . tunga' evokes a vulgar tongue. The 'chase' will then acquire overtones of Dante's hunt for the illustrious vulgar language while already in exile – Dante himself was, after all, a wild goose of his time. Finally, the words 'Let manner and matter . . . be cloaked up' suggests the method of fourfold interpretation, according to which the literal meaning 'clothes' or 'cloaks' the allegorical; as we saw in the first chapter, the metaphor of clothing is used in the analysis of the 'letter' or 'mamafesta' ('clothiering', *FW* 109.31) and was a usual one in medieval explanations of allegory.

Having fed on artificial, processed aliments, Shem now reprocesses his food by digesting it, and from the by-products he concocts his synthetic ink as the artist who, making use of all the elements at his disposal, including the basest ones, re-elaborates them, digesting them as it were, and transforming them into an indelible and eternal work of art (though the reader knows that Shaun's ironic narrative voice in I.7 throws some doubt over the 'eternal' value of Shem's synthetic/digestive process. More about this later). This process, described in a long Latin passage (*FW* 185.14–26), is thus connected to the complete biological-physiological cycle of nutrition (eating, digestion and defecation) and fertilisation, or re-employment of the wastes of digestion (and of the intellect: 'out of his wit's waste', *FW* 185.07–8) as nourishment for the artist's creation of the work of art. Significantly, Shem, the twin associated with the tree in the *Wake*, lives on the humus of the earth, and needs the soil to be fertilised. Thus, the numerous allusions in *Finnegans Wake* to defecation and excrement may often also imply an allusion to the production, or product, of art. At the same time as it celebrates a process of distillation (and therefore renovation), the episode seems to carry over some echoes from the implicitly ambiguous position which I have already described for Dante, who seeks a noble, redemptive language while taking up Nimrod's role as hunter and builder of the tower of Babel and sharing his sinful pride. Like Dante and Nimrod, Shem, called 'divi Orionis' (*FW* 185.24; we have seen above that HCE was associated with the mythical hunter Orion at 107.14), also shares traits of the hunter: he sounds a trumpet and sings a psalm, rather like Nimrod who sounds a horn (*Inf* XXXI, 12, 71) and whose confused babble is ironically described by Dante as a 'psalm' (*Inf* XXXI, 69).

It is relevant that Shem's distillation episode is written in Latin: as set passages in a foreign language within the *Wake* are often precise references or 'quotations', one may wonder whether this Latin account of Shem's distillation of vulgar matter may refer to Dante's Latin account of the history and 'distillation' of the *vulgares*. One could however also be reminded of the custom, still widespread until the first part of the century, of masking obscene or saucy passages under the appearance of a learned language which not everyone would be able to read, or, in the case of translations, of leaving them in the original language.[22] Following the exactly opposite convention, when Shem fabricates his excremental ink, the short but very explicit English interpolations '(Highly prosy, crap in his hand, sorry!) . . . (did a piss, says he was dejected, asks to be exonerated)' (*FW* 185.17–23) give us the down-to-earth substance of the Latin descriptions.

Not unlike Dante's 'synthetic' universalising of the *vulgare* into an illustrious redemption of Babel, Shem's production of the indelible ink would perform an alchemical act of linguistic distillation and prepare one of literary production, while at the same time performing a eucharistic transubstantiation that would transform bodily matter into something transcendent and eternal. Like his avatar Stephen, Shem poses as the 'priest of eternal imagination, transmuting the daily bread of experience into the radiant body of everliving life'. These words, excerpted from *A Portrait* (221), echo Stanislaus Joyce's description of how his brother saw himself giving spiritual enjoyment by converting 'the bread of everyday life into something that has a permanent artistic life of its own'.[23] This eucharistic theme is present also in Dante, especially in the *Convivio*, where, as we have seen, the author provides his readers with some 'crumbs' of the 'table where the bread of angels is consumed' (*Conv* 1.i); however, while the third English interpolation in the Latin passage, '(faked O'Ryan's, the indelible ink)' (*FW* 185.25–6), makes explicit the link between the poet's desire to forge an eternal literature (or maybe the as yet uncreated conscience of his Irish race) and the transformation of reality that this forging/faking will entail, it also shows the rather dubious transformations through which an 'original' language (here the Latin *divi Orionis*) can be assimilated as the convincingly Anglo-Irish, but not quite authentic, brand name O'Ryan.

The process of depuration described above can be especially performed and achieved by the artist who has purged himself by flying into exile 'across the kathartic ocean'; at the same time, it can be argued that Shaun's ironic voice, deflating Shem's eternalising desire, trashes his aesthetic and turns it back into nothing more than an aesthetic of trash, or an early form of *merdismo*. Is Shaun's irony in portraying his brother then comparable to that of the narrator of *A Portrait of the Artist as a Young Man*, who methodically deflates Stephen's highest artistic visions? Yet Joyce himself had been accused of vulgarity, of pornography, of writing the 'literature of the latrine';[24] is then Shaun's obtuse critique of the vulgarity of the Artist as a Young Man in turn ironised to satirise the writer's own critics? How seriously are we to take Shem's vulgar sources and his use of them? And Joyce's? If it is true that in the Middle Ages 'Whatever gold one might sift *ex sterco Vergilii*, excrement was still excrement', yet the modernist Shem-like Joyce, in distilling his 'golden' poetry from the precious 'excrement' of Dante's theories, was also transubstantiating the poet's remedial linguistics into a new technique of characterisation, a narrative of fall and rebirth, of sons overturning fathers (a point I shall illustrate in the next sections of this chapter), and into a plot of artistic redemption of the commonplace or trivial (literally, what is found at the *trivium* or crossroads and, by extension, the encounter between different texts and traditions – one could actually say 'the intertextual') through a gigantic epiphany of language. In both cases, the common (and trivial) Irish expletive 'Holy shit' becomes highly and uncannily appropriate.

PARLEYGLUTTON

Shem's artistic distillation of excrement is counterbalanced by his father's more prosaic brewing and drinking of alcohol, but the linguistic substratum is still there; the similarity between 'gluttony', or 'glutton' and words related to language and production of sounds ('glottal', 'polyglot', 'glottology', etc.), and the fact that the acts of eating, drinking and speaking use the same organs make it possible in the *Wake* to flow easily from the one aspect to the other. Thus, HCE is a 'parleyglutton' (*FW* 240.27–8), and the men in his pub drink 'through their grooves of blarneying' (*FW* 371.15–16), that is, through channels of eloquence and drinking. At the end of chapter II.3, after the closing of the pub, HCE uses all the dregs left in his customers' glasses (and not the noblest parts from each glass, as Dante would certainly have recommended) and mixes them – recycles them, as it were – in a new alcoholic concoction produced from 'pre-distilled' material. Carole Brown has identified several theories of language in the last pages of the chapter; beside Grimm's Law ('Gramm's laws', *FW* 378.28), these include three humorous speculations on the origins of speech formulated by philologists at the turn of the century: the Pooh-pooh theory, the Bow-wow theory and the Ding-Dong, Tick-Tock, Bang-Bong, or Knock-Knock theory.[25] To this list of fanciful theories we can add Dante's rather more serious but equally debunked *vulgare illustre*.

As HCE drinks his composite brew, he is 'thruming through all to himself with diversed tonguesed' (*FW* 381.19–20, remindful of Dante's 'diverse tongues' in *Inf* III, 25), 'like a blurney Cashelmagh crooner' (*FW* 381.22), and sending it down 'his woolly throat' (*FW* 381.26), 'in some particular cases with the assistance of his venerated tongue' (*FW* 381.31–2) – after all, Dante's defence of the vulgar tongue does employ tones of veneration. Among other dregs, HCE drinks the remnants from a product of the 'Phoenix brewery' (*FW* 382.04), thus bringing together the theme of the rebirth in and of language by now indistinguishable from the motif of the linguistic and spiritual *felix culpa*.

The echo of 'blarney' is interesting in this context, as it is related to Blarney Castle and its famous Blarney stone, said to confer the gift of eloquence on those who kiss it lying supine and bending backward. Blarney (eloquence) and vulgarity also come together in chapter 1.8, when, among the gifts that ALP distributes to the children, she gives 'a pair of Blarney braggs' to one of them and 'a hairpin slatepencil' to another 'doing her best with her *volgar* fractions' (*FW* 211.11–13, my italics), where the 'fractions' suggests, beyond the obvious mathematical term, the fragmentary nature of the 'vulgar' language (*volgare* in Italian) and its analysis in a work on vulgar, or vernacular, eloquence.

Ironically, it is at the end of II.3, after drinking all the leftovers in his customers' glasses – after distilling as it were his own synthetic language/drink – that the 'folkenfather of familyans' (*FW* 382.18), saturated with his alcoholic mixture, drops down to the floor (this is also what happens to all the languages in *Finnegans Wake*, 'collapsed' and 'put to sleep', as Joyce is reported to have said of the technique of his last novel[26]), in his drunken fall evoking both Tim Finnegan and Dante, who is not immune from this treatment in his own *Divine Comedy*: in canto III of the *Inferno*, as an earthquake strikes and a high wind rises, Dante falls down 'come l'uom cui sonno piglia' ('like a man who is seized by sleep', *Inf* III, 136) and, at the beginning of the next canto, he is wakened up again by a 'greve truono' ('a heavy thunderclap broke the deep sleep in my head', *Inf* IV, 1–2; shortly after Dante, moved by Francesca's story, drops down 'come corpo morto cade', 'as a dead body falls', *Inf* V, 142), whereas HCE, his mind clouded by alcohol, 'just slumped to throne' (*FW* 382.26).

MANUREVRING IN OPEN ORDURE

Sitting on the throne, or slumping on it, brings us back to Shem's distillation of his excrement;[27] but the best-known instance of defecation in *Finnegans Wake* is in the episode of 'How Buckley Shot the Russian General', in chapter II.3.[28] Butt/Buckley, who narrates the story in the first person, tells about the moment when, during the battle of Sebastopol, he saw the Russian general defecate and did not have the 'arts' (skill, heart, arse) to shoot:

But when I seeing him in his oneship fetch along within hail that tourrible tall with his nitshnykopfgoknob and attempting like a brandylogged rudeman cathargic, lugging up and laiding down his livepelts so cruschinly . . . and expousing his old skinful self tailtottom by manurevring in open ordure to renewmurature with the cowruads in their airish pleasantry I thanked he was recovering breadth . . . But when I got inoccupation of a full new of his old basemiddelism, in ackshan, pagne pogne, by the veereyed lights of the stormtrooping clouds and in the sheenflare of the battleaxes of the heroim and mid the shieldfails awail of the bitteraccents of the sorafim and caught the pfierce tsmell of his aurals, orankastank, a suphead setrapped, like Peder the Greste, altipaltar, my bill it forsooks allegiance (gut bull it!) and, no lie is this, I was babbeing and yetaghain bubbering, bibbelboy . . . I confesses withould pridejealice . . . I adn't the arts to.   (*FW* 344.12–345.03)

    In the flare of the Babelic battle of Sebastopol, amid the clash of weapons and the 'wail' of 'bitteraccents' (also reminiscent of the *Inferno*'s words of woe and 'accenti d'ira' quoted above), Butt/Buckley stands 'babbeing' and 'bubbering', like a 'bibbelboy', watching the father-figure of the Russian general ('altipaltar') expose his bottom and defecate to produce dung-bricks ('manurevring in open ordure') with which to build anew ('to renewmurature') something that sounds suspiciously like a new, tall, terrible tower of Babel ('that tourrible tall'; there are several echoes here from other Babel passages; cf. for instance the up/down motif in 'lugging up and laiding down'). HCE as Russian General frequently appears as an embodiment of the Tsar ('Peder the Greste'), traditionally endowed with the title of 'little father of all the Russians', but the punning on the regal title through vocalic variations on the pan-Slavic root *ser*, 'shit',[29] ('Saur', *FW* 344.33; see also 'the sur of all Russers', *FW* 340.35) also circularly turns him into the excrement he produces. At the same time, if we follow up associations previously made, the general/HCE *is* that same 'tourrible tall', a towering gigantic Nimrod-figure, the 'Creman hunter' (*FW* 342.20) whose pride and jealousy ('pridejealice') led to his wish to emulate God.

    It is only when the general wipes himself with the 'Irish' sod of turf that Buckley shoots him, causing his death/fall: 'I shuttm . . . Hump to dump! Tumbleheaver!' (*FW* 352.14–15); 'At that instullt to Igorladns! . . . Sparro!' (*FW* 353.18–21; *sparo*, Italian 'I shoot').[30] The shooting of the Russian general/builder re-enacts God's 'thundering' punishment of Nimrod and of the builders of Babel. Buckley's shot and the general's fall are immediately followed by one of the chapter's interpolated passages, illustrating here the consequences of Babel, parallel to an atomic explosion:

[*The abnihilisation of the etym by the grisning of the grosning of the grinder of the grunder of the first lord of Hurtreford expolodotonates through Parsuralia with an ivanmorinthorrorumble fragoromboassity amidwhiches general uttermost confussion are perceivable moletons skaping with muliculoes . . . Similar scenatas are projectilised from Hullulullu, Bawlawayo, empyreal Raum and mordern Atems*] (*FW* 353.22–9)

Universal confusion, the result of God's blow from heaven ('cum celitus tanta confusione percussi sunt', *Dve* i.vii, 6; *rombo* is in Italian the loud, rolling noise of the thunder, *fragore* is a loud noise, often describing the thunderclap) coincides with the loss of the language shared until that moment, a loss which can be described as an 'annihilation of the etym' insofar as it consisted, according to the interpretation given by Dante in the *De vulgari eloquentia*, in the *oblivio* (forgetting) of the original tongue (which, in Wakean terms, takes place 'at this deleteful hour', *FW* 118.32). By annihilating the etym, the history of the language (its memory) is erased, and men are left in a condition of 'general uttermost confussion' (both 'confusion' and 'concussion'), scattered and escaping in all directions to reinvent new languages *ab nihilo*.[31]

The fusion of 'How Buckley Shot the Russian General' and the story of Babel patterned on Dante's linguistic narrative, and their insertion into the basic plot-structure of the *Wake* (the son overturning the father) involves yet another inversion of the Italian model. In the *De vulgari eloquentia*, at the precise moment when confusion sets in, hierarchical order is nevertheless reaffirmed in the punishment that God-the-Father 'mercifully' inflicts on his sons ('non hostili scutica, sed paterna . . . rebellantem filium pia correctione necnon memorabili castigavit'; 'not with the scourge of an enemy but that of a father . . . he chastised his rebellious son with a correction at once charitable and memorable', *Dve* i.vii, 5). In the story of the Russian general, however, it is the son who punishes the father, and ends by taking his role (see e.g. *FW* 352.23). Significantly, in the sentence 'His Cumbulent Embulence, the frustate fourstar Russkakruscam' (*FW* 352.32–3) the 'frustrated' general becomes 'frustate' (Italian *frusta*, 'whip', 'scourge'; *frustate*, 'whiplashes'), as if he was directly hit by the metaphorical 'scutica' of Dante's God. (In his role as the Hun Attila, literally 'the scourge of God', HCE had earlier appeared both as the scourge itself and its victim: 'Attilad! Attattilad! Get up, Goth's scourge on you!', *FW* 251.01–2.)

Jean-Michel Rabaté's powerful reading of the Russian general story has shown how oedipal, homosexual and incestuous themes and the father–son relationship interweave with the political significance of the episode, and how the political theme is indivisible from the linguistic one, linking together idiom, idiolect and ideology.[32] Glides between such similar words as 'arse', 'erse' or 'aerse', and 'ark' may transform the general defecating before Buckley's eyes into Noah's drunken exposition of himself, while implying that Erse 'plays in *Finnegans Wake* the role of a "father-tongue": it appears as the metamorphosis of a native language, voiced and soiled by the father, returning to the materiality of loam or humus. Only then can it really fertilize the earth.'[33]

Rabaté recalls that in Vico's *Scienza nuova* the giants at the beginning of human history were left by their mothers to roll in their own dirt in the post-diluvian primal forest. Excrement fertilised the earth and contributed to the origins of civilisation: 'it creates a new language, one blended with body products, that amalgamates "humus" and "human nature" in a type of very special "humor"'. As Rabaté comments, when Shem, who has inherited this language from his father, threatens to wipe the English language off the face of the earth/arse (*FW* 178.06–7) he is actually breaking down the (linguistic) English rule through the use of foreign languages: '*Arse* and *Erse* allied to a multinational *earth* both effect the murder of the mother language. The murder of the father is in fact only a dialectical climax in this indefinite struggle.'[34]

The story of Buckley and the Russian general and Rabaté's interpretation help to throw new light on Shem's production of a synthetic ink. Both Shem and the general (HCE) use excrement in order to produce something new and, in a sense, both turn themselves into ink (cf. the 'Homo Made Ink' of *FW* 342.23). However, whereas HCE uses the bricks to build what is fated to fall and 'abnihilate', or 'delete' the 'etym', Shem's 'indelible' ink will be used to write a poetry which is supposedly destined to remain eternally undeleted. Dante's performance of a role analogous to that of Nimrod's but with opposite results is reflected in HCE and Shem both performing the same action but to opposite ends. Furthermore, the analogies discussed above between HCE's vicissitudes and the post-Babelic vulgar, fragmented tongues imply that he is fated to be superseded by the 'synthetic' creative act of the son.

Shem extracting a synthetic ink from excrement parallels the hen digging out the letter from the dung heap, but Biddy Doran extracting the letter from the dung of the battlefield during a truce in chapter I.1 (*FW* 11.08–28) also anticipates the episode of Buckley and the Russian general. When chapter 1.2, retracing the genesis of HCE, asks, 'No dung on the road?' (31.36–32.01), then, the answer must be 'yes' – and a lot of it too! HCE, builder of Babel, tower of Babel and fragmented consequence of Babel, will himself return to the earth when dead in order to be dug up again as letter by the hen, and purified into gold by his alchemist-poet son. The son, that is, has to kill the father (and the 'father-language') and turn to his own biological origin and generation in order to find, there, the materials and instruments to 'forge' his own original creation and his individual poetic language. Through this process, the 'sodomitic' gun of his obscene defeat of the father can be transformed into the 'fertile' pen/penis of the poet.

However, part of Shem's activity as creator also implies transforming himself into a written-over 'integument' (*FW* 186.01), a polysemic text which will finally coincide with the letter and will thereby grant him the (unstable) status of 'father'. Although dispossessing the father will lead to the inevitability of one's own further displacement in the (Vichian) 'cyclewheeling history' (*FW* 186.02) of the *Wake*, what is stressed in this phase of the oedipal struggle are the differences implicit in the parallel between father and son: whereas the underlined features of the father-aspect are the fragmentation, the burial and the reduction to dung before being extracted/recreated, the son-aspect of the theme emphasises this synthetic, creative (and idealised) phase, the extraction and writing. Thus the letter and all it stands for – literature, and *Finnegans Wake* in particular – becomes the *locus* of both literary creation and biological generation and transformation – in the sense of filiation, but also of life-producing and life-giving discourse[35] (cf. Stephen forging the conscience of his race in *A Portrait*) which is, in one sense, also the transmission of literary and linguistic material, transformation (and appropriation) of previous literary/linguistic sources (such as, for instance, Dante's) in order to generate a new, independent text/language (such as *Finnegans Wake*/Wakese). Babel is thus, as it is in the *De vulgari eloquentia*, a linguistic 'happy fault' which can afford the poet the role of redeemer, and at the same time enable the later writer to retrace his origin back to his medieval 'father' while defeating him through his superior artistic achievement. All these threads are brought together in chapter III.4 when the child Shem/ Jerry wakes up from a wet dream in the middle of the night:

Hush! The other, twined on codliverside, has been crying in his sleep, making sharpshape his inscissors on some first choice sweets fished out of the muck. A stake in our mead. What a teething wretch! How his book of craven images! Here are posthumious tears on his intimelle. And he has pipettishly bespilled himself from his foundingpen as illspent from inking-horn.[36]   (*FW* 563.01–6)

The child, teething and chewing on sweets extracted from the muck, having spilled tears from his eyes and (ink)drops from his pen(is), and already betraying a predilection for inebriating drinks ('mead'), anticipates the activities of his grown-up self, turning his own body into writing material, spending his bodily fluids to write (indelible) poetry.

The treatment of Erse in the *Wake* and its relationship to Anglo-Irish[37] find a correlative in Dante's theory of the vernacular. The poet's project of transcending regional or municipal linguistic differences is expressed in terms which enable the reader to see it, at the same time, as a project of the political and cultural unification of Italy. Dante's argument runs thus: Italy has no royal court, therefore the Italian vernacular has no seat; but if Italy had a court, this would be the place where the *vulgare illustre* would rightfully reside and be spoken (*Dve* I.xviii, 4–5). The illustrious vernacular is furthermore the language that belongs to that dismembered *curia* which exists but has no permanent abode. As dialectal particularism needs to be transcended and governed by a superior, noble language, so the fragmented Italian nation must also be reunited in a superior political structure. Dante chooses the *vulgare illustre* rather than Latin as the common language: Latin is an 'artificial' tongue, spoken by no Italian at birth – in fact, in Dante's interpretation, it was never natural for anyone. The *vulgare* (although refined and therefore vaguely suspicious of 'artificiality') is on the contrary the language that babies 'suckle' with their nurses' milk at birth (*Dve* I.i, 2), the language spoken by 'muliercolae'[38] (see the washerwomen's gossip in *FW* I.8 and ALP's frequent description as a small woman), the common language of any street-corner or crossroads – the trivial language of the 'triv and quad' (*FW* 306.12–13) learned by the children in their Nightlesson in chapter II.2. Given the fundamental role attributed to language in the political and cultural unification of Italy, it follows that, for the poet who has taken upon himself the mighty task of redeeming the language, every instance of linguistic use – not only the choice of subject-matter but even the choice of words and structures – is also a political act: fragmentation and municipalism are rejected in the name of a linguistic and political universalism.

While Joyce may not have shared the religious implications of Dante's project (except perhaps in order to exploit them jocularly for a pun), the linguistic-political significance of the treatise would have held greater appeal for him. Joyce had always rejected the Celtic Revivalists' plea for a return to Gaelic language and culture as artificial: the language 'suckled' by the majority of the Irish children with their mothers' milk and the language of modern emancipated Ireland was not Gaelic, and it could only be Anglo-Irish. Ireland could be a bilingual nation, but could not turn back to a language that would have been as artificial as any imposed one. If Erse, as Rabaté has shown, is the 'father-language', the language to be defeated and overturned, HCE can be called 'Emancipator, the Creman hunter' (*FW* 342.19–20) only ironically, through an inversion similar to the one that makes him see the Wellington monument as a sign of redemption (*FW* 36.24–5).

But the politics of Dante's medieval linguistics may have crystallised what a rather paradoxical circumstance was perhaps already suggesting. As Giorgio Melchiori has pointed out, Joyce's 'only public pronouncements in the political field on the state of Ireland and of the world in general, are in Italian', and, at the time of these public political statements – the articles in the Triestine paper *Il Piccolo della sera* – Joyce was living in an environment where the variegated Italian of the Triestine 'cross-roads of civilization' was commonly used as lingua franca.[39] Joyce himself, as a consequence of his decision to leave Ireland, used the Triestine melting-pot version of Italian as the lingua franca of the exile both in taking his 'political' position about his country and within his family, arguably turning into a personal truth Dante's metaphorical statement about Italian as the language that babies learn from their nurses. Personal circumstances and medieval linguistics appear to intersect from early on, but by the time Stephen Dedalus had left the stage to Shem the Penman, 'Father Dante' had also been overturned in the battle for literary dominance, trivialised and reduced, in true medieval tradition, to 'excrement' from which gold could be sifted in order for the poet-son to re-create himself and his race. At the crossroads between literary borrowing, aesthetic inspiration and biographical model – if Shem turns his own body, the only foolscap available to him (*FW* 185.35–6), into 'one continuous present tense integument' (*FW* 185.36–186.01), Dante had already produced what is probably the greatest continuous self-textualisation of the western world – Joyce's *oeuvre* and its relationship with Dante's may then remind us that 'intertextuality' need not be conceived of as only the pure and a-chronic textuality that, for instance, Barthes's theorisations opposed to old-fashioned studies of sources and influence (nor need the latter be restricted to Harold Bloom's doomed oedipal struggle); it may be more fruitful to see it instead as an intentional and historically grounded practice in which artistic choices reveal political/ideological implications and inscribe within the (inter)text the author's negotiations (also in terms of metaphorical filiation and of dispossession of the 'father') of his/her own place within the literary tradition.

THE HAUNTED INKBOTTLE

As I said in the introduction to this chapter, while the language theorised by Dante can be put to such strikingly different use in *Finnegans Wake* that it can even become a model for the characterisation of the novel's unusual and protean 'protagonists', it can also be used by the critic as a descriptive metaphor for the language of the *Wake*; as with the four levels of meaning, this is not a case of 'borrowing the terminology of the Middle Ages' to make up for our lack of 'critical equipment',[40] but a critical approach legitimised by the text itself.

When Dante explains why the *vulgare illustre* deserves to be called *cardinale*, he stresses that it functions as a hinge (Latin *cardo*) around which the other dialects turn, like a door: the door turns towards the inside and towards the outside, its movement 'governed' by the hinge, and so do the local vernaculars, governed by the illustrious and cardinal language. 'Wakese' 'governs' the multiple languages that contribute, in different degrees, to its composition; it is the idiom that, like the *vulgare illustre*, 'illuminans et illuminatum prefulgens', throws light on the other languages, showing how they can be interpreted and to what new conventions of reading they must be subjected. This also applies to the single word and the *portmanteau*. The term 'word' is of course ambiguous in this context, and it oscillates between the standard definition as 'sound or combination of sounds that expresses a meaning and forms an independent unit of the grammar or vocabulary of a language' (*Oxford English Dictionary*) and an *ad hoc* very general meaning of any sequence of letters between two blank spaces. Thus, maintaining this ambiguity, we can say that each word has in the *Wake* multiple valencies,[41] directed towards the inside and towards the outside ('seu introrsum seu extrorsum flectatur'): towards the inside, in the manifold meanings layered within the word, as well as in the etymology (often etymologies) which provides more ramifications in the root; and towards the outside in the many ramifications and associations (phonic, semantic, graphic) which branch off from the word in many different directions. When the word is a *portmanteau*, all the meanings inscribed in it, towards the inside and the outside, are of course multiplied, and they combine among themselves to produce potentially endless strings of meanings. The word is thus the hinge at the centre of a multiplicity of meanings: these meanings 'are there', but they are the result of an interpretation, a 'processing' of the text, and therefore 'are not there', not actually printed black on white on the page. The word or *portmanteau* only contains a trace of them, a spoor, or, to take up Dante's metaphor more explicitly, a scent of them, 'redolentem ubique et necubi apparentem'.

The language of the *Wake*, like that of Dante's theory, is a language which, in actual fact, exists nowhere except in the book that 'creates' it. As the *vulgare illustre* can be described as the super-regional language of a hypothetical *aula*, so can the language of *Finnegans Wake* be described as the synthetic (fictional) translation of a language which 'resides' in a (fictional) sleeping or dreaming mind, a 'museyroom' (*FW* 8.09; 10.22), the room where one 'muses' (*Oxford English Dictionary*: 'to muse, to think deeply or dreamily'), where all the past and present, history and legend, reality and fancies are exposed as in a museum; the *aula* where the language of the court, the King's English, is put to sleep or even murdered by (the) King himself (*FW* 93.01–2).

The Italian language becomes in Dante the shelter for the poet and the members of the *curia*. The political and personal significance of Dante's treatment of the language – dismembered, exiled and homeless – is reflected in the Wakean word and in the metatextual references of the *Wake* to itself. The exiled post-Babelic languages find in the text a common ground where they can meet and fuse together in a sort of regained unity[42] which simultaneously also reiterates their differences, and the pun or *portmanteau* becomes a shelter for words and meanings that have been exiled from the univocal correspondence with the thing they describe. These languages and meanings wander like pilgrims from one 'word' (in the sense of sequence of letters between two spaces) to another and (temporarily) inhabit it by deploying themselves in various layers of significance.

If the words are shelters, the book itself is a house: question 3 in chapter 1.6 begins, 'Which title is the true-to-type motto-in-lieu for that Tick for Teac thatchment painted witt wheth one darkness' (*FW* 139.29–30; Irish *Tig* or *teach*, house). One possible reading suggests that the title is the word or word-place for the house-thatch, i.e., that the title is the book's roof (it is on the cover, a sort of roof for the book/house). Although the answer in this case is one of the several versions of the motto of the coat of arms of Dublin City (*FW* 140.06–7), the title which was for a long time the actual object of a riddle is '*Finnegans Wake*' itself, which Joyce kept secret and sheltered under the provisional '*Work in Progress*' until Eugene Jolas guessed it in 1938 (*JJ*II 708).

The siglum which Joyce used until Jolas's discovery was a square: □,[43] a receptacle or container for all the materials of the text. Its four sides may indicate the four provinces of Ireland, or the four old men, or the four books of the *Wake*, or any fourfold pattern which contributes to its structure – including I would suggest the four levels of meaning and the four qualities of its 'illustrious' language. The four corners of the square may also be its cardinal points (which correspond sometimes to the four old men) and – if the book is meant to represent the world – the cardinal points of the earth. This may also be part of the paradoxical attempt to reconcile the square and the circle in the *Wake*, described by James Joyce in one of his letters as a wheel in the form of a perfect square (*Letters* I 251; I shall discuss this aspect at length in chapter 4); this both humorously counters and reflects Dante's explanation of *cardinale*, according to which the 'cardinal' point of the language is its centre, and the rest of the world of languages turn around it.

Shem's house, 'known as the Haunted Inkbottle' (*FW* 182.30–1), has many points in common with the book *Finnegans Wake* (a bottle of flowing ink containing practically everything, haunted by ghostly meanings that keep appearing but are never quite caught), with the ink and excrement theme and with literature in general. Of the house we read that 'this was a stinksome inkenstink, quite puzzonal to the wrottel' (*FW* 183.06–7). Thus, the vulgarity of his materials and the excrement-made-ink process are inscribed in the building where the poet lives, and where the stench inverts the fragrant scent of the 'beautiful panther' of Dante's treatise. The floor and the walls of Shem's lair, we are told, were covered by literary objects, love letters, tales, stories, quills and ink, borrowed idioms and Latin syntax and several other elements (*FW* 183.09–184.02). The list concludes with a category of items interesting in a Dantean context: 'ahs ohs ouis sis jas jos gias neys thaws sos, yeses and yeses and yeses' (184.01–2); this long series of words for 'yes' in different languages, as well as reminding Joycean readers of the end of Molly's mono-logue in *Ulysses*, may also evoke for the trained Dante reader the poet's criterion for distinguishing languages through the word used for 'yes': 'sì' (Italian), 'oc' (Provençal) and 'oïl' (French) (*Dve* I.viii, 6–9); this distinction is clearly echoed again in the *Wake* when the children are trying to discover the solution to the geometrical problem of the mother's sex: 'Oc, tell it to oui, do, Sem! Well, 'tis oil thusly' (*FW* 286.31). The same affirmative identification of language and country is employed by Dante when he refers to Italy as the 'bel paese là dove 'l sì suona' ('the fair land where the *sì* is heard', *Inf* XXXIII, 80), a line that appears in *Finnegans Wake* as 'Illbelpaese' (*FW* 129.27).

The inventory of the items of furniture in Shem's house ends with 'breakages, upheavals, distortions, inversions' (*FW* 184.03–4) – of course outstanding characteristics also of the *Wake*. To confirm finally that as we talk about the house we are talking about *Finnegans Wake*, we learn that the poet Shem is 'writing the mystery of himsel in furniture' (*FW* 184.09–10). The furniture, in other words, is part of the writing of the text and of the self performed by the poet; it is the material in/on which the work is written, and the environment in which the transformation of the vulgar matter into indelible ink is performed, Shem himself being part of this process. As he finds that his skin is the only 'foolscap' available, he transubstantiates into the text which will be lost, forgotten, found again and interpreted, and in which the entire (hi)story unfolds itself (*FW* 185.28–186.08). Shem, through (al)chemical processes, transaccidentates himself into paper, ink, and, finally, an 'integumental', all-enveloping text. 'In-tegumentum' is one of the terms used in the Middle Ages to refer to the 'external' meaning of a text, or literal level: Shem, in other words, transforms himself into the letter (its exterior, its interior: letter and envelope) which stands in *Finnegans Wake* for all literature and, in particular, for the *Wake* itself and which is in 1.5 and through most of the *Wake* identified with HCE. Yet again, the son is working on himself to dispossess the father.

ASK KAVYA FOR THE KAY

The murdering of the King's English mentioned above takes place in chapter 1.4, where the trial of Festy King (one of the many 'curial' situations of the *Wake*) is celebrated. The situation is very confused and it is difficult to distinguish the identities of the figures involved, who constantly tend to merge (see especially *FW* 92.06–11, which evokes Giordano Bruno's theory of the identity of opposites and recalls the 'tristitia-hilaritate' epigraph of his comedy *Candelaio*).[44] At the conclusion of the trial the text instructs the reader to 'Ask Kavya for the kay' (*FW* 93.22–3). One of the poets (Sanskrit *Kavya*, 'poet') we can ask for the key is perhaps Dante: after Festy King's 'murder' of English, several converging elements suggest that 'obvious' references to Bruno and Vico's philosophies may in fact also conceal allusions to Dante's theory of the *vulgare illustre*. The judges (the Four Old Men) 'laid their wigs together' (*FW* 92.35) in order to

promulgate their standing verdict of *Nolans Brumans* whereoneafter *King, having murdered all the English* he knew, picked out his pockets and left the tribunal scotfree . . . proudly showing off the blink pitch to his britgits to prove himself . . . *a rael genteel*. To the Switz bobbyguard's *curial but courtlike* . . . the firewaterloover *returted* with such a vinesmelling fortytudor . . . as would *turn* the latten stomach even of a *tumass equinous* . . . so that all the twofromthirty advocatesses within echo, pulling up their briefs at the krikgry: Shun the Punman! . . . where . . . *he shat* . . . the chassetitties belles conclaiming: You and your gift of your gaft of your garbage abaht our Farvver! and gaingridando: Hon! Verg! Nau! Putor! Skam! Schams! Shames!   (*FW* 92.36–93.21, my emphases)

King/Shem the Penman, the poet who circularly writes the book in which he appears, *Finnegans Wake*, murders English, picks his pockets and shows his 'blink pitch' (blank/blind patch, like the one that Joyce wore for a time) in order to prove himself a 'rael genteel'. Ennobling is achieved through the subversion of the standard of the English language and of the *illustre* and *aulicum* noble vernacular that

Dante would have liked to hear spoken in the court. 'Curial' and 'courtlike', justified by the fact that they describe the speech of the Swiss guard of the Vatican and of the 'Curia' (the Papal Court), may thus betray references to the Italian vernacular *aulicum et curiale*. Elements that would normally be interpreted as referring to the recurring patterns of the Vichian cycle of *corsi* and *ricorsi*, like 'returted . . . turn', or to Bruno the Nolan ('Nolans Brumans') acquire a new layer of meaning when read in the context of the description of Dante's illustrious vulgar language, capable of swaying hearts, making the willing unwilling and the unwilling willing ('nolentem volentem et volentem nolentem faciat', *Dve* I.XVII, 4), and situated at the centre of a *grex vulgarium* which turns and returns as it moves around. The hearts of the twenty-eight girls are certainly swayed, as they shun Shem at the 'krigcry' (war cry) 'Shun the Punman!', while Shem sat/defecated ('shat'), perhaps already planning to 'produce' the 'indelible ink' from his excrement or 'garbage' in order to express the eloquence of his 'gift of [the] gaft' (= gab).

Even the 'latten stomach' of Thomas Aquinas ('tumass equinous') would turn at Shem's 'vinesmelling fortytudor', or drunken fortitude – a trait that associates him with his father. That the stomach chosen to be turned is precisely that of Aquinas may be justified by the fact the Angelic Doctor would surely be disgusted and turn in his grave on seeing Joyce rather arbitrarily overturn his words and theories through his literary *personae* Stephen D(a)edalus and Shem the Penman. However, another reason to call Aquinas in question may be that the illustriousness that makes it possible for Dante's redolent vernacular to turn the hearts of men, 'volentem nolentem' or 'nolentem volentem', may have borrowed its name from Thomas Aquinas's theory of art and the *claritas* that makes an object beautiful.[45] In Aquinas's famous theory, *pulchritudo* (beauty) manifests itself through *integritas sive perfectio* (integrity or completeness), *debita proportio sive consonantia* (due proportion of the parts or harmony), and, finally, *claritas* (splendour).[46]

In *Stephen Hero* and in *A Portrait of the Artist as a Young Man*, Stephen appropriates Aquinas's theory in order to found his own. The lengthier discussion is in the former novel, where the young artist plans to collect epiphanies in a book, carefully recording what he saw as delicate, evanescent moments (*SH* 216; Joyce did actually record these epiphanies and later included them in his work[47]).

Talking to his friend Cranly, Stephen explains the meaning of the first two requisites of beauty ('integrity' and 'symmetry'), and says of the third that for a long time he had not been able to make out what Aquinas had meant by it, but that he had now finally solved this puzzle: '*Claritas* is *quidditas*' (*SH* 218), or, as it were, 'the thing itself', the mind's only logically possible final synthesis. This, Stephen concludes, is the moment of the epiphany (*SH* 218). Only one or two pages earlier Stephen had given the well-known definition of the epiphany: 'By an epiphany he meant a sudden spiritual manifestation, whether in the vulgarity of speech or of gesture, or in a memorable phase of the mind itself' (*SH* 216). This definition comes as the culmination of Stephen's logical argument, identifying the moment when the mind reaches the final phase of the apprehension of beauty, and thus constitutes a 'memorable phase of the mind itself' (in other words, one could say that the discovery of the epiphany is an epiphany in its own right). The source of the word 'epiphany' was first identified by Umberto Eco in Gabriele D'Annunzio's work,[48] and the D'Annunzian connection has been further explored by Corinna del Greco Lobner in her interesting study of the role of Italian and Italian literature in the development of Joyce's writing techniques.[49] Lobner emphasises the analogy between the *trasognamento* of D'Annunzio's *Venturiero senza ventura* (1911), where vision is 'a kind of practical magic exercised upon the most common objects with associations of appearances and of essences', and Stephen's definition of the epiphany. Lobner (who does not claim that Joyce would necessarily have been acquainted with D'Annunzio's novel and prefers to point out the similarity of their conceptions), comments that the only apparent alteration between the two definitions is 'Joyce's substitution of "vulgarity of speech" for D'Annunzio's "common objects." '[50]

Tentatively, I would suggest that if Dante is added to the sources of Stephen's theory, the substitution in the definition of the epiphany of 'common object' with 'vulgarity of speech' can be accounted for. 'Vulgarity of speech' closely recalls Dante's *De vulgari eloquentia*, the title and subject of the treatise in which Dante demonstrates the worthiness of a vulgar tongue purified, refined, chosen from the noblest elements of the local dialects, made capable of treating of any noble or spiritual matter. One of the characteristics of the Dantean ideal literary language is that it is *illustre*: luminous, radiant, bestowing splendour on those who use it and receiving it from them.

This 'splendour' derives from the same Aquinian *claritas* that leads, in Stephen's theory, to the epiphanic moment: 'The soul of the commonest object seems to us radiant. The object achieves its epiphany' (*SH* 218). The conclusion of Stephen's argument restores the D'Annunzian element – the most common objects – which had been dropped from the definition of the epiphany, possibly to bind it to the linguistic theories of the *De vulgari eloquentia*; all Thomistic, D'Annunzian and Dantean elements would thus finally be drawn together.[51] The elaboration and choice of the epiphanic moments in language will then develop in Joyce's production through *Ulysses* and *Finnegans Wake* to include increasingly 'vulgar' instances of words or events, until the artist is shown to produce the primary material of his writing by starting from excrement and distilling from it the 'indelible ink' that will enable him to write an indelible art.

Lobner also explores the parallel between Joyce's idea of art as 'eucharistic' transmutation and D'Annunzio's vision of the artist as the 'high priest of nature'. Linking this aspect to the theory of the epiphany, Lobner writes:

Although Stephen's 'sudden spiritual manifestation' includes 'vulgarity of speech' and thus offsets D'Annunzio's exalted mysticism (Aristotle, St. Augustine, and St. Thomas Aquinas play an important role in Joyce's demystification of D'Annunzio's epiphany), the stress on words as the ultimate goal of 'the priest of the imagination' is inextricably bound to D'Annunzio's aesthetics.[52]

But if 'vulgarity of speech' is accepted as an echo of the *De vulgari eloquentia* and its illustrious vernacular, the D'Annunzian 'exalted mysticism' appears no longer 'offset' but, rather, 'reset' in a new perspective which, after all, contrasts neither with D'Annunzio's poetics of the word nor with his and Dante's exalted linguistic mysticism.

Stephen discusses his theory again in *A Portrait*, this time with his friend Lynch. The theory is expounded now with greater economy of words and rejected as 'literary talk' (after all, Dante's talk too is 'literary talk'). The definition of the epiphany is also dropped; however, the several references to light, splendour, radiance and luminosity are carried over from *Stephen Hero* (*P* 212–13). When Joyce writes *Finnegans Wake*, he has travelled a long way from the early novels and the collection of epiphanies. These had already been treated dismissively by Stephen in his musings in 'Proteus' (*U* 50); now the epiphanic revelation ceases to emerge only from vulgarity of speech, of gesture, or from memorable phases of the mind. In the language of the *Wake*, every word, theme, motif, and the book as a whole can be the occasion of an epiphany, the revelation of the essential nature of what is known, what pertains to everyday reality, to history, to myth. Any element can acquire deeper and more comprehensive meanings thanks to the network of linguistic links that throws light on them ('illuminans et illuminatum prefulgens') and shows them all to be intimately related. It is the very concept of epiphany that has undergone a profound re-elaboration – presumably also causing the 'latten stomach' of Thomas Aquinas to turn. 'Vulgarity' (perhaps owing its name to Dante) is now more properly 'triviality' (maybe still partly thanks to Dante's theories or, more generally, to the medieval cast of Joyce's aesthetic imagination[53]), the encounter of many common and peregrine (exilic, migratory) words and meanings at the crossroads or *trivium* of the Wakean 'words' and of the text; the object is no longer selected in a 'luminous silent stasis' (*P* 213) but in a dynamic apprehension of its being part of larger systems, in the discovery of common roots and analogous patterns of development. As Giorgio Melchiori writes, 'What else is the language of Joyce's last work if not the epiphanisation of what is known, familiar, banal in our language, through its projection into a metalanguage which intensifies its semantic contents to its extreme limit, so that banality becomes memorable? *Finnegans Wake* is a single, gigantic epiphany: the epiphany of the human language.'[54]

Walton Litz, who describes the evolution of the concept of epiphany in Joyce's work as a 'movement from "centripetal" to "centrifugal" writing', gives us a lead to interpret Joyce's continuing appeal to Dante's linguistic theory, despite the profound change in his method of composition and in his writing techniques. Litz emphasises the 'process of selectivity' on which the earlier conception of epiphany is founded, and which assumes that experience can be revealed through single gestures or phrases. Thus *A Portrait* works mainly by 'a stringent process of exclusion', whereas Joyce's work subsequently became more attuned to a 'process of inclusion' in which meaning is established through multiple references and relationships. 'The earlier method', Litz writes, 'implies that there is a significance, a "quidditas", residing in each thing, and that the task of the artist is to discover this significance by *a process of distillation*. In the later method it is the artist who creates the significance through language.'[55]

The principle of selectivity and the process of distillation which characterise Joyce's early work may partly explain why Dante's theory of linguistic selection and 'distillation' from the *vulgares* was needed. In *Finnegans Wake* 'distillation' becomes one of the central themes and a symbol for poetic creativity, while the accretional method of composition still continues to resort to Dante's synthetic theory in order both to accommodate the technique of drawing materials from different linguistic sources and, at the same time, to undermine it by applying to it Dante's own weapon of the law of analogy and *contrapasso*. *Claritas* is thus a quality also of the obscure 'nat language' of the *Wake*, where meanings 'shine forth' through the surface and 'radiate' in all directions, spreading from the central 'cardinal' point, combining with other 'illustrious' words, illuminating them and receiving light from them and from the whole.

CHAPTER 4

Figures of ineffability

e così, figurando il paradiso,
convien saltar lo sacrato poema[1]

(*Par* XXIII, 61–2)

imeffible tries at speech unasyllabled

(*FW* 183.14–15)

The *Divine Comedy* has been variously interpreted as a vision,[2] a mystic *itinerarium mentis a Deo*,[3] a fiction based on the assumption that it is not a fiction.[4] It is also a dream or dream-like experience that starts in the sleepy atmosphere of *Inferno* I ('Io non so ben ridir com'i' v'intrai, / tant'era pien di sonno'; 'I cannot well retell how I entered it, I was so full of sleep', *Inf* I, 10–11) and ends with a similarly dream-like vision and the loss of individual will and consciousness in *Paradiso* XXXIII ('Qual è colui che sognando vede', 'As is he who dreaming sees', *Par* XXXIII, 58; 'ma già volgeva il mio disio e 'l *velle*', 'but already my desire and my will were turned', *Par* XXXIII, 143). Within this dream, vision, or journey, what we find is a *summa* of medieval culture, an epic in which Dante meets and talks to historical, legendary and fictitious people from different times and cultures and who tell their stories, revealing unknown truths and unfolding unseen, arcane connections between the different phases of the history of mankind; they explain the laws of nature, illustrate the divine rules that regulate this and the other world, prophesy future events. Erich Auerbach has thus encapsulated the encyclopaedism of Dante's 'vision':

The *Comedy*, among other things, is a didactic poem of encyclopedic dimensions, in which the physico-cosmological, the ethical, and the historico-political order of the universe is collectively presented; it is, further, a literary work which imitates reality and in which all imaginable spheres of reality appear: past and present, sublime grandeur and vile vulgarity, history and legend, tragic and comic occurrences, man and nature; finally, it is the story of Dante's – i.e., one single individual's – life and salvation, and thus a figure of the story of mankind's salvation in general. Its dramatis personae include figures from antique mythology, often (but not always) in the guise of fantastic demons; allegorical personifications and symbolic animals stemming from late antiquity and the Middle Ages; bearers of specific significations chosen from among the angels, the saints, and the blessed in the hierarchy of Christianity; Apollo, Lucifer, and Christ, Fortuna and Lady Poverty, Medusa as an emblem of the deeper circles of Hell, and Cato of Utica as the guardian of Purgatory.[5]

The danger is in the neatness of identifications, Samuel Beckett warned the readers of *Work in Progress* and the future critic who would follow in his steps and try to investigate the function of Dante's (as well as Bruno's and Vico's) work in *Finnegans Wake*. It is not an exercise in 'analogymongering', I hope, to point out that, with a few adjustments, it would not be difficult to read the above paragraph as a description of *Finnegans Wake* as well as of the *Divine Comedy*. Dante's all-encompassing, epic journey of salvation and of metamorphosis is in fact one of the closest antecedents of the encyclopaedic nocturnal epic of mankind and of the universal laws of death and rebirth embodied, at one of the several levels of the *Wake*, in the transformed events of the ordinary day of a Dublin man, at once an individual and Everyman. Indeed, Auerbach's description of the *Comedy* proposes a reading that is strikingly similar to the one suggested by Levin's attempt at a fourfold interpretation of *Finnegans Wake*, which I discussed in chapter 1.

Allusions to the *Divine Comedy* are scattered throughout the *Wake* but it is not my intention here to trace as many of them as I can. The densest chapters are probably the 'Mime' (*FW* II.1) and the 'Night-lesson', or 'Geometry Lesson' (*FW* II.2). Many of the allusions to Dante in the latter chapter have been discussed by Mary Reynolds and James Atherton; Atherton for instance points out that one of the main reasons for this wealth of references is that this chapter, as a 'lesson', wants to impart 'all' knowledge, and Reynolds shows that the geometry problem of the mother-triangle, the 'eternal geomater' (*FW* 296.31–297.01), was inspired by Dante's analogy in *Paradiso* XXXIII between the incapacity of man to comprehend God and the doomed effort of the geometer that tries to solve the mystery of the squaring of the circle (I shall discuss this geometrical simile later in the chapter). Atherton in particular finds in *FW* II.2 several echoes of *Inferno* V and its moving story of the adulterous love of Paolo and

Francesca, perhaps Joyce's favourite canto[6] and also one of the best known by English-speaking poets and critics.[7] The Wakean motifs of the warring brothers and Issy's attempts at seduction are a fitting context for the episode of Francesca's adultery with her husband's brother. Atherton identifies two quotations from this canto in *FW* II.2:[8]

Finnegans Wake	*Divine Comedy*
lamoor that of gentle breast rathe is intaken seems circling toward out yondest (it's life that's all chokered by that batch of grim rushers) . . . (*FW* 292.01–3)	Amor, ch'al cor gentil ratto s'apprende . . . (*Inf* v, 100) (Love, which quickly takes hold in a gentle heart . . .) + cf. the souls whirled in *Inf* v by the wind of Hell, and the bird similes of the canto
And the greater the patrarc the griefer the pinch. And that's what your doctor knows. (*FW* 269.24–6)	Nessun maggior dolore che ricordarsi del tempo felice ne la miseria; e ciò sa 'l tuo dottore. (*Inf* v, 121–3) (There is no greater sorrow than to remember the happy time in wretchedness; and this your doctor knows.)

It is worth recalling Atherton's perceptive discussion of the allusions: Joyce would have been aware of the disagreement among Dante's editors on the interpretation of 'tuo dottore', which could mean doctor, guide, teacher; according to some, the lines refer to Virgil's 'Infandum, regina, jubes renovare dolorem' (*Aeneid*, II, 3), while others point out that Virgil's situation is the exact opposite of the one described by Dante, as the former is asked to remember sorrow in the midst of joy; Dante would therefore be more likely to be referring to a passage from Boethius' *Consolatio Philosophiae* (II, iv, 4). But all interpreters would agree that any other occurrence of the phrase 'tuo dottore' in the *Commedia* refers to Virgil. Joyce, Atherton argues, is creating one of his typical mirror effects, and his words cannot be fully comprehended if one is not aware of a hidden quotation which itself contains a hidden quotation about which interpreters differ. 'Patrarc', which as Atherton says is explained by Adaline Glasheen's *Census to Finnegans Wake* as referring to Petrarch, is one of Joyce's mischievous false leads, a key to the wrong Italian poet (a technique which, as I argued earlier, is typical also of Beckett's *Exagmination* essay). 'Logically', says Atherton, 'the trope could be described thus: as Dante says *tuo dottore* which in his work should mean Virgil, to follow a quotation from Boethius; so Joyce says "Patrarc", which in his language should mean Petrarch, to precede a quotation from Dante.'[9] Incidentally the intertextual situation is in fact complicated by the possibility that a reference to Petrarch is indeed there, and in particular to his lines in the *Trionfi*, 'Al tempo che rinnova i miei sospiri / per la dolce memoria di quel giorno / che fu principio a sì lunghi martiri' ('At the time that renews my sighs for the sweet memory of that day which was the start of such long sufferings').[10] But this does not at all invalidate Atherton's argument.

Allusions and misquotations, in short, are selected for their context and function in the original and then recontextualised and given a new function in the *Wake*. My point however is that the presence of Dantean allusions in *Finnegans Wake* is much more wide-ranging than has been suggested by either Atherton or Reynolds. Some allusions may simply serve to support a textual point within a limited context and do not necessarily take part in a wider system of thematic or structural cross-references, but they also contribute to a more general purpose: that of distributing through the *Wake* examples of Dante's poetic figuration of the other-world and of his poetics of ineffability – in fact his self-celebration of the poet's success in saying the unsayable, an issue that is also central to the *Wake*'s experimentations with 'nat language'. With some degree of simplification, it is correct to say, I think, that Dante's and Joyce's problem is the same: how to express what language cannot say, how to mediate successfully between the linguistically representable and the unrepresentable. Thus, the echoes, references and irreverently – or even self-annulling – 'quashed quotatoes' (*FW* 183.22) scattered through the text point in fact to a common conception of poetics and of the artist's task.

No one before Dante had ever attempted a poetic representation of the other-world which would account for its complete and complex structure, its parts and its laws, with such a profusion of precise and coherent detail: the world posited by Dante for his pilgrimage is totally heterogeneous to our day-to-day experience, and it requires therefore much more than the usual repertoire of words and idioms – the more so since at the beginning of the fourteenth century vernacular Italian was still a young and limited language. Thus, the poet must compose or invent (Latin *invenio*, 'I find', hence the *inventio* of classical rhetoric and its precept to 'find' in the *loci* of one's mind and one's culture the material for the literary work) a 'new' language which can, not so much describe – since the reality of the other-world is immaterial and certainly beyond the human faculties of representation – as, rather, evoke the supernatural experience. This is encapsulated in Dante's coinage 'trasumanar' (*Par* I, 70), an untranslatable word that Charles Singleton renders through a periphrasis, 'the passing beyond humanity'[11] but which also suggests going 'through' humanity. To this end, Dante embarks on a poetic pilgrimage that ventures to the extreme reaches of the language (rather similarly to Joyce's claim to be 'au bout de l'anglais', *JJ*II 546) in order to convey to his readers 'a shadow' of the truth (*Par* I, 23; XIII, 19), so that they can, in turn, 'recreate' or re-experience the extraordinary journey into the world of eternity. I would argue that this necessary renewal of language and the construction of a poetics of the 'ineffable' (which, as we shall see, may be turned in Joyce's text into a poetics of the unspeakable), rather than the *Wake*'s use of precise themes and images from Dante's epic, is the *Comedy*'s most significant contribution to the *Wake*. Thus, although Beckett implied in 'Dante. . . Bruno. Vico. . Joyce' that the greatest similarity exists between *Finnegans Wake* and the *Purgatorio*, and although the night world and obscure language of the *Wake* would intuitively suggest a greater analogy with the *Inferno*, it is on the *Paradiso* – the apex of Dante's linguistic battle with the ineffable – that I shall concentrate in the final stage of this pilgrimage through Dante's and Joyce's works.

If the Word cannot be spoken, the journey towards God will have to be a quest for the words to fill the silence, to make silence itself speak. I shall therefore look at the dialectic of speech and silence and at the function that vowels – 'the soul and juncture of every word' (*Conv* IV.vi, 3–5), what allows words to be voiced that would otherwise be silent – acquire in this dialectic. To follow this thread, it will be necessary to go back to Stephen's articulation of his theory of literary creation, of authorial identity, of literary, biographical and material debts in 'Scylla and Charybdis', the chapter of *Ulysses* in which, as Jean-Michel Rabaté has demonstrated,[12] Stephen is in turn indebted to Dante's vocalic bond in the *Convivio*. We shall then look at how Issy's vocalic ties in *Finnegans Wake* may be seen to offset Stephen's weaving together of these issues; in fact, I will argue that Stephen's attempts at expressing a theory of artistic creation in

'Scylla and Charybdis' – and, even earlier, in *A Portrait* and *Stephen Hero* – are part of a subtext that crosses most of Joyce's works, a transversal text-in-progress that Joyce never stopped writing and rewriting, and which he continually ironised as he was writing it. Stephen's theory finally resolves itself in a deluding and unconvincing French triangle, dismissed by Stephen himself: '"You are a delusion," said roundly John Eglinton to Stephen. "You have brought us all this way to show us a French triangle. Do you believe your own theory?" "No", Stephen said promptly' (*U* 274). As we shall see, Eglinton's 'round' remark not only wraps up and dismisses Stephen's theory but also paves the way for the *Wake*'s inscription of the triangle within the circle. Stephen's theory will thus serve as a starting point for an examination of the geometrical problems of *FW* 1.6 and 11.2 (originating in Dante's simile of the geometer in *Paradiso* XXXIII) in order to tie together Joyce's and Dante's articulations of vowels and letters, figures of speech and of geometry, quests for the origin and the end, and the two writers' ongoing quests for the language that endeavours to voice the ineffable or the unspeakable but whose words are ultimately condemned to remain silent.[13]

TO DISLOCATE IF NECESSARY LANGUAGE INTO MEANING

Although the issue of the (in)expressible may be said to stand at the centre of the two writers' poetics, the concept of ineffability and its value are different for Joyce and for Dante: for the latter the ineffable is the divine, the transcendent, the eternal, what is immutable; it cannot be said because it is incommensurate with language and with the human mind. For Joyce, on the contrary, the ineffable derives from the inexhaustibility, transience and fluidity of the real which cannot be grasped, and from the (modernist) awareness and thematisation of the 'mismatch' between the real and any linguistic representation of it, but also, as I have argued in chapter 1, from an uncontrollable polysemy that drowns single and referential meanings into an excess of signification.

For Dante, words and referents do not correspond perfectly because, as we have seen in the previous chapters, post-Edenic language is an improper, insufficient means of communication which can never hope to bridge the immeasurable gap between the human and the divine, and has therefore to rely on a polysemic conception of writing and reading. For Joyce, on the contrary, it is language itself that creates its own subject(s), just as style creates the subject-matter of the individual chapters of *Ulysses*. The unrestrainable proliferation of meanings that issue from the materiality of language can transubstantiate into ever-deferred, evanescent meanings – as in Dante's allegories ('other' sense) – but only because, unlike for the medieval poet, these meanings are a result of, and do not pre-exist, the verbal creation of the artist.

The paradox of representation is of course that language may be insufficient for and incommensurate with the reality it tries to represent, but it is the only means the poet or the novelist can use. Writing thus becomes a struggle against language and its limits, an effort to stretch those limits, expand boundaries, bend what is scarcely flexible. Overcoming this resistance means 'inventing' a way of using language to signify in a different, novel way. It is in this sense that the poetics of the ineffable has to become an experimental poetics of the *novum* (the new, the marvellous, the extraordinary):[14] a poetics, that is, of the as yet unattempted, undiscovered, undiscoverable in the *loci* of one's mind, almost the contrary of *invenio*, a paradoxical search for what cannot be found.

This renewal of poetic language takes several forms: for Dante, one of them is the technical 'invention' of the *terza rima*, a structure that can be read as 'one and triune', like the Trinity conflating oneness and multiplicity, which enables the poet to join the discrete parts in a linear continuous chain that is however also circular and that reflects therefore both the structure of the whole (one poem, made of three enchained *cantiche*) and the final vision of God, both linear (the river) and circular (*Par* xxx–xxxiii).

This rhythmical mirror-reflection of the parts in the whole and the whole into the parts is typical of *Finnegans Wake* too, but Joyce's fascination with Dante's *terza rima* was already explicit in Stephen Dedalus' musings in 'Aeolus':

South, pout, out, shout, drouth. Rhymes: two men dressed the same, looking the same, two by two:

        . . . . *la tua pace*
        . . . . *che parlar ti piace*
        . . . . *mentre che il vento, come fa, si tace.*

He saw them three by three, approaching girls, in green, in rose, in russet, entwining, *per l'aer perso* in mauve, in purple, *quella pacifica oriafiamma*, in gold of oriflamme, *di rimirar fè più ardenti*. But I old men, penintent, leadenfooted, underdarkneath the night : mouth south : tomb womb. (*U* 175)[15]

Stephen's masculine, old, sad rhymes, too monotonously similar, dark and heavy, do not stand up to Dante's lithe, varied, young, feminine and colourful model. Three by three, Dante's girlish entwining rhymes nearly form the rainbow that Issy and her six friends will come to embody in *Finnegans Wake*, lovely and leaping and lissom, lightly dancing, like the angels in Dante's *Paradiso* going round and round in the circles and garlands of the 'Mime of Mick, Nick and the Maggies', fresh, coy and seductive, joining the rhythms of rhymes with the grace of flowers (of speech) and the variety of their clothes (*FW* 226.21–35).

To win Issy's graces – her letters, rhymes and colours, 'including science of sonorous silence' (*FW* 230.22–3) – Nick/Shem will have to try poetry – 'have recourse of course to poetry' (*FW* 230.23–4). But his quest in the Mime is, as any quest in the *Wake*, as any attempt to say the ineffable, doomed to failure, and Nick will not guess the heliotropic colour of the Maggies' drawers. In the *Divine Comedy* Dante stresses time and time again the problem of insufficiency and the inevitability of failure: the failure of the human language to represent adequately the divine; of his intellect to apprehend the sublime; of his memory to comprehend, to contain and retain the excess of the other-worldly experience. Versions of the topos of ineffability[16] punctuate Dante's ascent towards God and his progress towards the completion of the book, and become the main framework of the third *cantica*; there are of course earlier examples of the topos, starting from the very first canto ('quanto a dir qual era è cosa dura', 'how hard it is to tell what it [that wood] was like', *Inf* I, 4), but it is in *Paradiso*, as Dante approaches the Empyrean, that it becomes the leading motif. As it happens with the four levels of meaning that Dante borrowed from both the literary and the Biblical traditions and transformed into a completely new interpretative and poetic system, in the case of ineffability too he completely transforms the topos. An index of the novelty is the word *ineffabile* itself, used for the first time in vernacular Italian by Dante, in the phrase 'ineffabile cortesia' (*VN* III, 1). As Manuela Colombo has pointed out, although this may not strike a modern reader as unusual, the conflation of a term canonised by the tradition of the *trouvères* and of the Italian love lyric with one that had until then belonged only to the writings of the mystics would have been quite unsettling to Dante's contemporaries.[17]

If in the *Vita Nuova* the association was unexpected, in the *Comedy* the use of a mystical lexicon may appear justified and legitimised by the context and the theme. However, even in the *Divine Comedy* the concept is used in a disturbing manner: its referent is no longer exclusively the divine, and the attribute is now applied to the poem itself and the poetic activity of the author – a move potentially as risky as applying the four levels of meaning of Biblical exegesis to his own worldly poetry. Thus, the polysemic exegesis of his *canzoni*, the elevation of the vernacular to illustriousness and the renovation of language I have dealt with separately come together and must be seen as various facets of the same activity: the construction of a new role for the poet and a new function for his work. Dante's theme and technique, then, are inseparable, as they are in *Ulysses* and *Finnegans Wake*, where style and subject-matter coincide – or, even further, where style creates its own subject-matter: it is not so much the choice of the theme that entails a stylistic adaptation of the topos of ineffability, but the project of the modernisation and elevation of the poetics that requires such a theme. The stress shifts in other words from the exceptionality of the topic to the uniqueness of the poetic enterprise, from the 'vista nova' (*Par* xxxiii, 136) to the 'novelty' of the work, and the *Comedy* can call itself 'sacred poem' (*Par* xxiii, 62; xxv, 1) and be labelled *Divine*.

The poetics of ineffability of the *Paradiso*, however, involves serious consequences for the tenability of the fourfold exegetical/interpretative model. If the divine cannot be rendered in language, the literal level of the poetic construction inevitably fails: any attempt at a literal description of what 'actually' happened or what Dante 'actually' saw and heard can only be an evocation or a trope: 'Trasumanar significar per verba / non si poria' ('The passing beyond [or through] humanity could not be signified in words', *Par* i, 70–1, my emphasis). As Peter Hawkins has pointed out, a literal 'significar' is out of the question from the start of the *cantica*,[18] and the process of signification can therefore only be founded on a conception of language as pure tropology: language can be endowed with the three layers of meaning that in the *Epistle to Can Grande* are united under the more general label of 'allegorical', but no 'literal', 'historical', 'enveloping' or 'anterior' sense may exist as such. The impasse reached by Dante's theory and which, as we have seen in chapter 1, Joyce exposes in the 'mamafesta' chapter of the *Wake*, is therefore a consequence already implicit in Dante's evolving poetics. In fact, the poetics of *Paradiso* points to what modern hermeneutics has indicated as the inevitable condition of language: the unbridgeable gap between any semiotic system and its referent. What Paul deMan has described as being caught in the tropological system of language is what Dante experiences in his poem and makes his readers experience with him through a progressive intensification of the rhetorical density and difficulty of the poem. This is however also what makes it possible for the poet to arouse in his readers a suggestion of the unutterable vision, and the foregrounding of the ineluctable representational mismatch, the exploitation of the 'tropological' ('other', 'alien',[19] or even 'alienating') nature of language, is finally what enables Dante to circumvent the problem of representation and the impossibility of a literal level: the poem refuses to represent, and language becomes an experience rather than a mediation of meaning. This may explain to a large extent the modernists' fascination with Dante's work (one is reminded of Eliot's dictum that poets 'must be *difficult*' and that the poet must 'force . . . dislocate if necessary, language into his meaning'[20]), and may suggest why such writers as Joyce, Eliot and Pound felt the need to return to the medieval roots of modern European culture in order, as Pound's slogan goes, to 'make it new'.

SILENT LEAPS

Dante tries to remember and to say, but cannot, memory and language do not suffice – like Shem, he is 'in his bardic memory low' (*FW* 172.28), and the *Comedy* thus takes the form of an imperfect copy from the book of memory,[21] which in turn is only an imperfect copy from the book that Dante has seen in his final vision (*Par* XXXIII, 85–7). His 13,000-plus lines of poetry are a huge effort to remember the vision while creating it (*invenio*), just as the 600-plus pages of the *Wake* are a huge effort to both remember the dream and invent it. Both works are the equivalent of a post-Babelian effort to remember what cannot be remembered, to 'balbly call to memory' (*FW* 37.16) the original forgotten language while inventing new ones, a remedy to and an exploitation of the linguistic fall and the limits of memory.[22]

The reader, then, shares with the poet a (fictional) awareness of inadequacy, of not being able to 'retell' and, consequently, the need for an extraordinary creative effort; paradoxically, the (fictionally) failed attempt to retell, or, to borrow a word from the *Wake*, 'retale' (cf. *FW* 3.17), is the main activity of the *Comedy* since its very first lines: 'Io non so ben ridir com'i' v'entrai' ('I cannot well retell how I entered it', *Inf* I, 10). The rhetorical depth of the text grows significantly in conjunction with the protests of poetic or mnemonic inadequacy, exhibiting an exceptional concentration of figures and tropes as if to underscore the disjunction between the referent and the tropological system of language of which the poem is part. In fact, the poet's assertions of incapacity that punctuate all the cantos of the *Paradiso* can be read as a massive instance of *praeteritio*, the metadiscursive figure through which the speaker explicitly announces his intention not to deal with a certain subject. But the preterition is soon transformed into a performative form of litotes in that, while it asserts that something is not going to be dealt with, it actually deals with it through its negation. Ineffability becomes a challenge which the author declares to be insurmountable but which is in fact taken up, fought against and at each occurrence overcome throughout the poem.

Despite its length, it is worth quoting the following passage in its entirety, as it is one of the most complete and interesting instances of the topos of ineffability in the *Divine Comedy*:

> Come foco di nube si diserra
> per dilatarsi sì che non vi cape,
> e fuor di sua natura in giù s'atterra,
>   la mente mia così, tra quelle dape
> fatta più grande, di sé stessa uscìo,
> e che si fesse rimembrar non sape.
>   'Apri li occhi e riguarda qual son io;
> tu hai vedute cose, che possente
> se' fatto a sostener lo riso mio'.
>   Io era come quei che si risente
> di visione oblita e che s'ingegna
> indarno di ridurlasi a la mente,
>   quand'io udi' questa proferta, degna
> di tanto grato, che mai non si stingue
> del libro che 'l preterito rassegna.
>   Se mo sonasser tutte quelle lingue
> che Polimnia con le suore fero
> del latte lor dolcissimo più pingue,
>   per aiutarmi, al millesmo del vero
> non si verria, cantando il santo riso
> e quanto il santo aspetto facea mero;
>   e così, figurando il paradiso,

convien saltar lo sacrato poema,
come chi trova suo cammin riciso.
    Ma chi pensasse il ponderoso tema
e l'omero mortal che se ne carca,
nol biasmerebbe se sott'esso trema:
    non è pareggio da picciola barca
quel che fendendo va l'ardita prora,
né da nocchier ch'a sé medesmo parca.   (*Par* xxiii, 40–69)

(As fire breaks from a cloud, because it dilates so that it does not fit there, and against its nature comes down to earth, so my mind, made greater amid those feasts, went out of itself, and what it became it cannot remember. 'Open your eyes and look at what I am: you have seen such things that you have become able to sustain my smile.' I was like someone that wakes from a forgotten vision [dream], and who strives in vain to bring it back to mind, when I heard this proffer, worthy of such gratitude that it can never be dimmed in the book that records the past. Even if all those tongues that Polyhymnia and her sisters made most rich with their sweetest milk sounded now to come to my aid, it would not come to a thousandth of the truth in singing the holy smile, and how it brightened the holy aspect; and so, figuring Paradise, the sacred poem must make a leap, just like him who finds his path cut off. But whoever thinks of the ponderous theme and of the mortal shoulder [lit.: *humerus*] which is burdened with it, will not blame it [the shoulder] if it tremble beneath it [the load]. It is no voyage for a little boat, this one which the daring prow parts as it goes, nor for a pilot who would spare himself.)

These lines begin with a simile drawn from the natural world in order to compare the meteorological phenomenon of the lightning with the *excessus mentis* provoked by the vision of Christ, immediately followed by the first assertion of the inadequacy of the poet's memory that cannot retain the experience. Beatrice then calls Dante, inviting him to look at her (46–8), and this gives the occasion for another claim of the insufficiency of memory through a second simile (49–51) followed by a *terzina* in which Beatrice's words are described as such that they can never be forgotten. The contrast is striking: the *excessus mentis* is such that memory will not contain it, but at the same time the intellective, mnemonic and sensory powers of the poet have been so strengthened that he will from now on be able to apprehend and retain other similar experiences; the improvement explicitly described for the sense of sight (46–8) is implicitly affirmed for memory too, but the capacity just acquired is immediately offset by a new version of the topos of ineffability which this time concerns language's incapacity to render the supernatural experience adequately. This new difficulty is conveyed through the opposition between 'tutte quelle lingue' and a 'millesmo del vero', with its pun on 'lingue' as both tongues – and with a further trope, poets' voices and poems – and natural languages. The disproportion between divine and human means, even when the greatest poets are appealed to, is overwhelming, and the hyperbole is resolved into a preterition, the abandonment of the attempt to describe the experience itself. Dante insists on the necessity for the poem to 'leap',[23] inviting the reader to reflect on the disproportion between the 'ponderous' theme and the 'omero mortale' – that is, the human shoulder that should support it, but the reader immediately perceives a reference to the poet Homer too; the successive metaphors of the boat and of the 'ferryman' are grafted on to this trope through a noun, 'pareggio', which can be translated as 'voyage' (as Singleton does) but which also suggests in Italian the inevitably doomed attempt to 'compare', make equal, be equal to the task.

Echoes of this figuration of ineffability resound in the following lines of *Paradiso* XXIII (77–8, 87, 97–102, 118–19, 129), while this expression of the topos in turn resounds with echoes from other cantos – the image of the boat that must sail a rough sea in order to arrive at a safe harbour which has been used to refer either to the poet or the reader, or both;[24] the metaphor of the book of memory;[25] the simile of the lightning.[26] And each of these echoes may, in turn, refer to other passages: the 'nocchiere' cannot but recall Dante's entrance into Hell, when he is ferried across the Acheron by Charon in *Inferno* III, or into Purgatory (the 'celestial nocchiero' of *Purg.* II, 43); the topos of the boat cannot fail to bring to mind the 'folle volo' ('mad flight', *Inf* XXVI, 125) of Ulysses, whose doomed, tragic voyage is often contrasted to Dante's successful 'flight' to God (we perceive in these words yet another instance of Dante's 'pride', and maybe also a premonition of Stephen's invocation of his artificer-father Dedalus at the end of *A Portrait*). Through these echoes and linguistic, rhetorical or thematic reprises, the poem builds an increasingly complex web which gives it a tighter unity than the linear disposition of the verse can offer – a trait which is typical of poetry in general but which in Dante's poem acquires a rarely achieved density and whose nearest parallel can probably be found in Joyce's work, from *Dubliners* onwards, but especially in the 'Echoland' of *Finnegans Wake* (13.05), whose 'meandertale' (*FW* 18.22) requires an equally meandering reading of the tale.

Taking the cue from the lines quoted above, one could say that Joyce takes up Dante's implicit challenge, 'Se mo sonasser tutte quelle lingue': all those tongues and languages seem to be literally made to resound in order to try to obtain, not 'a thousandth of the truth', but its totality. Unfortunately, this totality could only be comprehended by an ideal reader whose most important asset would be constant alertness and incapacity to sleep – 'that ideal reader suffering from an ideal insomnia' (*FW* 120.13–14) who could ideally decipher the 'letter' of *FW* 1.5. But this ideal reader, whose powers of concentration and retention must be so advanced, comes too close to resembling God, and the human minds of us non-ideal readers can only approach 'a thousandth of the truth'. Even Dante, whose powers have so increased in his ascent to the Empyrean, needs to rest from the lesson that St Bernard gives him on the composition of the 'rosa dei beati', because he is getting sleepy:

> Ma perché 'l tempo fugge che t'assonna,
> qui farem punto, come buon sartore
> che com'elli ha del panno fa la gonna . . . (*Par* xxxII, 139–41)

(But because the time flies that makes you sleepy, we shall stop here, like a good tailor that cuts the garment according to his cloth . . .)

In the simile of the tailor (a significant one in the *Comedy* that also appears in *Inferno* xv, when Dante and Virgil encounter the host of the sodomites among whom is Brunetto; see *Inf* xv, 16–21), the shortness of the cloth is the shortness of Dante's faculties, but it will soon become the 'shortness' of language itself, incapable of conveying the memory of his vision: 'Omai sarà più corta mia favella' ('Now will my speech be more short', *Par* xxxIII, 106; I shall come back again to the 'shortness' of language). The entire *Comedy* is indeed inscribed within a paradox: Dante enters the forest in a slumber that signifies sin ('tant'era pien di sonno a quel punto / che la verace via abbandonai'; 'I was so full of sleep at that moment that I abandoned the true way', *Inf* I, 11–12), but the salvific vision too is and can only be achieved in a dream-like experience: 'Qual è colui che sognando vede, / che dopo 'l sogno la passione impressa / rimane, e l'altro a la mente non riede' ('As is he who dreaming sees, and after the dream, the passion remains imprinted and the rest does not come back to the mind', *Par* xxxIII, 58–60). And yet Dante is prevented by St Bernard from falling asleep *in order that* he may see this vision. It is the same paradox of *Finnegans Wake*, whose ideal reader must suffer from insomnia and stay awake in order to experience what has been variously interpreted as the language of dream, the language caught between sleeping and waking, night-language, not-language.

Not many readers can fulfil these ideal requirements, whether of *Finnegans Wake* or of the *Divine Comedy*. While readers are made to participate in the signifying process of the text, they are also selected, streamed as it were, because of the difficulty of the task. The text is full of leaps that have to be taken, of gaps that have to be filled in; only some will be able to follow (in) the wake/*Wake* (see *Par* II, 1–18, quoted in the epigraph of the Introduction), and the artist, while requiring the co-operation of the readers, at the same time leaves them to fend for themselves:

> A descriver lor forme più non spargo
> rime, lettor; ch'altra spesa mi strigne,
> tanto ch'a questa non posso esser largo;
> ma leggi Ezechiel, che li dipigne
> come li vide . . .   (*Purg* XXIX, 97–101)

(To describe their forms I do not spread any more rhymes, reader, because another spending constrains me so that I cannot be lavish to this; but read Ezekiel, who depicts them as he saw them . . .)

The poet's concern is not explication but the form of his subject(-matter). The 'keys' are 'given' in the text (*FW* 628.15); it is up to the readers to find them and fill the gaps, 'put together again' the bits and pieces of these difficult, Humpty Dumpty-like, works. The text, then, is the result of a dialectic between the 'presence' of the words and the 'absence', the blanks, or gaps, or leaps which the reader has to (ful)fill. Where Dante's privileged trope for this is the 'leap', in the *Wake* it is more often a pun combining opposites: whole/hole, word/void, together with an insistence on gaps, holes, and on absence.[27] Critics have pointed out the importance of 'absence' in Joyce's work from the very first page of *Dubliners*, where the 'gnomon' – the term from Euclidean geometry that describes an incomplete figure, a parallelogram from which a smaller parallelogram has been cut out – becomes the symbol of the incomplete lives of the Dubliners, but also of Joyce's method of composition.[28]

This 'streaming' of the readership, however, should not be seen only as a writing for the happy few ('Voialtri pochi che drizzaste il collo / per tempo al pan de li angeli'; 'You other few who raised your necks in time for bread of angels', *Par* II, 10–11), the elitism which modernism too has often been accused of. In fact, it is exactly this difficulty and the presence of these gaps that makes it possible for the text to be *potentially* infinite, for every reader to experience directly the difficulty of comprehending infinity and the ultimate defeat of a poetics of the ineffable and of the truly *novum*: such a poetics will only finally allow for texts which, because they cannot tell, are ultimately silent.

If the poet is caught in the tropology of language, all he can do is catch his readers in the game. After all, this silent 'leaping' may just be a matter of deviously suggesting while avoiding the issue; it forces the reader to assume that beyond the text there is something else, something more, and that this 'something more' is indeed what matters. As Clive Hart put it in his classic study *Structure and Motif in Finnegans Wake*, one of Joyce's aims, and one of the reasons why the book has such a wealth of allusions and references, was to give his readers the impression that there was always something more beyond what they had understood, something more that they needed to strive for.[29] Some readers may refuse to be 'caught'; Ezra Pound – 'jaded, disillusioned, fastidious', to use the words Henry James employed to describe the type of 'difficult' reader he wanted to 'catch' in *The Turn of the Screw*[30] – complained of *Finnegans Wake*: 'Nothing so far as I make out, nothing *short* of *divine vision* or a new cure for the clapp can possibly be worth all the circumambient peripherization.'[31] Pound probably thought that he was being dismissive, but surely he was missing the irony of his own words: if neither the *Wake* nor the *Comedy* could offer a cure for 'the clapp', it is precisely a 'divine vision' that inspired Dante's leaps, and Dante's linguistic leaps that partly inspired Joyce's 'circumambient peripherizations'.

In the *Divine Comedy* the artifice whereby the artist claims not to be able to say the ineffable is part of a larger issue, the silence about or over certain topics, a preterition that in the course of the *Comedy* may take many different forms. In the *Paradiso* it appears mostly as dialectic between wanting or having to say vs. not being able or allowed to say. The prohibition to retell what Dante has learned remains episodic (there are only two examples of it in *Paradiso*[32]), but it is equally significant within the larger context of the 'silence' and the 'leaps', insofar as we know that something has been revealed to Dante, but this revelation is now withheld from us. The reader's co-operation seems no longer required here, and indeed s/he is excluded from the process of communication and creation of meaning. The 'leap' is now governed by a different logic: the issue is no longer one of ability but of licitness. Yet, the reader still has to attempt to fill in the blanks. As in the 'nominigentilisation' of HCE, the question will have to be asked: 'Are those their fata which we read in sibylline between the *fas* and its *nefas*?' (*FW* 31.35–6). And as in the case of the prophecies disclosed to Dante, which will not be explained for some years ('Taci e lascia muover li anni'; 'Keep silent, and let the years go by', *Par* IX, 4), 'We shall perhaps not so soon see' (*FW* 32.02). There is a striking coincidence between the 'nominigentilisation' in which HCE's name and rise are discussed, and Cacciaguida's 'parlar profondo' ('deep speech', or 'profound speaking'; cf. *Par* XV, 39). Cacciaguida is Dante's progenitor, and Dante learns from him about his fate (exile), about his own ascendancy and about the origins, decay and fate of Florentine society; it is he who predicts divine revenge and forbids Dante to reveal the content of his prophecy (one of the meanings of *fatum*). Likewise, sinful and obscene, illicit actions are suggested in the history of Humphrey Chimpden Earwicker's name and origins: *fas* is what is licit, rightful, it is (divine) law, and what one can say without fear of punishment (cf. Latin *fari*, I speak), etymologically related to *fatum*, *fata* (fate, destiny, what is written). Its contrary, *nefas*, denotes what is impossible, illicit, unjust because contrary to the divine word. Between the '*fas*' and the '*nefas*' stand both human existence and the text, all to be deciphered ('sibylline'). (There may be a more precise echo here of *Par* XXXIII 65–6: 'così al vento ne le foglie levi / si perdea la sentenza di Sibilla'; 'Thus in the wind, in the light leaves, the Sibyl's oracle was lost'. I shall come back to these lines later in this chapter.)

In a way, the *Divine Comedy* is the attempt to save as much as possible of the vision from the silence to which the failing of memory will otherwise consign it. Yet, it is only through silence that the final vision of the Word can be spoken: 'The silence speaks the scene' (*FW* 13.02–3), and it is to this silence that one must listen. The *Wake* tells us that one option may be to turn a blind eye and a deaf ear ('We may see and hear nothing if we choose', 12.25–6), but we cannot escape the archetypal quest for the origins and the mystery of life: 'But all they are all there scraping along to sneeze out a likelihood that will solve and salve life's robulous rebus' (12.32–4; *rebus* = word puzzle, or perhaps with only a slight twist, 'Word puzzle'. We shall encounter again Romulus and Remus, the fighting twins at the origin of Rome).

At the centre of this enquiry backwards and forwards again into genealogical origins (see also *FW* 14.16, 'parently') and into the book of history (see *FW* 13.29–14.27, where the pages of the 'boke of the deeds' are being turned by the wind and historical chronology is first reversed – 1132 AD, then 566 AD – and then, after a moment of silence, redressed into 566 AD followed by 1132 AD) stands the moment of silence between the ages ('(Silent)', *FW* 14.06), the Ginnunga-gap of Norse mythology in which the scroll (the letter, the text, the book of history itself) disappears, stolen (or saved?) by the copyist, to resurface again in the midden heap of history, in fragments, incomplete, to be endlessly re-interpreted:

Somewhere, parently, in the ginnandgo gap between antediluvious and annadominant the copyist must have fled with his scroll. The billy flood rose or an elk charged him or the sultrup worldwright from the excelsissimost empyrean (bolt, in sum) earthspake or the Dannamen gallous banged pan the bliddy duran. A scribicide then and there is led off . . .

(FW 14.16–21)

In the silent gap, something happened: a flood, an elk charging, or a bolt from heaven (like the one that struck the builders of the tower of Babel, or the one that signals the end of a cycle and the start of the next one in Vico's view of history); or else, a hen (Biddy Doran) was laid by a cock (Lat. *gallus*), or killed, or 'banged' into a pan (one almost wants to ask, what came first, fried chicken or the omelette? and, what was laid first, the hen or the egg? In the cheekiness of the questions is yet again the quest for the origin); or perhaps 'Dannamen gallous' just banged shut the 'bloody door', closing the gap, thereby also preventing any recovery of the scroll. Shortly after, we are given the hint that closing the door shuts out polysemy, maybe even meaningfulness: 'So you need hardly spell me how every word will be bound over to carry three score and ten toptypsical readings throughout the book of Doublends Jined . . . till Daleth, mahomahouma, who oped it closeth thereof the. Dor' *(FW* 20.13–18). Indeed, by the time the scribe is killed and the scribicide is led off, the scroll of history – the book where the memory of mankind is recorded – is lost. The silence between the ages, the dark ages between the stealing of the text and its reappearance in the midden heap, are also the silent gap between the end of the *Wake* and its (re-)beginning, the moment of silence in the *Divine Comedy* between the vision of God and the writing of the poem which leads to (indeed, *is*) the vision.

The origin of HCE in *FW* 1.2 – the origin of man – is equally obscured by a mysterious silence: '(One still hears that pebble crusted laughta . . . and still one feels the amossive silence of the cladstone allegibelling . . .)' (*FW* 31.29–32). There has to be an enquiry into the shadows of the past, with their sinister laughter, into the shadowy past of alleged crimes and intestine wars ('allegibelling', also evoking the Ghibellines of medieval, and Florentine, memory; but if alleged, is it smear or guilt?) so that the questions come to mind again, 'are these the facts of his nominigentilisation . . . Are those their fata which we read in sibylline . . . ? No dung on the road?' (*FW* 31.33–32.01).

After the meeting with the cad and the enquiry that does not dispel the doubts despite the disclaimers (cf. *FW* 33.18–35; 36.33–4) the cad himself becomes 'Gaping Gill'[33] (*FW* 36.35) and 'gildthegap Gaper' (*FW* 37.08), the gap into which the memory of the truth – HCE's story and words – disappears to resurface in broken and badly remembered talk: 'repeated in his secondmouth language as many of the bigtimer's verbaten words which he could balbly call to memory' (*FW* 37.14–16), like the sinners' striving to speak in corrupt languages after their 'big time' at Babel or Dante's futile attempt at recalling his vision.

In the very different plots of the *Divine Comedy* and *Finnegans Wake*, the origins and the end are in silence, and need silent leaps to be 'retaled'. That is why the 'girl detective' who helps in the quest for the truth about HCE in chapter 1.3 is called 'Sylvia Silence':

Sylvia Silence, the girl detective . . . when supplied with informations as to the several facets of the case in her cozydozy bachelure's flat, quite overlooking John a'Dream's mews, leaned back in her really truly easy chair to query restfully through her vowelthreaded syllabelles: Have you evew thought, wepowtew, that sheew gweatness was his twadgedy?

(*FW* 61.01–7)

The 'several facets of the case' anticipate the description of the 'mamafesta' as a 'polyhedron of scripture' (*FW* 107.08) and the many facets of ALP (*FW* 298.30–1; I shall discuss these later). (Sylvia) Silence may help to solve the mystery, find ('invent') the solution, 'solvere il nodo' (untie or loosen the knot[34]) of the quest through poetic tropes. This vocal, dreaming Sylvia Silence who threads together beautiful syllables and who clearly is an emanation of Issy – but whose syllabic attempts to voice the silence may also approximate the 'imeffible tries at speech unasyllabled' of my second epigraph – once again presents us with another paradox: vowels are the 'voice' of otherwise mute, silent words whose consonants could not be pronounced, but it is this vocal silence that weaves, threads or binds together voices and vowels to form resonant words and sentences. Sylvia Silence will resurface later, in chapter II.3, when her beautiful syllables are recast into beautiful thoughts: 'Suppwose you get a beautiful thought and cull them sylvias sub silence' (*FW* 337.16–17). Issy, in the meantime, has been herself threading or tying together syllables, vowels and semi-vowels in chapter II.2:

Where flash becomes word and silents selfloud. To brace congeners, trebly bounden and asservaged twainly. Adamman, Emhe, Issossianusheen and sometypes Yggely ogs Weib. Uwayoei! So mag this sybilette be our shibboleth that we may syllable her well!   (*FW* 267.16–21)

These 'silents selfloud' (German *Selbstlaut*: 'vowel'), the silent vowels that Sylvia can thread together in 'syllabelles' and that we wish Issy may 'syllable' well, reverse the Incarnation (flesh now becomes (the) (W)ord) and add to the list of vowels the two semivocalic W and Y to form the rainbow-like 'Uwayoei'. Through this addition, the splitting of the U (you) into the W (double U) and the of I into the bifurcating Y both suggests Issy's split identity and implicitly poses the fundamental interrogation of identity, subjecting the 'I' to the question 'why' ('Y').[35] Issy's vocalic operations and questioning of identity in her 'sybilette', and Sylvia's corresponding vocalic silence may also be seen as an elaboration or a supplanting of Stephen's earlier binding together of vowels in 'Scylla and Charybdis' in the middle of his exposition of his theory of literary and biographical/biological creation and of his discussion with the Dublin Platonists, when his 'I' had been inscribed at the centre of a bond of material and literary debts:

– But this prying into the family life of a great man, Russell began impatiently.

. . .

How now, sirrah, that pound he lent you when you were hungry?
    Marry, I wanted it.
    Take thou this noble.
    Go to! You spent most of it in Georgina Johnson's bed, clergyman's daughter. Agenbite of inwit.
    Do you intend to pay it back?
    O, yes.
    When? Now?
    Well... no.

When, then?

I paid my way. I paid my way.

Steady on. He's from beyant Boyne water. The northeast corner. You owe it.

Wait. Five months. Molecules all change. I am other I now. Other I got pound.

Buzz. Buzz.

But I, entelechy, form of forms, am I by memory because under everchanging forms.

I that sinned and prayed and fasted.

A child Conmee saved from pandies.

I, I and I. I.

A. E. I. O. U.   (*U* 241–3)

Stephen's I.O.U. acknowledges his material debt of a pound to A.E. (George Russell) but at the same time he releases himself, at least hypothetically, from the obligation of paying it through a casuistic argument that relies on a pseudo-biological negation of identity ('Molecules all change. I am other I now. Other I got pound'). In so doing, however, as Jean-Michel Rabaté has shown in his 'Portrait of the Author as a Bogeyman',[36] Stephen incurs a literary debt to Dante's formulation of literary authority and authenticity through the vocalic bond in the fourth book of the *Convivio*, where the word *autore* is made to derive either from the Latin *auieo*, 'I tie' or 'bind', or from the Greek *autentin*, 'trustworthy' (hence 'authentic'):

> E chi ben guarda lui, ne la sua prima voce apertammente vedrà che elli stesso lo dimostra, che solo di legame di parole è fatto, cioè di sole cinque vocali, che sono anima e legame d'ogni parola, e composto d'esse per modo volubile, a figurare imagine di legame. Chè, cominciando con l'A, ne l'U quindi si rivolve e viene dritto per l'I ne l'E, quindi si rivolve e torna ne l'O; sì che veramente imagina questa figura: A, E, I, O, U, la quale è figura di legame. E in quanto 'autore' viene e discende da questo verbo, si prende solo per li poeti, che con l'arte musaica le loro parole hanno legate.
>
> (*Conv* IV.vi, 3–5)

(And who looks at it carefully in its first person form will clearly see that it shows its own meaning, for it is made up only of the bonds of words, that is to say of the five vowels alone, which are the soul and tie of every word, and it is composed of them in changing manner, to figure the image of a bond [tie]. For beginning with A it turns from there to U, and then goes straight by I to E, from where it turns back and returns to O, so that they truly image forth this figure, A, E, I, O, U, which is the figure of a bond [tie]. And insofar as 'author' is derived and descends from this verb, it is used only for poets, who have bound their words with the art of the muses.)

Dante's argument is indeed a threading together of the vowels A E I O U, the 'the soul and tie of every word'. Stephen's – and the chapter's – weaving of literary references to Dante, among other poets, is in a way an accretion of literary interests; but, disregarding Mr Deasy's earlier advice in 'Nestor' that the proudest words an Englishman can say are 'I paid my way' (*U* 37, 242), Stephen is however not going to pay his way: this 'immense debtorship' (*U* 255) is of a kind that cannot be paid off; it can only be worded away through casuistry (or, as Buck Mulligan would have it, by algebra, *U* 21). Stephen uses the vocalic bond to reject his biological and material debt through a Cartesian neat separation of the bodily I from the I of memory, thus hoping to preserve his psychological identity and integrity. Stephen himself acknowledges the untenability of this position ('But I, entelechy, form of forms, am I by memory because under everchanging forms'); in the later novel, Issy will subvert this theory by asserting her split identity through the vocalic and semivocalic multiple knot; as Laurent Milesi has argued, Issy's 'female grammar' also voices her desire of a (sexual) binding to the father through the unlawful knot of incest.[37] The *Wake*'s incestuous version of Dante's spiritual 'maker mates with made' (*FW* 261.08) echoes St Bernard's chaste prayer to the Virgin:

> 'Vergine madre, figlia del tuo figlio,
> umile e alta più che creatura,
> termine fisso d'etterno consiglio,
>   tu se' colei che l'umana natura
> nobilitasti sì, che 'l suo fattore
> non disdegnò di farsi sua fattura.'   (*Par* xxxiii, 1–6)

('Virgin Mother, daughter of your Son, humble and exalted more than any creature, fixed goal of the eternal counsel, you are she who ennobled human nature so that its maker did not disdain to become its made.')

Unlike the *Commedia*, whose stress falls on the paradoxical nature of the mystery of the Incarnation, Joyce's text brings out the incestuous nature of the oedipal relation, foreshadowing an illicit mating of 'maker' with 'made', father with 'maid', which the following bracketed, slightly outraged exclamation '(O my!)' (*FW* 261.08), also betrays.

But with Stephen's theory of literary creation and fatherhood as self-engendering, the vocalic ties or knots of 'Scylla and Charybdis' and Issy's vocalic desire of the Father, we are already 'prying into the

family life' (*U* 241), getting embroiled in an increasingly entangled
'family umbroglia' (*FW* 284.04), and in order to solve this rebus we
shall have to venture even deeper into it by following the thread of
the twins' quest for the mother-as-origin (the mother's sex as their
origin) in the geometry lesson of chapter II.2, an episode which, in its
exploration of familial, literary, linguistic and sexual issues must be
seen both as a complement and a counterpoint to the father/son
oedipal, literary and Babelian battle analysed in the previous
chapter. As Dante knew, the shortest way may not be the right one,
and this enquiry will therefore have to take a detour back through
various phases of Stephen's poetics from *A Portrait* to *Ulysses*.

UNSPEAKABLE GEOMETRIES

Modern philosophical enquiry into or about geometry has often
been – as in the work of Kant and Husserl for instance[38] – an
enquiry into its origin as well as into its function of mediating
between the transcendent and the immanent, the ideal and the
material. However, already in the Middle Ages geometry had served
the purpose of mediating origin and end, transcendence and human
perception. At the height of his pilgrimage and great feat of linguistic
invention, Dante strives to convey to the reader his effort to see God
(in the journey) and represent him (in the poem) through the image
of the geometer who gazes into the mystery of the squaring of the
circle and yet cannot find the solution:

> Qual è 'l geomètra che tutto s'affige
> per misurar lo cerchio, e non ritrova,
> pensando, quel principio ond'elli indige,
>   tal era io a quella vista nova:
> veder volea come si convenne
> l'imago al cerchio e come vi s'indova . . .
>
> (*Par* XXXIII, 133–8)

(As is the geometer who wholly fixes himself to measure the circle, and does
not find, in thinking, that principle of which he is in need, such was I at
that new [marvellous] sight. I wished to see how the image conformed to
the circle and how it finds its place there [literally: how it inwheres itself
there] . . .)

The comparison with this frustrated geometer is both appropriate to
Dante's impossible attempt to see God, and paradoxical, as the
geometer is, literally, he who measures the earth, whereas Dante is

trying to encompass linguistically concepts that are by definition beyond the earthly and beyond any measure.

In an equally paradoxical way, the image of the geometer who strives to see into the mystery of the squaring of the circle, a metaphor for the divine radiance of the vision, also recalls an earlier episode of striving to see into the darkness: in *Inferno* xv Dante and Virgil meet a host of souls,

> e ciascuna
> ci riguardava come suol da sera
>   guardare uno altro sotto nuova luna;
> e sì ver' noi aguzzavan le ciglia
> come 'l vecchio sartor fa ne la cruna.   (*Inf* xv, 17–21)

(and each looked at us as men look at one another under a new moon at dusk; and they knit [lit.: sharpen] their brows towards us as the old tailor does at the eye of the needle.)

I have argued elsewhere[39] that this image may have been used by Joyce for the first paragraph of the short story 'The Sisters', where the desire to learn and the mystery of words and of death are associated with that puzzling concept of Euclidean geometry, the 'gnomon', which suggests incompleteness but is also etymologically related to knowledge. The simile of the tailor is, as I suggested earlier, also important in the context of Dante's final vision. As for the tailor in the image used by St Bernard in *Paradiso* xxxii to allude to Dante's limited powers (*Par* xxxii, 140–1, quoted earlier), the measure of Dante's human 'favella' (speech, language) is too 'short' to convey even the memory of his vision – let alone the vision itself:

> Omai sarà più corta mia favella,
> pur a quel ch'io ricordo, che d'un fante
> che bagni ancor la lingua a la mammella.
>   (*Par* xxxiii, 106–8)

(Now will my speech be more short, even for what I remember, than that of a child who still bathes his tongue at the breast.)

> Oh quanto è corto il dire e come fioco
> al mio concetto!   (*Par* xxxiii, 121–2)

(O how short is speech, and how feeble to my conception!)

The geometer's efforts fall short of solving the mystery, Dante's speech is short: the poet must end his poetic journey here because his measure – his length of cloth – is finished. At the height of his journey to God, the 'father' of the Italian language cannot grasp the mystery of the Son, the Father and the Word, nor invent a language to 'say' it, and has to revert to the condition of a small child who is just learning to say his words ('fante', just one linguistic step ahead, as it were, of the '*infant*' with which Singleton translates the word; but if one keeps in mind Statius' discussion of the generation and development of the embryo in *Purgatorio* xxv which I outlined in chapter 2, 'fante' also signifies the divinely infused moral, rational and linguistic potentiality of the child). St Bernard thus has to ask for the Virgin Mother's intercession to grant Dante the vision his limited powers cannot give him, while Beatrice is already praying God that he may grant this gift: from the man Dante to God the Father, from the author of words to the Word, the necessary bridging measure can be granted only through the agency of saintly, virginal, motherly women.

In the 'geometry lesson' of *Finnegans Wake* – Joyce's own attempt at 'circling the square' (*FW* 186.12), structurally realised in the transposition of the siglum for the book, a square (also the polygon ideally formed by any fourfold pattern of interpretation, whether linguistic, historical or other) into the circle formed by the continuation of the last sentence into the first – the children learn their 'triv and quad' (*FW* 306.12–13), and Dante's questing geometer is transformed into the quested 'geomater'[40] – mother earth, mother of the earth – whose 'whome' (the womb, the origin, the telos: a feminised alpha and omega) Shem/Dolph wants to reveal to Shaun/Kev: 'I'll make you to see figuratleavely the whome of your eternal geomater' (*FW* 296.30–297.01). At the same time, the inscription of the river Liffey/ALP, figured through the triangle of her delta, in the circle (see the diagram on page 293 of the *Wake*) may also transpose Dante's inscription of the river into the circle of the one and triune face of God the Father, Son and Holy Ghost in the last cantos of *Paradiso*.

In a brief discussion of Joyce's allusions in the *Wake* to the last canto of *Paradiso*, Mary Reynolds comments that in the adaptation of the geometry problem to the *Wake*, Dante's 'geometra' is made to undergo a 'grotesque' and 'ludicrous distortion'. The transformation may be comical, but its premises and function are too serious and far-reaching I believe to be reduced to a mere distortion which 'In part . . . can be traced to the free-association of the dream, and in part is a reminder that Dante's own sublimity includes and poetically uses grotesque components'.[41] But before we proceed in this direction, Joyce's geometrical steps must be retraced briefly; a checklist leading up to II.2 would include at least the gnomon in 'The Sisters', the French triangle in 'Scylla and Charybdis', Miss Portinari as an isosceles triangle in 'Eumaeus' and the 'isoscelating biangle' (*FW* 165.13) constructed by the twins within the story of Burrus, Caseous and Margareen (*FW* I.6).

The 'gnomon' did not appear in the first version of 'The Sisters', published in 1904 in *The Irish Homestead*; it was added, together with the words 'paralysis' and 'simony' and the entire Dantean intertext, when Joyce radically rewrote the story in 1906.[42] Perhaps one could identify this as the period in which Joyce developed an insight into the uses to which Euclidean geometry might be put for literary ends, and one way of looking at this issue may be to see it in the context of the use of scientific metaphors for the literary activity by several artists at the turn of the century and in the first decades of the twentieth century. Apart from Cubist and Futurist uses of geometrical drawings and metaphors and their centrality in abstract art, one can think for instance of Eliot's image of poetic activity as a chemical process, which he condensed in the well-known simile of the 'catalyst',[43] or of Conrad's process of 'crystallisation'.[44] Another important example would be Pound's reliance on scientific theories of energy, including Cartesian geometry, for his vorticist poetics and for his later writings.[45] In this sense, Joyce's gnomon and, later, the circles and triangles of *Finnegans Wake*, would be related to the use of other scientific images, such as Luigi Galvani's 'enchantment of the heart', analogous for Stephen to the epiphanic moment when the Aquinian radiance of the aesthetic object arrests the mind (*P* 213). It is certainly possible that some geometrical/literary figures in Joyce's work may have been favoured by this widespread attempt to redefine art as a scientific and precise activity rather than one inspired by a kind of Romantic and unaccountable genius, and that Pound's reliance on geometry in the definition of his poetics and in his criticism in the 1910s (especially the analogy between the *Divine Comedy* and the equation that relates the right-angled triangle to the circle in analytical geometry, quoted below), may have offered a more or less conscious source for some of Joyce's own geometrical images in *Ulysses* and especially in *Finnegans Wake*.[46] In *The Spirit of Romance* (1910) Pound wrote:

The *Commedia*, as Dante has explained in the Epistle to Can Grande, is written in four senses: the literal, the allegorical, the anagogical, and the ethical. For this form of arcana we find the best parallel in the expressions of mathematics. Thus, when we are able to see that one general law governs such a series of equations as $3 \times 3 + 4 \times 4 = 5 \times 5$, or written more simply, $3^2 + 4^2 = 5^2$, $6^2 + 8^2 = 10^2$, $12^2 + 16^2 = 20^2$, etc., express the common relation algebraically $a^2 + b^2 = c^2$. When one has learned common and analytical geometry, one understands that this relation, $a^2 + b^2 = c^2$, exists between two sides of the right angle triangle and its hypotenuse, and that likewise in analytics for the points forming the circumference of any circle. Thus to a trained mathematician the cryptic $a^2 + b^2 = c^2$ expresses:

1*st*. A series of abstract numbers in a certain relation to each other.

2*nd*. A relation between certain abstract numbers.

3*rd*. The relative dimensions of a figure; in this case a triangle.

4*th*. The idea or ideal of the circle.

Thus the *Commedia* is, in the literal sense, a description of Dante's vision of a journey through the realms inhabited by the spirits of men after death; in a further sense, it is the journey of Dante's intelligence through the states of mind wherein dwell all sorts of conditions of men before death; beyond this, Dante or Dante's intelligence may come to mean 'Everyman' or 'Mankind', whereat his journey becomes a symbol of mankind's struggle upward out of ignorance into the clear light of philosophy. In the second sense I give here, the journey is Dante's own mental and spiritual development. In a fourth sense, the *Commedia* is an expression of the laws of eternal justice.[47]

It is evident that for Pound, at this stage, analytical geometry provided a system which, thanks to its abstract formulas, could account for what he saw as the 'arcane' relations within the literary work, in this particular case Dante's four levels of meaning. The parallel however remains quite mechanical, and in no way is the geometrical example brought to bear on Dante's poem. As Pound himself admits in the quotation above, he is interested in *general laws* and the relationship between the triangle and the circle is one of analogy and parallel rather than interaction or necessary relation between the two. Similarly, the meanings of the cryptic algebraic formula are distributed in four points but there is no direct relation between these and the four levels of meaning of the *Commedia* (which moreover, in Pound's formulation, refer only loosely to the ones described in the *Convivio* or in the *Epistle to Can Grande*).[48]

On the contrary, Joyce's use of geometry in his works seems to suggest, rather than a metaphor or an analogy *for* the poetic activity, a field that is woven *into* the reflection on the poetic and opens up the possibility of an enquiry into the broader question of origins and of the potentiality as well as limitations of language. It is therefore fitting that the use of geometry should be part of an intertextual practice (which, it should be clear by now, I understand as a practice in which the issues at stake also need to include the relationships between source and outcome, literary fathers and necessarily irreverent sons, original model and transformed rewriting) in which one of the main sources, Dante, also used geometry in his attempt to 'stretch' language beyond its limitations and, in the process, had to admit his own limitations, his own regression to a state of near-infancy, and the ineluctable 'shortness' of language.

It will not come as a surprise, then, that Joyce's use of geometrical figures very often appears in a context where Dante is also appealed to in one form or another. Stephen's rather puzzling definition of Dante's historical referent for his poetic Beatrice, Bice Portinari ('Then, Stephen said . . . we have the impetuosity of Dante and the isosceles triangle, Miss Portinari, he fell in love with', *U* 737, anticipated by Lynch's preference for the hypotenuse of the Venus of Praxiteles over the hypotenuse of a rightangled triangle, *P* 208[49]), can thus be read retrospectively as the first appearance of a motif that Joyce would develop in *Finnegans Wake*, the female (sex) as triangle and the opposition between isosceles and equilateral (I shall return to this contrast later). Translated into a less sophisticated idiom, Stephen's words would have to read something like, 'the impetuosity of Dante and that cunt, Miss Portinari, he fell in love with'. As Stephen's previous mention of Dante's (platonic) love of Beatrice was put in terms of 'the spiritual-heroic refrigerating apparatus, invented and patented in all countries by Dante Alighieri' (*P* 252), one notices how that frigidity is now transposed into the perhaps cold logic of a geometrical figure, yet one cannot but be struck also by the incongruity of Dante's 'impetuosity', which suggests something rather more passionate than a refrigerator. 'Isosceles', defined in 'the Euclid' (*D* 9) as 'that which has two equal sides',[50] etymologically means 'equal-legged' and can therefore evoke the image of the compasses (as in *FW* 295.27, where the 'daintical pair of accomplasses' encompasses a pair of dainty and accomplished lasses, as well as the – Dantean? – pair of compasses needed to encircle the triangle in the problem set to the twins and illustrated in the diagram on *FW* 293), but it also suggests, perhaps more appropriately in the context of Stephen's bitter remark, the triangle at the apex of the lower half of that equal-legged, if spiritualised, creature loved by Dante.[51]

No wonder it is misogynist Stephen who uses this (tri)angular image for Beatrice, while Bloom's rejoinder, admiring the splendid proportions of the hips and bosom of the antique statues of the Kildare Street Museum, draws attention again to the rotundity of 'the female form' (*U* 737; one can also think of 'Ithaca', where Bloom's attention is drawn to the round shape of Molly's buttocks). One suggestion comes to mind: if ALP is the triangle inscribed within the circularity of a river-like flow of words in turn inscribed within the square that is the book according to Joyce's siglum for *Finnegans Wake*, then it is possible to see the *Wake* as offering a compromising and encompassing solution to the alternative between Stephen's and Bloom's figurations of the female form. But the *Wake*'s trigonometry extends and redefines the relationship between the female and the geometric in other ways too, which include the relationship between the maternal and the paternal, the linguistic and the ineffable and/or unspeakable. It is necessary therefore to take a further digressive path through Stephen's musings in 'Proteus' and in 'Scylla and Charybdis'; in the former chapter the navelcord constitutes a universal, transhistorical biological link through all generations, back to the navel-less Eve, and a direct (phone) line to Eden; it is what also enables the monks' mystic vision, but Eve's unblemished belly is swiftly turned into a 'womb of sin' that brings Stephen's thoughts back to his own conception (*U* 46).[52] The materiality of this maternal connection symbolised by the umbilical cord shifts in 'Scylla and Charybdis' to the immateriality of the paternal link – a progressive shift that can be seen also in the diverse associations that towers and pillars evoke in Stephen: first the umbilical Martello tower, the 'omphalos' (*U* 20) from which he is evicted, and then, in 'Aeolus', the phallic Nelson Pillar of his Parable of the Plums, from which the two 'Dublin vestals' spit plum stones on to the city (*U* 187–8). The link of fatherhood is for Stephen a void, a legal fiction but nevertheless now more stable and resistant – because uncertain – than any maternal cord, at least in the processes of literary, rather than biological, creation:

– A father, Stephen said, battling against hopelessness, is a necessary evil. He wrote the play in the months that followed his father's death. If you hold that he, a greying man with two marriageable daughters, with thirtyfive years of life, *nel mezzo del cammin di nostra vita*, with fifty of experience, is the beardless undergraduate from Wittenberg then you must hold that his seventyyear old mother is the lustful queen. No. The corpse of John Shakespeare does not walk the night. From hour to hour it rots and rots. He rests, disarmed of fatherhood, having devised that mystical estate upon his son . . . Fatherhood, in the sense of conscious begetting, is unknown to man. It is a mystical estate, an apostolic succession, from only begetter to only begotten. On that mystery and not on the madonna which the cunning Italian intellect flung to the mob of Europe the church is founded and founded irremovably because founded, like the world, macro and microcosm, upon the void. Upon incertitude, upon unlikelihood.

(*U* 265–6)

Like the navelcords of 'Proteus', fatherhood thus acquires the status of a (mystic) apostolic chain leading back to the origin, but this time without any material ties; in this widely commented passage which also links Shakespeare's predicament to Dante's (both thirty-five years old, an age at which, we have seen earlier, Joyce was keen to join them by modifying his own), the shift from motherhood to fatherhood is also a shift from the concrete to the nebulous, from the clear identifiable origin to the incertitude of authority. The maternal is now reserved only for the biological relationship, but as we have seen, Stephen has already (Cartesianly) rejected the contintuity of his biological and corporeal self ('Molecules all change. I am other I now. Other I got pound', *U* 242) in favour of a psychological, immaterial identity based solely on memory or on a 'ghostly' continuity of the body's image (*U* 249).

Stephen's battling also links him to Dante's struggle to combat despair when, *nel mezzo del cammin*, he finds himself in the dark forest; Stephen can thus join the noble company of bards – Dante, Shakespeare (and Joyce). His words, hopelessly cast against the Platonism of Dublin's intellectual circle, should be seen as a further development of the theory of the artist's 'impersonalisation' that emerged in *A Portrait* out of Stephen's (Aristotelian) 'true scholastic stink' (*P* 214) – a stench that may even unwittingly prefigure Shem's stinking house and practices. In the earlier novel, literature is for Stephen the most spiritual of arts, in which forms are not, but should be, clearly distinguished: 'Even in literature, the highest and most spiritual art, the forms are often confused' (*P* 214). It is perhaps in response to Russell's echo of these words in his Platonist advocacy of literature as the expression of the 'formless spiritual essences' (a phrase Stephen mentally repeats in conjunction with other theo-

sophist concepts, *U* 236) that Stephen is spurred into reworking the
Aristotelian-Scholastic theory in which he had defended to his friend
Lynch the clear definition and separation of literary forms. In his
morphogenesis of literary genres, Stephen identifies the lyrical as the
most primitive, instinctual and purely expressive phase or form; the
epical figures as an extension of the lyrical, when a self-reflexive
attitude emerges in the subject and the subject knows himself as a
subject, and this progression finally leads to the third step, the
dramatic, with the artist de-centring himself, becoming only a point
in the circle of the literary work, when the narrative is no longer
purely personal (*P* 214–15). Stephen continues:

> The personality of the artist passes into the narration itself, flowing round
> and round the persons and the action like a vital sea . . . The personality of
> the artist, at first a cry or a cadence or a mood and then a fluid and
> lambent narrative, finally refines itself out of existence, impersonalises
> itself, so to speak. The esthetic image in the dramatic form is life purified in
> and reprojected from the human imagination.   (*P* 215)

Narrative form and narrative personality are interdependent, and
even the impersonalisation is an active purification and projection of
the narrative subjectivity: the movement is from unconscious presence of personality to a conscious concealment of it. Stephen's words
in *A Portrait* are thus re-elaborated in 'Scylla and Charybdis':

> As we . . . weave and unweave our bodies . . . from day to day, their
> molecules shuttled to and fro, so does the artist weave and unweave his
> image. And as the mole on my right breast is where it was when I was
> born, though all my body has been woven of new stuff time after time, so
> through the ghost of the unquiet father the image of the unliving son looks
> forth.   (*U* 249)

Stephen's weaving of bodily, genealogical and literary images continues, from his earlier self's theories of the poet's projection of his
personality into the narrative, through his later (half-hearted) claim
in 'Scylla and Charybdis' that he is another self because the
molecules of his body have changed, to his admission of an
immaterial but nonetheless actual artistic and personal continuity
and the conception of the immaterial mystical link of fatherhood.

Betraying his reliance on the theory explained to Lynch in *A
Portrait* ('This supreme quality is felt by the artist when the esthetic
image is first conceived in his imagination. The mind in that
mysterious instant Shelley likened beautifully to a fading coal',
P 213), which in turn is a re-elaboration of the theory of the

epiphany illustrated to Cranly in *Stephen Hero*,[53] Stephen continues: 'In the intense instant of imagination, when the mind, Shelley says, is a fading coal, that which I was is that which I am and that which in possibility I may come to be. So in the future, the sister of the past, I may see myself as I sit here now but by reflection from that which then I shall be' (*U* 249).[54] Typically, Stephen has already undermined his theory of the artist weaving and unweaving his images to become a father unto himself when, in his history lesson in 'Nestor', his own musing on time's relation to the infinite possiblities of being are treated as futile weavings of wind (*U* 30). In the previous chapter, 'Telemachus', when he thinks of the theory he will not expound until 'Scylla and Charybdis', Stephen prophesies: 'The void awaits surely all them that weave the wind' (*U* 25); retrospectively, Penelope/Molly's weavings in the last chapter of the book also provide a female counterpoint to Stephen's 'male' weavings.[55]

In *A Portrait*, Stephen's conclusion:

The mystery of esthetic like that of material creation is accomplished. The artist, like the God of the creation, remains within or behind or beyond or above his handiwork, invisible, refined out of existence, indifferent, paring his fingernails. (*P* 215)

– perhaps one of the most quoted sentences from Joyce's works – anticipates both the link of literary and biological creation and the theme of the mystical and the necessity of the 'void', of the unstable, the unlikely of 'Scylla and Charybdis'.

Stephen's shift to the disembodied essence of the paternal in matters aesthetic in *Ulysses* has then already been prepared by *A Portrait*. But to go further back, Stephen's theory of the epiphany in *Stephen Hero* intriguingly emerges, as Jacques Aubert has noted, from the narration of the conflict between the young artist and his family, a conflict that leads him to the decision to work out in his own way what he calls 'the enigma of his position', free of the 'bond of association or impulse or tradition' (*SH* 214) and to a 'fierce criticism of women in general and of one Emma in particular'.[56] Stephen's misogyny in *Ulysses* appears thus to be closely and genealogically linked to his own desire, from *Stephen Hero* through *A Portrait*, not to incur – or, rather, to deny – any biological or literary debts.

It is therefore because of the artist's need to impersonalise and authorise himself that biological generation (female, material) cannot constitute the model for Stephen and a mystical, trinitarian and all-male one has to be relied upon, one in which the woman – the 'madonna' invented by the 'cunning Italian intellect' – plays a merely marginal role and can safely be 'flung to the mob of Europe', her status demoted from Virgin to Adulteress, her form from the circular (of which Bloom remains a champion) to the angular. If this is so, it is in the context of this shift of allegiances from the material to the 'void' that Stephen's later definition of Beatrice as isosceles triangle in *Ulysses* should be read: a Platonically ideal but sterile form, frigid despite Dante's impetuosity, incapable of (Aristotelian) generation and therefore, because fruitless, a sexual being unredeemable by any spiritualisation (but unexplicitly sexual: the unmentionable is figured, not said).

In fact, to continue this quest back into the origins and evolution of aesthetic theories, Joyce's early essay 'Drama and Life' (1900) encapsulated the core of the principle of impersonality in ways which already foreshadowed the linking of poetics and of authorship with the problem of the ineffable, the divine, and the need to mediate between the transcendent and the immanent: 'The artist forgoes his very self and stands as a mediator in awful truth before the veiled face of God.'[57] In order to mediate, the artist has to void his self and diffuse it – weave and unweave it – into language; but the veiled face of God, which the artist's mediation desires to unveil, will become for the mature artist the veiled equilateral sex of the mother which the artist-child, Shem/Dolph, promises to unveil by lifting her skirt in his 'maieutic' quest for knowledge.[58]

But does *Ulysses* in fact support Stephen's claim for an all-male fiction of creation, or does the novel ironise his artist-protagonist's speculations – as *A Portrait* had done, for instance by reverting from the third-person impersonal narration to the first-person, lyrical (more primitive) form of the diary in the last pages? I would suggest that *Ulysses* indeed undermines the theory of art as male gestation and (re)production, and not only because the mythical weaver and unweaver, Penelope, a woman, has the last word through Molly's concrete, corporeal, round form. *Ulysses* is a book of many climaxes: in 'Sirens', when, during Bloom's imagined seduction of Molly by Boylan, the seductions of the sirens at the bar include Simon Dedalus' song, transformed by Bloom's monologue ('Come . . . She ought to. Come. To me, to him, to her, you too, me, us', *U* 356) into an intersubjective, communal orgasm or orgasmic communion; in 'Nausicaa' for Bloom, Gerty, the Roman candle and the crowds watching it, the congregation in the church, the narration in its rhythms, even the readers in their voyeurism of Gerty's and Bloom's voyeurism; in 'Ithaca' in the libretto's final indications for *Love's Old Sweet Song* sung together by Boylan and Molly: '*ad libitum, forte*, pedal, *animato*, sustained, pedal, *ritirando*, close' (*U* 830). *Ulysses* is also a book that denies its readers a single narrative climax, when Bloom and Stephen come together but do not stay together, when the Blooms may be reconciled but perhaps are not reconciled, and so on. *Ulysses* is a book without an individual culmination because it allows for multiple climaxes. Some years after the publication of *Ulysses*, Orlando's biographer in Virginia Woolf's novel has to admit, finally:

and we must snatch space to remark how discomposing it is for her biographer that this culmination to which the whole book moved, this peroration with which the book was to end, should be dashed from us on a laugh casually like this; but the truth is that when we write of a woman, everything is out of place – culminations and perorations; the accent never falls where it does with a man.[59]

In a novel that centres on its protagonist's gender and sex such as *Orlando*, narrative and sexual climaxes can only come together; in *Ulysses*, Bloom is 'the new womanly man' (*U* 614), the man who menstruates (in 'Circe'), who experiences in 'Ithaca' the 'surety of the sense of touch in his firm full masculine feminine passive active hand' (*U* 788). Bloom, less than Orlando, less than Tiresias, but certainly more than Stephen, is one of the several androgynous or semi-androgynous figures of modernism (Shakespeare too is briefly discussed in 'Scylla and Charybdis' as an androgynous figure). Can one suggest that, like its semi-androgynous protagonist, *Ulysses* itself, with its possibility of multiple 'culminations and perorations', becomes a semi-androgynous narrative that undercuts in its literary practice the literary theory of its other, misogynist, protagonist who would see literary creation as founded on a mystical and nebulous male fiction of fatherhood and male self-engendering proved by algebra and figured in a French triangle? Does the poly-climactic narrative structure of *Ulysses* suggest that this is, precisely, a fiction?

If this is the case, the female geometry of *Finnegans Wake* may be seen as yet another extension (and by implication an undercutting) of Stephen's reflection on maternal and paternal origins, on the divinity of engendering and self-engendering, and an ulterior exploration of the need to go in search of the origins – one's own

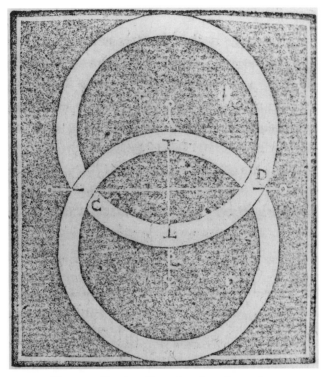

Figure 1. Giordano Bruno's union of opposites

origins, as well as the origins (but also the end) of an author's authority and language; but also in search of how much language can be stretched, and when it becomes 'too short'. In fact, there is a possibility that what I have just called 'female geometry' – the (double) triangle inscribed within the double circles in the diagram on p. 293 of *Finnegans Wake* – should be reinterpreted as 'androgynous geometry',[60] if we observe the striking similarity between the *Wake*'s diagram and Giordano Bruno's figuration of the unity of opposites, which has also been interpreted as the simplest figuration of androgyny[61] and which also consists of two interlocking circles, vertically juxtaposed and sharing – like the *Wake*'s diagram – a common radius as well as a common single chord that cuts the arc of both circles from the points where the circles juxtapose (figure 1).[62]

(The area common to the two circles is in both Bruno's and Joyce's cases the *vescica piscis*;[63] 'at the centre of this area artists used to represent both the Virgin and Christ because it is the space where two are one'.[64])

During the various pseudo-geometrical demonstrations of *FW* II.2,[65] the logarithmic 'Quarrellary' of an 'unpassible' (*FW* 298.18–19) proposition in which eternal self-reproduction turns into poetic self-propagation ('returnally reprodictive of themselves', *FW* 298.17–18) is that 'The logos of somewome to that base anything, when most characteristically mantissa minus, comes to nullum in the endth' (*FW* 298.19–21). The expression 'returnally reprodictive of themselves' suggests 'reproductive' of the word, of poetry (Latin and early Italian *dictare*, to dictate, to compose poetry; German *Dichtung*, poetry, *Dichter*, poet), also recalling the world's (and the *Wake*'s) mysterious and self-engendering writing ('But the world, mind, is, was and will be writing its own wrunes for ever', *FW* 19.35–6); 'somewome' suggests someone, some woman, some womb, and therefore also some 'whome', since the aim of the whole geometrical exercise is to show the 'whome' of the 'eternal geomater'. 'The logos of somewome' points then to the possibility of a feminine logos, or *Logos*, through which ALP would achieve the status not only of a pagan mother-earth goddess, but also of a feminised version of the Christian God as Word – a word which now transcends the gossip of the washerwomen and of the *muliercolae*[66] in order to become the divine Logos for which human language eventually fails, falls short and inevitably therefore fades away into silence ('comes to nullum in the endth').

Stephen's theory of filiation, patterned both on the French triangle of *Hamlet* and Shakespeare's biography and on the triangle of the Trinity to which the female is only instrumental, is finally transformed in *Finnegans Wake* and refocused on to a female Word Goddess endowed with attributes that appear to be the same as those of an ever-expanding divinity whose centre is everywhere and whose circumference is infinite:

to expense herselfs as sphere as possible, paradismic perimutter, in all directions on the bend of the unbridalled, the infinisissimalls of her facets becoming manier and manier as the calicolum of her umdescribables (one has thoughts of that eternal Rome) shrinks from schurtiness to scherts.

(*FW* 298.27–299.01)

The 'umdescribability', unmeasurability, ineffability of the divinity is mixed, as always, with the unmentionable, the sexual, here the shrinking of the shirt/skirt (which will be lifted by Dolph to show the mother's sex to Kev) as well as the shortness of the words to tell about it. This female Logos – comparable to the definition that Love gives of himself in the *Vita Nuova*, denying Dante a similar complete- ness and centrality: 'Ego tanquam centrum circuli, cui simili modo se habent circumferentie partes; tu autem non sic' ('I am like the centre of a circle, from which all points are always at the same distance; but you are not the same', *Vita Nuova* XII) – is now incarnated in the ever-expanding, all-comprehending god/dess and the (sexually) spending mother, her perimeter encompassing all – not just the earth, but the spheres, the heaven, and is therefore literally paradisal: 'paradismic perimutter'. It is in fact ALP's 'holy' nature that mediates between divinity and the hole, gap or void of the triangle, and it is significant that already in 'The Sisters' the geometrical had the function of mediating between the materiality of the word ('I longed to be nearer to it and to look upon its deadly work', *D* 9) and the void or incompleteness of the gnomon.[67] At the same time, the infinity and smallness ('infinisissimalls') of the mother's 'facets' make her into that voluminous figure, the 'polyhe- dron of scripture' (*FW* 107.08) that is the *Mama*festa, thus explicitly recovering the feminine nature of a document that, under the scrutinising eye of the exegete, had appeared mainly as the male HCE. (Incidentally, this lead is borne out if we follow up the implications of the words 'paradismic perimutter': 'paradise' derives from the the ancient Persian *pairidaeza*, 'park', from *pairi*, 'around', and *diz*, 'shape' (*Oxford English Dictionary*); the mother's association with the 'park' requires us to reconsider the traditional identification of the Dublin territory, including Phoenix Park, with the male character HCE, an identification that we were already led to question in chapter 1 through the *Wake*'s confusion between the literal and the allegorical.)

It is possible then to surmise that this creation and expansion of a 'divine' mother-language (as well as of a divine mother) is what enables the transcendence of the paternal into the maternal (and maybe further into the androgynous), and what allows, on the one hand, the overcoming and the overturning of the father and the father-language (Erse) in *FW* II.3 (in the episode of Buckley and the Russian general I have discussed in chapter 3) and, on the other hand, retrospectively, the reversal of the trajectory delineated by Stephen which now moves back again from the paternal to the maternal. This reversal also goes through the necessary redefinition of the feminine as nebulous (Issy is Nuvoletta, ALP is and has been a cloud too) and, like Stephen's artist-God, as continually refining itself out of existence (through evaporation, rain, disappearance into the sea) in order to pervade the entire creation.

As we know, however, Joyce's texts are never straightforward, and despite the reversal of gender relations with regard to poetic as well as biological and biographical engendering, the treatment of the geometrical problems of chapters 1.6 and II.2 suggests a much more complex answer for the schoolboys in this text. The risk is that the hi/story will not change and will go on repeating itself: if Stephen's French triangle in 'Scylla and Charybdis' was a story of adultery and betrayal, of broken promises and unpaid debts, *FW* 1.6 involves an 'obsoletely unadulterous' Burrus and a Caseous who is 'obversely the revise of him' (*FW* 161.17–18), while *FW* II.2 is also a tale of 'trifid tongues' (*FW* 281.16) and of a 'bifurking calamum' (*FW* 302.15–16), of double if not even treble talk, of forked tongues, of betrayal – Joyce's version perhaps of Dante's post-babelian *ydioma tripharium* (*Dve* I.viii, 2), a threefold or 'trifid' tongue.

As the grammatical form suggests, the 'isoscelat*ing* biangle' of *FW* 165.13 (my italics)[68] is a triangle in progress, as yet endowed with only two angles; thus its only possible actual representation (figure 2):

Figure 2. The 'isoscelating biangle'

seems to offer the exact opposite of what its name ('equal-legged') suggests (and which would, incidentally, correspond to the shape of the siglum Joyce used for Shaun, figure 3):

Figure 3. Equal-legged

The twins' 'isoscelating biangle' is then a contradiction in terms, and it is only through the conjunction of the actual drawings suggested on the one hand by the description and, on the other, by the literal interpretation of its name, that we can obtain a Euclidean isosceles triangle. Seen in another way, the 'isoscelating biangle' is also a gnomonic figure, an isosceles triangle from which an isosceles triangle has been cut out (figure 4):

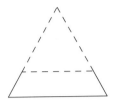

Figure 4. The 'isoscelating biangle' as gnomonic triangle

The 'isoscelating biangle', or even the more complete but still Platonically limited isosceles triangle, will have to grow into a full-blown and equilateral triangle in order to graduate from the frigid, two-legged and incomplete (in progress) or purely spiritual and sterile one (like Beatrice) to the earthly and motherly triangle of the 'geomater'.

If *FW* I.6 begets a figure which is a contradiction in terms, similarly the problem in chapter II.2 has no solution: it is, as it were, a 'family umbroglia' (Italian *imbroglio*, both 'swindle' and muddled, confused, entangled situation):

Show that the median, hce che ech, interecting at royde angles the parilegs of a given obtuse one biscuts both the arcs that are in curveachord behind. Brickbaths. The family umbroglia.   (*FW* 283.32–284.04)

It is impossible to draw the figure as requested: we are asked to draw a median line (and are given three points for it, 'hce che ech', which is either misleading or useless, because a straight line only needs two points to be drawn) that intersects at right angles the obtuse angle of an isosceles triangle ('the parilegs [= equal legs, = isosceles] of a given obtuse'), but the only possible median of an obtuse angle will form two equal angles that can only be acute (figure 5):

Figure 5. 'The median . . . interecting . . .
the parilegs of a given obtuse one'

These equal angles resulting from the bisecting of an obtuse angle certainly cannot be right because only an angle of 180° can be bisected into two right ones – in which case the original angle would no longer be an angle (certainly not part of a triangle) but a straight line (figure 6):[69]

Figure 6. 'The median . . . interecting at royde angles'

The only way one can form right angles from an obtuse one is through *two* secting lines (figure 7):

Figure 7

The median should also bisect the arc behind ('curveachord': in fact another contradiction in terms, because the chord is straight and cuts the curvilinear arc), or bis-cut it, i.e., cut it twice, which, again, is impossible: for two arcs to exist they need to meet the angle at the apex, and in that case the median, or whichever line secting the angle, can only cut them once (figure 8):

Figure 8

(The angle, the arcs and the possible medians of this figure form a shape that looks like an umbrella: is this a version of the 'family umbroglia'?).

To make it possible for the median to cut the arc twice, the arc itself needs to be extended into a circle, so that the median can cut it again at the opposite side (figure 9):

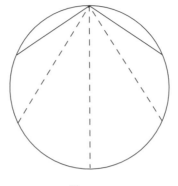

Figure 9

The situation is again that of the contradictory 'isoscelating biangle' of 1.6. The other solution, of course, is to have two interlocking circles (or buttocks, the 'curveachord *behind*'), like those of the diagram on p. 293, so that a single median, coinciding with the circles' common radius (A-L or α-λ), can cut both arcs (i.e. the arcs of both circles) – but still it won't form right angles with the obtuse angles of the possible isosceles triangles A-P-π and L-P-π. The only other chord that can 'bis-cut' each of the circles – the line drawn between the points where the two circles juxtapose (or P-π), as in Bruno's diagram – can cut at right angles not the obtuse angles but their median – i.e., the common radius of the two circles (A-L or α-λ). The *Wake* consistently creates problems which are impossible to solve ('cruxes'), just like the one faced by the geometer of Dante's *Paradiso* – or indeed, problems that require a leap of the imagination from the purely geometrical to the physical, quite unlike the one faced by Dante, who needs to leap from the physical to the metaphysical.

That three letters are given for the median which would only need two also reproduces the pattern of incommensurable twos and threes (the isosceles triangle having two legs, etc.), of 'bifurking calamums' and 'trifid tongues' that has haunted Stephen first, the twins next, in the attempt perhaps somehow to reconcile the irreducible opposition between the number of the ideal couple – two – and the number of the adulterous couple – three – which is also, inevitably, the number of the trinitarian deity (and of course two and three – the two prostitutes and the three soldiers – are also the numbers that recur in conjunction with HCE's hetero- or homosexual sin in Phoenix Park).

As in 'The Sisters', where the child is 'learning' from Father Flynn and is fascinated by the power and action of words, 'Scylla and Charybdis', *FW* I.6 and *FW* II.2 all evoke a context of learning, of seeking to know, and perhaps, like in *Paradiso* XXXIII, of regression to a state of near-infancy. In the Library chapter, to Russell's retort that 'Art has to reveal to us ideas, formless spiritual essences . . . All the rest is the speculation of schoolboys for schoolboys', Stephen responds 'superpolitely' that 'The schoolmen were schoolboys first . . . Aristotle was once Plato's schoolboy' (*U* 237). In this chain of philosophical teachers and pupils, Stephen too proves himself a good disciple of Socrates, who in turn had been a good disciple of his wife, from whom he had learned dialectics, and of his mother, from whom he had learned maieutics (*U* 243). Maieutics can, in this context, be defined as drawing knowledge out of the mother's womb, which is, figuratively, or 'figuratleavely' (*FW* 296.31), what the children are also attempting in chapter II.2: to know about their origins, about origins, to learn (out) of their mother's womb. (One of the midwife's tasks during childbirth is to measure the size of the mother's womb – she too is a geometer of sorts.)

However good a disciple Stephen is in 'Scylla and Charybdis', there is a lesson in Dante that he has not learned. Stephen wants to become his own father, thus forgoing his status as the son of an unknowable father. Yet what Stephen is missing in Dante's model – what in the last analysis makes his theory as sterile as Miss Portinari's Platonic isosceles triangle – is that Dante himself can become the father of the Italian language only by reverting to the condition of a child, a barely speaking son (cf. e.g. 'fantolin', *Par* XXIII, 121; 'fantin', XXX, 82; 'fante', XXXIII, 107). Indeed, the vernacular is consistently for Dante the language of babies: 'vulgarem locutionem asserimus, quam sine omni regula nutricem imitantes accipimus' ('we assert that the vulgar tongue is that which we acquire without any rule by imitating our nurses', *Dve* I.i, 2). In what could be read as a complete reversal of Stephen's model, Dante – himself claiming the title of 'miglior fabbro del parlar materno' ('a better craftsman of the mother tongue', the title that Dante bestows on Arnaut Daniel in *Purg* XXVI, 117) – turns himself into a son in order to become the father of the mother-language. As Robert Hollander has shown, in so doing Dante also turns both Virgil, otherwise consistently treated as father, and the *Aeneid*, into 'mothers'.[70] Was Dante (unwittingly) already constructing semi-androgynous figures?

If the *Wake*'s 'geomater' is traced back to the 'geometra' of *Paradiso* XXXIII, one inevitably wants to pursue the Dantean intertext and read in 'figuratleavely' yet another echo. Not long before the image of the geometer, and just before the vision of the universe as a book whose scattered leaves are bound together by love,[71] the fading of the divine vision in the poet's memory is rendered through the image of the scattering of the leaves in whose mysterious figurations the Sibyl read her prophecies:[72]

> Così la neve al sol si disigilla;
> così al vento ne le foglie levi
> si perdea la sentenza di Sibilla.   (*Par* XXXIII, 64–6)

(Thus is the snow unsealed by the sun; thus in the wind, in the light leaves, the Sibyl's oracle was lost.)

These sibylline leaves of mystery that have come to us through at least the classics, the medievals (Dante) and the Romantics (Coleridge) and have become in *Finnegans Wake* the sibyl-lines of obscene, therefore unspeakable meanings ('Are those their fata which we read in sibylline between the *fas* and its *nefas*?', *FW* 31.35–6: that is, between the speakable and the unspeakable) may then reappear (in) 'figuratleavely' in the children's attempt to discover the mystery written in the leaves of their mother's book, their mother's equilateral sex.

It appears then that the science whose aim is to measure the earth – the physical world – becomes necessary when the end is to look for the origin, for the metaphysical, the alpha and the omega – but also the essentially and originally physical: the sexual. Geometry has to be relied upon when the end is to speak of the unspeakable – the ineffable, the mysterious, the mystic, the obscene; it offers the metalanguage (the language about language, the language beyond language) when language fails, falls short, when language itself is found to be 'short'.

I would suggest that perhaps this is one of the main reasons why, despite the striking analogies in the choice of theme and figures, Pound's and Joyce's uses of geometry are essentially different, and why, while Pound's allegiance goes to the Cartesian analytical geometry through which, in his own words, 'one is able *actually* to create' by forgoing the reliance of Euclidean geometry on figures and thus achieving an independence from the material world,[73] Joyce also continued to rely in his works on the more concrete and 'figural' Euclidean geometry that mediates between ideal, perfect forms and their actual manifestations, and can therefore be adopted by the artist in his own attempt to mediate between the transcendent and the immanent, language and the ineffable, but can also, in the artist's weaving together of figures and letters that evoke the ineffable, be itself the means through which 'one is able *actually* to create'.

The equilateral triangle restored in II.2 and inscribed within a perfect circle is indeed both a geometrical figure and a *letteral* (literary, literal) one, woven on a problematic 'loom' that has ceased to weave simple threads, like Penelope's, in favour of vowel- and letter-threads, and which prefers weaving water to Stephen's weaving of wind (and which may emphatically side with Bloom's preference for the rounded forms and backside views against Stephen's favouring of the frontal and the angular if we twist 'Probe loom' into 'pro-Bloom'): 'Problem ye ferst, construct ann aquilittoral dryankle Probe loom! With his primal handstoe in his sole salivarium. Concoct an equoangular trillitter' (*FW* 286.20–3).

Issy's note to the problem, 'As Rhombulus and Rhebus went building rhomes one day' (*FW* 286.F1), ties up again the origins of Rome (cf. also 'one has thoughts of that eternal Rome', *FW* 298.32–3) with the mother's sex – a triangle here doubled into a rhomb – from which the children originate and to which their quest leads. While the Euclidean problem and its explication by Dolph to Kev may suggest the boys' oedipal desire for the mother (equivalent to Issy's desire for the father), these letters/litters (the three children) complement Issy's vocalic and semivocalic bond by linking vowel (A) with liquid (semi-)consonant (L) and consonant (P) in a double alphabet (A L P and α λ π) and in a stereoscopic[74] system of relations ('The doubleviewed seeds', *FW* 296.01[75]) that, on the one hand, transforms the plane geometry of page surfaces into the solid geometry of volumes (the book as 'polyhedron of scripture'), and, on the other, articulates identity (sameness, equality) into variable linguistic and figural weavings by combining geometrical grammar (a figural linking of letters in geometrical shapes, such as the sigla) with grammatical geometry (a wording of geometrical figures and (unsolvable) problems).

However, in Joyce's works, geometry is used not only to hint at issues of origin, sexuality and transcendence; it also becomes a means through which to express one's frustrations, antagonism

(Stephen's bitterness and misogyny, the twins' antagonism in their eternal battle, the adulterous triangle of 'Scylla and Charybdis' but also of *Exiles*; the 'quarrellary' discussed above, whose familiar corollary is the eternal quarrel between brothers, or fathers and sons). Is it because, as was shown in chapter 1, anagogic transcendence always implies in the Wakean system a literal baseness: 'A baser meaning has been read into these characters the literal sense of which decency can safely scarcely hint' (*FW* 33.14–15)? Because whatever transcendence we try to read in these characters (graphic signs or letters as well as narratological entities) and between these lines is in fact written in 'sibylline[s]', in the evanescent lines of mystery? Is it because to the problem of transcendence there is no possible transcendent solution, and the only answer can be an attempt at mediation (maybe, like Dante's *geometra*, doomed from the start)? Is this why the geometrical problem needs not just one but several medians aspiring to be 'right' but doomed to be imprecise?

The speculation on Dante's levels of meanings led us, as I argued in chapter 1, to acknowledge the impossibility of distinguishing the 'sense other' (allegory) from the 'letter' because, among other things, the figurative use of language could be ascribed neither exclusively to the letter nor exclusively to the allegory. We come now to yet another paradox: in this polymorphic, polysemic, polyhedral articulation of letters and figures, only language and '*letter*ature' can supply the alternative to the identity of geometry, the repetition of the same as same which is necessary to Euclidean geometry but which the *Wake* rejects by proposing problems impossible to solve and incomplete shapes (as shown above, even when the shape is complete, like the mother's equilateral triangle, there is no simple solution to the geometrical exercise). Thus if 'gnomonic' geometry offers, as I have suggested, the meta-language when language fails, the necessary length when language is 'short', then language and its 'sonorous silence' must conversely provide the necessary depth when geometry itself falls short of solving the problem, of filling the voluminous gaps.

Another reason why Euclidean geometry on its own cannot suffice is that *Finnegans Wake* is, like the *Divine Comedy*, a book of changing shapes, of metamorphoses: of the object observed, but also and more importantly perhaps, of the observing subject. Metamorphosis is a two-way movement which leaves neither side untouched, in which identity is a process of becoming and of mutual influences, and in which the 'truth', even for Dante who finally would ground it in a transcendent God, is constantly displaced by the necessity of inter-pretation, of finding the 'sense other'. The 'truth' can only be approached when the 'I' becomes a 'you' and a 'he' (*intuarsi, inluiarsi*) and opens itself up to the other (*immiarsi*) – as in 'Dio vede tutto, e tuo veder s'inluia' (*Par* IX, 73) and 's'io m'intuassi, come tu t'inmii' (*Par* IX, 81); these lines are translated by Singleton as 'God sees all, and into Him your vision sinks' and 'were I in you, even as you are in me'; but a literal rendering of Dante's lines would have to sound positively Wakese: 'God sees all, and your vision inhims', and 'if I inyoued myself as you inme yourself'. The truth can only be approached, that is, when the 'I' ceases to be *either* a subject *or* an object, and is both, relinquishing its boundaries and individuality: 'you're changing from me, I can feel. Or is it me is? I'm getting mixed' (*FW* 626.35–6), as Anna Livia wonders towards the end of her course, as she flows into the sea, mixing with her other, with her father.

In at least two episodes in the *Divine Comedy* – *Purgatorio* XIX and *Paradiso* XXX–XXXIII – Dante's vision changes as he watches, but indeed it is Dante who changes *because* he is watching; the objects of his visions, the 'femmina balba' in *Purgatorio* and God and the Empyrean in *Paradiso*, transform as an effect of Dante's own metamorphosis. A vision of sin and one of God, joined by the metamorphosis of the observing subject: 'così lo sguardo mio le facea scorta / la lingua' ('so my gaze made her tongue ready', *Purg* XIX, 12–13); 'ma per la vista che s'avvalorava / in me guardando, una sola parvenza, / mutandom'io, a me si travagliava' ('but through my sight, which was gaining value [strength] in me as I looked, one sole appearance, as I changed, was altering itself to me', *Par* XXXIII, 112–14). The object, in fact, 'tal è sempre qual s'era davante' ('is ever such as it was before', *Par* XXXIII, 111), always remains the same.

The goal – salvation in Dante's *itinerario a Deo*, but also and especially poetic success – can be achieved only through the relinquishing of one's subjectivity ('immiarsi', 'inluiarsi', 'intuarsi'), the recognition of the necessity of one's psychological permutations – and this may be another lesson that Stephen has not learned. When in 'Scylla and Charybdis' Stephen claims to be biologically another because 'molecules all change' but the same psychologically thanks to the agency of memory, he is in effect advocating a serial form of the self and of identity: 'everchanging forms' (self-images) threaded together by memory (*U* 242). In the *Wake*, memory does not have the stability that could grant even this serial notion of the self. Memory is 'm'm'ry' (*FW* 460.20, a silent mummery[76]), deprived of the vowels that signal authenticity, authority, subjectivity. As after Babel, the effort to remember comes up against the wall of inevitable oblivion: no permanence of a unified self is possible because Stephen's conception of a stable memory fails: 'm'm'ry's leaves are falling' (*FW* 460.20).

CONCLUSION: ONLY A LEAF, JUST A LEAF AND THEN LEAVES

Anna Livia of the multiple beauties is, like Dante's Virgin Mother, 'a lively fountain of hope' ('di speranza fontana vivace', *Par* XXXIII, 12, echoed in 'Elpis, thou fountain of the greeces', *FW* 267.04; Greek *elpis*, 'hope'), a Brook of Life (*FW* 264.06) adorned with leaves who has however equilaterally lost her virginity; she is then herself a book, the b(r)ook of life and hope, a 'babbling brook' (*FW* 306.F1). And the flowing and babbling, 'hitherandthithering' (*FW* 216.04) waters of the brook are also the flowing, turning and returning leaves and words of the book, turned by the wind (*FW* 13.29–31), scattered sibylline leaves slipping into silence (*FW* 13.29–14.27) 'before the bookflood or after her ebb' (*FW* 118.11–12). The quests for/questionings of the origins or sources of the river foregrounded throughout the *Wake*[77] are ultimately unachievable – like the problem of the squaring of the circle, like the Nightlesson's several unanswerable problems, like the origin of 'that eternal Rome' whose history should go back to the twins fed by the she-wolf but which is transformed once again into a riddle ('robulous rebus', *FW* 12.34; 'As Rhombulus and Rhebus went building rhomes one day', *FW* 286.F1): the rebus of the triangle, the circle and the rhomb of the mother's sex.

The quest for ALP as the origin is then also a journey, like Dante's, towards the river (Alpheus, or Coleridge's sacred Alph, which lends to the *Wake* the first two words), the form under which God (Alpha) and the blessed in the Empyrean first appear to Dante (*Par* XXX, 61 ff.). As Dante bathes his eyes in the stream, once again reverting to a small child, the river turns into a circle:

> Non è fantin che sì sùbito rua
> col volto verso il latte, se si svegli
> molto tardato da l'usanza sua,

> come fec'io, per far migliori spegli
> ancor de li occhi, chinandomi a l'onda
> che si deriva perché vi s'immegli;
>   e sì come di lei bevve la gronda
> de le palpebre mie, così mi parve
> di sua lunghezza divenuta tonda'.   (*Par* xxx, 82–90)

(No infant who wakes much later than his usual hour, so suddenly rushes with his face toward the milk as I did then, to make yet better mirrors of my eyes, stooping to the wave which flows from there, so that we may be bettered in it; and even as the eaves of my eyelids drank of it, so it appeared to me out of its length to have become round.)

The boundless circle will become first the vision of the universe as scattered leaves gathered together in a book by Love (*Par* xxxiii, 85–7), and then, binding together the river and the Word, the circular and triple vision of the Trinity:

>   una sola parvenza,
> mutandom'io, a me si travagliava.
>   Ne la profonda e chiara sussistenza
> de l'alto lume parvermi tre giri
> di tre colori e d'una contenenza;
>   e l'un da l'altro come iri da iri
> parea riflesso, e 'l terzo parea foco
> che quinci e quindi igualmente si spiri.   (*Par* xxxiii, 113–20)

(one sole appearance, as I changed, was altering itself to me. In the profound and luminous subsistence of the noble light appeared to me three circles of three colours and one dimension; and one by the other, as rainbow by rainbow, seemed reflected, and the third seemed fire that from the one and from the other equally breathes forth.)

But the metaphor of the river as word was introduced in the *Commedia* much earlier, in the first canto of the *Inferno*, when the pagan Virgil – allegorically, reason without grace, to whom the final vision of God is forbidden – had appeared to Dante as an envoy of Beatrice in order to save him from the dark forest of sin:

> 'Or se' tu quel Virgilio e quella fonte
> che spandi di parlar sì largo fiume?'   (*Inf* i, 79–80)

('Are you then that Virgil, that fount which pours forth so broad a stream of speech?')

Dante's poem is then a journey between two rivers, the river of words and the river of the Word:[78] the former is the river whose words are interpreted in the allegorical tradition and in order to see one's fate, as in the practice of the *sortes virgilianae* that Issy also tries ('volve the virgil page and view', *FW* 270.25) only to find that 'the O of woman is long' (*FW* 270.25–6): a long 'o', like the omega (ω) – stretched maybe into the symbol of infinity (∞) – or perhaps not quite a perfect circle, elliptical therefore like the celestial courses of the planets and the stars, but if elliptical then perhaps also 'gnomonic', incomplete. The latter is the Word (also, and more legitimately, symbolised by the omega) which the exegetes have to interpret and which can make things mean 'this and that'.

Dante's poem is a journey between the scattered leaves of the souls waiting to cross the Acheron, one by one falling away as from a bough in autumn –

> Come d'autunno si levan le foglie
> l'una appresso de l'altra, fin che 'l ramo
> vede a la terra tutte le sue spoglie,
>   similemente il mal seme d'Adamo
> gittansi di quel lito ad una ad una,
> per cenni come augel per suo richiamo.   (*Inf* III, 112–17)

(As the leaves fall away in autumn, one after the other, till the bough sees all its spoils upon the ground, similarly the evil seed of Adam cast themselves one by one from that shore at the signals, like a bird at its call.)

– the scattered leaves of the Sibyl's oracle, and the leaves of the book of the universe gathered together in the book of God. Anna Liffey, the leafy, the 'leafiest', unlike the God of Dante's vision, sheds her leaves in her final flowing into the sea, as she approaches the end of her course, as the book has used up all its leaves. Anna Livia, the female goddess posited by II.2, is more like the immanent universe in which the book 'si squaderna' than the God in whom the leaves are bound together: as she leaves, Anna Liffey's leaves are shed and lost. As God 'unquires' himself in the universe, so that its meaning has to be sought for through a fourfold method and yet can never be fully recovered, so do the sentences of the Sibyl, written in light leaves, disperse their truths at the opening of the door that lets the wind in, at the banging of the door that shuts the meanings out. The dispersal of the leaves is the fading of truth into silence, and the silence can only be filled, partially, by the umpteenth quest for the origin that will always only lead to a hole, a gap, another silence, which will always 'come to nullum in the endth'.

Dante's poem is a journey between the bitterness of the dark wood ('Tant'è amara che poco è più morte'; 'It is so bitter that death is hardly more', *Inf.* I, 7) and the sweetness of the final vision:[79]

> cotal son io, ché quasi tutta cessa
> mia visione, e ancor mi distilla
> nel core il dolce che nacque da essa.   (*Par* XXXIII, 61–3)

(such am I, for my vision almost wholly fades away, and yet the sweetness that was born of it still drips [is distilled] within my heart.)

From the sleepiness of *Inferno* I to the awakening of *Paradiso* XXXIII, Dante has been to God, but the vision is lost and only its sweetness lingers on, an imperfect memory, the dreamer's imperfect desire to recall upon awakening (*Par* XXXIII, 58–63) an experience 'Impossible to remember' but 'improbable to forget' (*FW* 617.08–9). As for ALP in her final moments before coming to 'nullum', the confusing orders are 'Forget, remember!' (*FW* 614.22); 'Forget!' (*FW* 614.26); 'Don't forget! . . . Remember' (*FW* 617.25–6), as the sun rises and the dream is fading while its sweetness lingers on.

Notes

INTRODUCTION: IN THE WAKE OF THE DIVINE COMIC

1 'The water which I take was never coursed before . . . You few who
lifted up your necks in time to the bread of angels, which we live on
here but are never sated of, you may commit your vessel to the deep
salt, keeping to my wake before the water that turns smooth again.'

2 See Ellmann, *JJ*II, and Mary T. Reynolds, *Joyce and Dante: The Shaping
Imagination* (Princeton: Princeton University Press, 1981), which also
gives a very useful account of the presence of Italian language and
literature in Joyce's curriculum as a student; this also included Latin,
and a study of the history of Italian. See esp. chapter 1, 'The presence of
Dante in Joyce's fiction'. In *Stephen Hero*, probably written as early as
1903 (cf. *SH*, Introduction by Theodore Spencer), Stephen thinks of
Dante as Europe's first poet (*SH* 46), discusses Dante with the President
of the school's Debating Society (*SH* 97), chooses Italian at university in
order to read the medieval poet seriously (*SH* 152), and even plans to
model his scattered love poems on the wreath-like structure of the *Vita
Nuova* (*SH* 179).

3 Cf. Michael Caesar (ed.), *Dante: The Critical Heritage, 1314(?)–1870*
(London: Routledge, 1989), 40.

4 Quoted in Thomas L. Cooksey, 'The Central Man of the World: The
Victorian Myth of Dante', in Leslie J. Workman (ed.), *Medievalism in
England. Studies in Medievalism* IV (Cambridge: Brewer, 1992), 187. See
also Alison Milbank, *Dante and the Victorians* (Manchester: Manchester
University Press, 1998).

5 On this see also Steve Ellis, *Dante and English Poetry: Shelley to T. S. Eliot*
(Cambridge: Cambridge University Press, 1983).

6 Stuart Y. McDougal (ed.), *Dante Among the Moderns* (Chapel Hill and
London: University of North Carolina Press, 1985), ix.

7 Reed Way Dasenbrock, *Imitating the Italians: Wyatt, Spenser, Synge, Pound,
Joyce* (Baltimore and London: Johns Hopkins University Press, 1991),
209. On Dante and other modernists cf. also, beside the books already
cited in the previous footnotes, James J. Wilhelm, *Dante and Pound: The*

Epic of Judgement (Orono, ME: University of Maine Press, 1974) and Dominic Manganiello, *T. S. Eliot and Dante* (Basingstoke and London: Macmillan, 1989).

8 Bruno Migliorini, *Storia della lingua italiana* (Florence: Sansoni, 1962), 153.

9 Ettore Settanni, *James Joyce e la prima versione italiana del Finnegan's* [sic] *Wake* (Venice: Cavallino, 1965), 30, my translation.

10 Records exist of Joyce's visit to Marsh's Library on 22 and 23 October 1902 when he asked for this book.

11 On the fortunes of Dante's *De vulgari eloquentia* and its role in the *questione della lingua* see A. Marigo's notes in his introduction of the treatise, esp. xvii–xxi, and the useful account by Angelo Mazzocco in chapter 8 of his *Linguistic Theories in Dante and the Humanists: Studies in Language and Intellectual History in Late Medieval and Early Renaissance Italy* (Leiden, New York and Cologne: E. J. Brill, 1993).

12 Reynolds, *Joyce and Dante*, 21–2.

13 This volume is stamped and dated with the National Library stamp NLI 4 December 1890.

14 Stamped and dated NLI 11 June 1889.

15 On Joyce's interest in the Italian Risorgimento cf. in particular Dominic Manganiello's *Joyce's Politics* (London, Boston and Henley: Routledge and Kegan Paul, 1980), esp. chapter 2, 'Young Europe'.

16 Cf. e.g. the works of Francesco D'Ovidio – for instance his *Dante e la filosofia del linguaggio* (Naples: Tipografia della Regia Università, 1892) – and those of Pio Rajna, one of the most eminent Dantean scholars at the turn of the century, whose 'Il primo capitolo del trattato "De vulgari eloquentia" tradotto e commentato' was published in Trieste in the *Miscellanea di studi in onore di A. Hortis* in 1910.

17 Nino Frank, 'The Shadow That Had Lost Its Man' (1967), in Willard Potts (ed.), *Portraits of the Artist in Exile: Recollections of James Joyce by Europeans* (Portmarnock: Wolfhound Press, 1979), 80.

18 'There was no hope for him this time' evokes Dante's 'Lasciate ogne speranza, voi ch'intrate' ('Abandon every hope, you who enter', *Inf* III, 9). See Jackson Cope, 'An Epigraph for *Dubliners*', *James Joyce Quarterly* 7 (1970), 362–4. For the Dantean substratum of the story and of the collection as a whole cf. Mary Reynolds, 'The Dantean Design of Joyce's *Dubliners*', in Bernard Benstock (ed.), *The Seventh of Joyce: Essays from the 7th International James Joyce Symposium, Zurich, June 1979* (Bloomington: Indiana University Press, 1982), 124–30 (reprinted in an expanded version in *Joyce and Dante*, 156–65); and Francesco Gozzi, 'Dante nell'inferno di Joyce', *English Miscellany* 23 (1972), 195–229. See also Jackson Cope, *Joyce's Cities: Archaeologies of the Soul* (Baltimore and London: Johns Hopkins University Press, 1981).

19 'The Artist Paring His Quotations: Aesthetic and Ethical Implications of the Dantean Intertext in *Dubliners*,' in Rosa M. Bollettieri Bosinelli

and Harold F. Mosher, Jr. (eds.), *ReJoycing: New Readings of* Dubliners (Lexington: University Press of Kentucky, 1998), 228–46.

20 Cf. Harold Bloom, *The Anxiety of Influence: A Theory of Poetry* (Oxford: Oxford University Press, 1973), 30, 94–5; and *A Map of Misreading* (Oxford: Oxford University Press, 1975).

21 On the canto of Oderisi in relation to Ovid's *Metamorphoses* and the question of Dante's pride cf. also Teodolinda Barolini, *The Undivine Comedy: Detheologizing Dante* (Princeton: Princeton University Press, 1992), chapter 6.

22 T. S. Eliot claimed that trying to imitate Dante would do less harm to the aspiring poet than imitating Shakespeare, because the latter – like any other great English poet – writes in his own language and is therefore 'inimitable', whereas Dante's is 'the perfection of a common language'. Cf. T. S. Eliot, 'Dante', in *Selected Essays* (London: Faber, 1951), 252.

23 *Imitating the Italians*, 218–19.

24 Jacqueline Risset, 'Joyce traduce Joyce', in Franca Ruggieri (ed.), *Joyce: Poesie e Prose* (Milan: Mondadori, 1992), 722.

25 Cf. e.g. 'The Renaissance', in *Literary Essays of Ezra Pound*, ed. T. S. Eliot (London: Faber, 1954), 214.

26 Ezra Pound, 'For T.S.E.', in *Selected Prose 1909–1965*, ed. Willliam Cookson (London: Faber, 1973), 434.

27 I have developed this aspect at more length in my introduction to L. Boldrini (ed.), *Middayevil Joyce: Essays on Joyce's Medieval Cultures* (Amsterdam and Atlanta: Rodopi, forthcoming). See also, in the same collection, R. Dasenbrock and R. Mines, ' "Quella vista nova": Dante, Mathematics and the Ending of *Ulysses*'.

28 See Ellis, *Dante and English Poetry*, 171–209 and 210–43, and Dasenbrock, *Imitating the Italians*, esp. 209–19.

29 T. S. Eliot, *The Complete Poems and Plays* (London: Faber, 1969), 198.

30 See e.g. Stanislaus Joyce, 'The Background to *Dubliners*', *Listener* 60 (25 March 1954), 526, and Robert Boyle, 'Swiftian Allegory and Dantean Parody in Joyce's "Grace" ', *James Joyce Quarterly* 7 (1969), 11–21.

31 Cf. Dasenbrock, *Imitating the Italians*, 6–7.

32 *Ibid.*, 11–12.

33 *Ibid.*, 11.

34 Cf. e.g. Roland Barthes, 'The Death of the Author' and 'From Work to Text', in *Image–Music–Text*, ed. and trans. Stephen Heath (London: Fontana, 1977), 146 and 160–1; 'Théorie du Texte', *Encyclopedia Universalis*, vol. xv, 1973, 1015.

35 Cf. Roland Barthes, *S/Z* (1970), (Oxford: Blackwell, 1990), 4.

36 Bloom, *The Anxiety of Influence*, 7.

37 *Ibid.*, 10.

38 Bloom, *A Map of Misreading*, 3.

39 Jay Clayton and Eric Rothstein, 'Figures in the Corpus: Theories of

Influence and Intertextuality', in Clayton and Rothstein (eds.), *Influence and Intertextuality in Literary History* (Madison: University of Wisconsin Press, 1991), 9.

40 A critique of Bloom's theory of influence in relation to Joyce's works is carried out by Patrick Colm Hogan in the introduction to his *Joyce, Milton, and the Theory of Influence* (Gainesville: University Press of Florida, 1995).

41 On reading as 'raiding' cf. Stephen Heath, 'Ambiviolences: Notes for Reading Joyce', in Derek Attridge and Daniel Ferrer (eds.), *Post-Structuralist Joyce: Essays from the French* (Cambridge: Cambridge University Press, 1984), esp. 41–5.

PRELUDE: 'BETHICKET ME'; OR, LOOKING FOR THE STRAIGHT
WAY IN THE WOOD OF SAMUEL BECKETT'S OBLIQUITY OF
EXAGMINATION

1 Cf. also Massimo Verdicchio, 'Exagmination Round the Fictification of Vico and Joyce', *James Joyce Quarterly* 26, 4 (1989), 531.

2 Cf. also *SL* 339–42.

3 For an example of this technique in *Finnegans Wake* cf. James Atherton's comments on Joyce's use of Dantean allusions in the 'Nightlesson', quoted below in chapter 4.

4 Suzette Henke, 'Exagmining Beckett & Company', in Janet Dunleavy (ed.), *Reviewing Classics of Joycean Criticism* (Urbana and Chicago: University of Illinois Press, 1991), 60.

5 *Ibid.*, 61.

6 Verdicchio, 'Exagmination', 531.

7 Henke, 'Exagmining', 66.

8 Linda Ben-Zvi, *Samuel Beckett*, quoted in Henke, 'Exagmining', 63.

9 W. C. Williams, 'A Point for American Criticism', *Exag*, 183.

10 Cf. Angelo Mazzocco, *Linguistic Theories in Dante and the Humanists: Studies in Language and Intellectual History in Late Medieval and Early Renaissance Italy* (Leiden, New York and Cologne: E. J. Brill, 1993), chapter 8; and Ileana Pagani, *La teoria linguistica di Dante* (Naples: Liguori, 1982).

11 Cf. Alessandro Francini Bruni, 'Joyce Stripped Naked in the Piazza', in W. Potts (ed.), *Portraits of the Artist in Exile: Recollections of James Joyce by Europeans* (Portmarnock: Wolfhound Press, 1979), 12.

12 See e.g. Giovanni Boccaccio, *Vita di Dante*, in *Vita di Dante e difesa della poesia*, ed. Carlo Muscetta (Rome: Edizioni dell'Ateneo, 1963).

13 Giambattista Vico, 'Discovery of the True Dante', in Irma Brandeis (ed.), *Discussions of the Divine Comedy* (Boston: Heath, 1966), 11; also in Michael Caesar (ed.), *Dante: The Critical Heritage, 1314(?)–1870* (London: Routledge, 1989), 352–5. Cf. also Vico's *Scienza Nuova*, trans. Thomas G. Bergin and Max H. Fish (Ithaca, NY: Cornell University Press, 1984), §786, §817; and, finally, Vico's letter to Gherardo degli Angioli, written

in 1725, on Dante and the nature of true poetry, in Caesar (ed.), *Dante: The Critical Heritage*, 348–52.

14 Vico, 'Discovery of the True Dante', 11. However, some years earlier, in the letter to Gherardo degli Angioli, Vico had been much more ambiguous: 'On account of such poverty of speech, Dante, in order to unfold his *Comedy*, had to assemble a language from those of all the people of Italy, in the same way that Homer had compiled his, using all those of Greece'; Caesar (ed.), *Dante: The Critical Heritage*, 351–2.

15 Boccaccio, *Vita di Dante*, 53–7.

16 The quotations are from *Conv* I.xi, 10–11 and I.xiii,12.

17 On the concept of *figura* cf. e.g. Erich Auerbach, 'Figura', in *Studi su Dante* (Milan: Feltrinelli, 1963), 176–226. I shall come back to it in chapter 1.

18 Adolf Hoffmeister, 'Portrait of Joyce', in Potts (ed.), *Portraits of the Artist in Exile*, 129–30. Padraic Colum, *Our Friend James Joyce* (New York: Doubleday, 1958), 124.

19 Thomas McGreevy also refers to *Work in Progress* as 'purgatorial', associating this quality to the composite nature of its 'transitional language' in a constant state of flux. But McGreevy adds that there is also a 'politically purgatorial side' to *Work in Progress* embodied in the 'intermediate' Anglo-Irish figure of Earwigger, or Perse O'Reilley; and suggests that there may furthermore be the 'personal purgatory of the author'. See his 'The Catholic Element in *Work in Progress*', *Exag*, 124.

I WORKING IN LAYERS

1 A. J. Minnis, *Medieval Theory of Authorship: Scholastic Literary Attitudes in the Later Middle Ages* (Aldershot: Wildwood House, 1988), 36.

2 *Ibid.*, 34.

3 Charles S. Singleton, 'Dante's Allegory', *Speculum* 25 (1950), 78, 80.

4 Minnis, *Medieval Theory*, 73.

5 Cf. e.g. J. A. Mazzeo, *Structure and Thought in the Paradiso* (Ithaca, NY: Cornell University Press, 1958), in particular the second chapter, 'Dante's Conception of Poetic Expression', 25–49; A. D'Andrea, ' "L'allegoria dei poeti". Nota a Convivio II.I', in M. Picone (ed.), *Dante e le forme dell'allegoresi* (Ravenna: Longo, 1987), 71–8; and C. Singleton, 'Dante's Allegory'.

6 *Structure and Thought*, 33–4.

7 Cf. Luis Jenaro-MacLennan, *The Trecento Commentaries on the Divina Commedia and the Epistle to Cangrande* (Oxford: Clarendon, 1974).

8 Cf. e.g. Louis Gillet, *Claybook for James Joyce* (London and New York: Abelard-Schuman, 1958).

9 *Epistola a Cangrande della Scala*, in *Dantis Aligherii Epistolae*, ed. and trans. Paget Toynbee (Oxford: Clarendon, 1920), pp. 160–211.

10 Cf. Peter Armour, 'The Theme of Exodus in the First Two Cantos of

the Purgatorio', in D. Nolan (ed.), *Dante Soundings: Eight Literary and Historical Essays* (Dublin: Irish University Press, 1981), 59–99; Erich Auerbach, 'Figura', in *Studi su Dante* (Milan: Feltrinelli, 1963), 176–226; Robert Hollander, 'Dante Theologus-Poeta', in *Studies in Dante* (Ravenna: Longo, 1980), 39–89.

11 *Expositio in librum B. Iob*, cap. i, lect. 2; quoted in Minnis, *Medieval Theory*, 74.

12 Jean Pépin, *Dante et la tradition de l'allégorie* (Montreal: Institut d'Etudes Médiévales; Paris: Librairie Vrin, 1970), 75. See also Giuseppe Mazzotta, *Dante, Poet of the Desert: History and Allegory in the* Divine Comedy (Princeton: Princeton University Press, 1979), 252.

13 As Giorgio Padoan interprets it, explaining that the *Commedia* has all the characteristics of the mystic vision. Cf. ' "La mirabile visione" di Dante e l'epistola a Can Grande', in *Il pio Enea, l'empio Ulisse* (Ravenna: Longo, 1977), 30–63.

14 *Structure and Thought in the Paradiso*, 34. See also Charles Singleton's well-known and successful encapsulation that 'the fiction of the *Divine Comedy* is that it is not fiction', in 'The Irreducible Dove', *Comparative Literature* 9 (1957), 129. Teodolinda Barolini discusses in chapter 1 of *The Undivine Comedy* how the question of the 'truth' or 'fiction' of the *Commedia* has determined and has been determined by differing interpetations of the allegorical issue and by the opposition between the modes of the poets and the theologians. *The Undivine Comedy: Detheologizing Dante* (Princeton: Princeton University Press, 1992).

15 A modified and much shorter version of the following two sections is forthcoming as ' "Let Dante be silent . . . ": *Finnegans Wake* and the Medieval Theory of Polysemy', in Lucia Boldrini (ed.), *Middayevil Joyce: Essays on Joyce's Medieval Cultures* (Amsterdam and Atlanta: Rodopi, forthcoming).

16 *Joyce and Dante: The Shaping Imagination* (Princeton: Princeton University Press, 1981), 323.

17 Cf. *James Joyce Archive* (New York: Garland, 1978), vol. XLVI, Preface.

18 Gillet, *Claybook for James Joyce*, 58.

19 Harry Levin, *James Joyce. A Critical Introduction* (London: Faber [1941], 1960), 133–4.

20 For instance, Marvin Magalaner and Robert M. Kain underline in their *James Joyce: The Man, The Work, The Reputation* (Oxford: Plantin [1956], 1990) the importance of Dante's four levels of meaning in *Ulysses* and find them particularly relevant to the 'Scylla and Charybdis' chapter (169–70), and Robert Boyle has found a quadripartite structure in the short story 'Grace', which he interprets as modelled on Dante's fourfold pattern ('Swiftian Allegory and Dantean Parody in Joyce's "Grace" ', *James Joyce Quarterly* 7 (1969), 11–21). Dante's theory has now long been accepted in Joycean criticism and references to it appear in many commentaries of Joyce's works; cf. e.g. the chapter on 'Joyce and Dante'

196 Notes to pages 38–49

in T. C. Theoharis's *Joyce's Ulysses: An Anatomy of the Soul* (Chapel Hill and London: University of North Carolina Press, 1988), and, more recently, M. Keith Booker, 'The Historicity of Language and Literature: Joyce, Dante, and the Poetics of Appropriation', chapter 3 in *Joyce, Bakhtin and the Literary Tradition. Toward a Comparative Cultural Poetics* (Ann Arbor: University of Michigan Press, 1995). Klaus Reichert is, as far as I am aware, the only one who has found a direct allusion in the *Wake* to the list of the levels of meaning, and in the paper 'The Theory of the Fourfold Meaning in Joyce' read at the 10th James Joyce International Symposium, Copenhagen, June 1986, he suggested that in the sentence 'scruting foreback into the fargoneahead to feel out what age in years tropical, ecclesiastic, civil or sidereal' (*FW* 426.22–4) 'tropical' refers to the tropological, or moral, sense; 'ecclesiastic' to the allegorical, also called 'mystic' by Dante in the *Convivio*; 'civil' is the literal sense, in which we see the 'public' life of HCE and his family; and finally, 'sidereal', with its reference to the stars above, alludes to the anagogical *sovrasenso*. I am grateful to Professor Reichert for pointing out to me this possible reference.

21 In a letter to J. S. Atherton of 30 August 1954, Harriet Shaw Weaver wrote: 'My view is that Mr Joyce did not intend the book to be looked upon as the dream of any one character, but that he regarded the dream form with its shiftings and changes and chances as a convenient device, allowing the freest scope to introduce any material he wished – and suited to a night-piece.' James S. Atherton, *The Books at the Wake* (Mamaroneck, NY: Appel, 1974), 17.

22 *A Skeleton Key to Finnegans Wake* (London: Faber, 1947).

23 Derek Attridge, 'Countlessness of Livestories: Narrativity in *Finnegans Wake*', in Morris Beja and David Norris (eds.), *Joyce in the Hibernian Metropolis* (Columbus: Ohio University Press, 1996), 290–6.

24 Chapter 1.5 and this longer version of the letter were planned and composed at the same time, but the letter was later relocated towards the end of the book, so as to make the 'actual' text of the missive the object of an ever-deferred quest. For an account of the genetic interlinked development of 1.5 and the letter in Book IV and their seminal importance in the conceptualisation of the structure of the book and the theme of the quest in *Finnegans Wake*, cf. Laurent Milesi, 'Metaphors of the Quest in *Finnegans Wake*', in Geert Lernout (ed.), *Finnegans Wake: Fifty Years. European Joyce Studies* 2 (Amsterdam and Atlanta: Rodopi, 1990), pp. 89–101.

25 Cf. also 'holypolygon' (*FW* 339.35) in the Butt and Taff episode of *FW* II.3, which associates HCE with a (holy) geometric polygonal figure. I shall deal with the implications of the *Wake*'s use of geometrical figures in chapter 4.

26 Joyce told Arthur Power that the Book of Kells is 'the most purely Irish thing we have, and some of the big initial letters which swing right across a page have the essential quality of a chapter of *Ulysses*. Indeed,

you can compare much of my work to the intricate illuminations. I would like it to be possible to pick up any page of my book and know at once what book it is' (*JJII* 545). On this cf. also Guillemette Bolens, 'Milly's Dream, Bloom's Body, and the Medieval Technique of Interlace', forthcoming in Boldrini (ed.), *Middayevil Joyce.*

27 Within 'scaliger' we also notice the presence of 'Aliger', i.e. Dante Alighieri.

28 Roland McHugh explains in *Annotations to Finnegans Wake* (Baltimore and London: Johns Hopkins University Press, 1980, 1991) that 'to slip the dinkum oil' means 'to tell all about it' (i.e., 'to tell the truth').

29 St Thomas's words had of course already been subjected to a shameless transformation in both *Stephen Hero* and *A Portrait*, where Stephen smuggles his own theories as 'applied Aquinas'. For a discussion of Stephen's aesthetic theories in relation to Aquinas's cf. Umberto Eco, *The Middle Ages of James Joyce: The Aesthetics of Chaosmos* (London: Hutchinson Radius, 1989), especially the first chapter, 'The Early Joyce'. See also 'L'Epistola XIII e l'allegorismo medievale', *Carte Semiotiche* 0 (1984), 13–31, where Eco relates Dante's theory of polysemy to Aquinas's thought. Cf. also William T. Noon's classic study *Joyce and Aquinas* (New Haven: Yale University Press, 1963), and Jacques Aubert, *The Aesthetics of James Joyce* (Baltimore and London: Johns Hopkins University Press, 1992), esp. chapter 6, 'The Pola Notebook and Aquinas'.

30 On the influence of aestheticism, Wagner and Nietzsche on Joyce, cf. Klaus Reichert, 'The European Background to Joyce's Writing', in Derek Attridge (ed.), *The Cambridge Companion to James Joyce* (Cambridge: Cambridge University Press, 1990), 55–82; on Joyce's assumed D'Annunzian attitudes, cf. Constantine Curran, *James Joyce Remembered* (London and New York: Oxford University Press, 1968) and Stanislaus Joyce, *My Brother's Keeper* (London: Faber, 1958); I relate Joyce's early modulations of the theory of impersonality to his intertextual use of the *Divine Comedy* in 'The Artist Paring his Quotations': Aesthetic and Ethical Implications of the Dantean Intertext in *Dubliners*', in Rosa M. Bollettieri Bosinelli and Harold Mosher Jr. (eds.), *ReJoycing: New Readings of* Dubliners (Lexington: University Press of Kentucky, 1998).

31 Several essays have been written about the mechanics of reading of the *Wake* and the new conventions it generates, thus forcing the reader to accept them and face the book in this new way. I found the following particularly stimulating: Jacques Aubert, 'riverrun', in D. Ferrer and D. Attridge (eds.), *Post-Structuralist Joyce: Essays from the French* (Cambridge: Cambridge University Press, 1984), 69–77; Roland McHugh, *The Finnegans Wake Experience* (Dublin: Irish Academic Press, 1981); and Pieter Bekker's 'Reading "Finnegans Wake"', in William McCormack and Alistair Stead (eds.), *James Joyce and Modern Literature* (London: Routledge and Kegan Paul, 1982), 185–201.

32 Reynolds, *Joyce and Dante*, 65.

33 Cf. Fritz Senn's brilliant 'The Challenge: *"ignotas animum"* ', in Senn, *Joyce's Dislocutions: Essays on Reading as Translation,* ed. John Paul Riquelme (Baltimore: Johns Hopkins University Press, 1984), 73–84, which shows how this method of cyclic reading is in fact required by Joyce's works from at least the epigraph of *A Portrait.* Cf. also, in the same collection, 'Book of Many Turns' (121–37), on *Ulysses* as a 'polytropic' book.

34 Harold Bloom, *The Anxiety of Influence: A Theory of Poetry* (Oxford: Oxford University Press, 1973), 14.

35 *Ibid.*

36 I shall come back to the (not) paying of debts and the tropology of the literary work in chapter 4.

37 Bruno's unity of all things in the one is present thoughout the *Wake* in the infinite number of coincidence of opposites, and specifically informs the relationship between the antagonist brothers Shem and Shaun; Quinet's theory is alluded to several times in the book (starting perhaps from the flow of the first word, 'riverrun'), but the most complete version of its key-sentence is in the 'Lesson' chapter (*FW* 281.04–13), a sentence parodied at regular intervals from this correct central version (the first and last chapters, and the chapters immediately before and immediately after the 'Nightlesson' reproduce it with several 'Wakese' distortions).

38 Mazzeo, *Structure and Thought,* 34.

2 THE CONFUSIONING OF HUMAN RACES

1 Warman Welliver has suggested in his introduction to *Dante in Hell: The De vulgari eloquentia. Introduction, Text, Translation, Commentary* (Ravenna: Longo, 1981), on the basis of some linguistic anomalies, internal contradictions, and distribution of key words in the treatise, that indeed the *De vulgari eloquentia* was intentionally conceived to *appear* as an 'unfinished' book of epic theme and design; its unfinishedness would support the inadequacy and unwholeness of post-Babelian languages and both reverse Dante's 'comic' attempt to redeem the language into the 'tragic' failure of humankind to challenge the divine decree that languages will be confused and, biographically, reflect Dante's 'hell', the nadir of his life at the moment when he was composing the work (Welliver, Introduction, 15–19). Like most Dante scholars, I am not convinced by Welliver's argument as to the intentionality of the unfinished project, and I do not share his reading of the treatise as a 'tragedy' that the *Convivio* will then reverse into a 'comedy'. But his interpretation of the epic scale of Dante's intent and his passing suggestion of an analogy between Dante and Nimrod (Introduction, 12–13) are uncommon readings of the treatise that I will also develop – in the context of a

different overall interpretation – in my discussion of the *De vulgari eloquentia* in this chapter and the next.

2 For a comprehensive discussion of critical tendencies and an assessment of the theories of the *De vulgari eloquentia*, cf. Ileana Pagani, *La teoria linguistica di Dante* (Naples: Liguori, 1982) and Angelo Mazzocco, *Linguistic Theories in Dante and the Humanists: Studies in Language and Intellectual History in Late Medieval and Early Renaissance Italy* (Leiden, New York and Cologne: E. J. Brill, 1993). Cf. also Umberto Eco's *The Search for the Perfect Language* (Oxford: Blackwell, 1995), esp. chapter 3, 'The Perfect Language of Dante'.

3 As pointed out in the Prelude, Samuel Beckett does not fail to draw the readers' attention to the importance of numbers (especially three and four) in Dante and Joyce ('DBVJ' 21). For a detailed discussion of the use of numbers in Dante, cf. Guglielmo Gorni, *Lettera nome numero: L'ordine delle cose in Dante* (Bologna: Il Mulino, 1990).

4 Cf. Eco, *The Search for the Perfect Language*, 38–46.

5 All references to Charles Singleton's translations of the *Commedia* are to Dante, *The Divine Comedy*, trans. and notes Charles S. Singleton, 6 vols. (Princeton: Princeton University Press, Bollingen Series, 1970–5).

6 On the problem of multiplicity and sameness in the treatise and the *Paradiso* cf. also Teodolinda Barolini, *The Undivine Comedy: Detheologizing Dante* (Princeton: Princeton University Press, 1992), 180–1. For a discussion of the language of Adam, the link between soul and language, and the differences between the *De vulgari eloquentia* and the *Divine Comedy* see Giuseppe Mazzotta's *Dante, Poet of the Desert: History and Allegory in the Divine Comedy* (Princeton: Princeton University Press, 1979), chapter 5, 'Literary History'.

7 Quoted in Patrick Boyde, *Night Thoughts on Italian Poetry and Art* (Cambridge: Cambridge University Press, 1985), 1.

8 A list of twenty occurrences of the *felix culpa* motif is offered by Niall Montgomery in 'The Pervigilium Phoenicis', *New Mexico Quarterly* 23 (1953), 470–1; Clive Hart lists twenty-four; cf. *Structure and Motif in Finnegans Wake* (London: Faber, 1962), 236. John Paul Riquelme interprets the act of writing itself as a *felix culpa*; see his *Teller and Tale in Joyce's Fiction: Oscillating Perspectives* (Baltimore and London: Johns Hopkins University Press, 1983), 4.

9 Cf. e.g., Aristide Marigo's introduction to his edition of the *De vulgari eloquentia* (Florence: Le Monnier, 1957); Francesco Di Capua, *Insegnamenti retorici medievali e dottrine estetiche moderne nel 'De vulgari eloquentia' di Dante* (Naples: Loffredo, 1945); Roger Dragonetti, 'La Conception du langage poétique dans le "De vulgari eloquentia" de Dante', *Romanica Gandensia* 9 (1961), 9–77; and Pier Vincenzo Mengaldo's introduction to his edition of the *De vulgari eloquentia* (Padua: Antenore, 1968).

10 Robert Hollander, 'Babytalk in Dante's *Commedia*', in *Studies in Dante* (Ravenna: Longo, 1980), 120.

11 *Ibid.*

12 Pagani, *La teoria linguistica*, 208–33.

13 Eco, *The Search for the Perfect Language*, 45–6.

14 There are several other contradictions or paradoxes: if Babel was the origin of the vernacular languages and their decay, and Latin was invented to make up for their deficiency, Latin should logically be the nobler of the two, rather than the vernacular that results from sin. Particularly intriguing is also the paradox of the use of Latin in the treatise that declares the vernacular the nobler language, and the use of vernacular in the book that asserts the greater nobility of Latin. Another 'curiosity' (which is by some critics interpreted as a further contradiction) is that the naturalness of the vernacular that signals its superiority over artificial Latin would be undermined by the project to fashion and 'fix' an illustrious language whose foundations would be provided by all the exisiting dialects, and which would therefore be a superior but in the last analysis 'artificialised' idiom modelled (at least in part) on the rational structure of Latin.

15 Matthew, 4.16: 'the people who sat in darkness have seen a great light, and for those who sat in the region and shadow of death light has dawned'. Cf. also Isaiah 9.2.

16 On this cf. also Laurent Milesi, 'Italian Studies in Musical Grammar', in Claude Jacquet and Jean-Michel Rabaté (eds.), *Scribble 3: Joyce et L'Italie* (Paris: Minard, 1994), 105–53.

17 There are countless instances of passages drawing together Babel and original sin in the *Wake*; cf. e.g. the description of HCE as 'swobbing broguen eeriesh myth brockendootsch, making his reporterage on Der Fall Adams' (*FW* 70.04–5, swapping broken Irish with broken Dutch/German while making his report on the fall or case [German *Fall*] of Adam). 'O'Phelim's Cutprice' (*FW* 72.04) and 'Swayed in his Falling' (*FW* 72.07) figure among the 'abusive names' he is called.

18 Cf. Roland McHugh, *Annotations to Finnegans Wake* (Baltimore and London: Johns Hopkins University Press, 1980, 1991).

19 Mary Reynolds finds in the 'Mime' chapter of the *Wake* a reference to the position of Lucifer at the bottom of Hell and Dante and Virgil's climbing down his body in order to go up (*FW* 227.19–23). Cf. Reynolds, *Joyce and Dante: The Shaping Imagination* (Princeton: Princeton University Press, 1981), 309.

20 *Ibid.*, 302.

21 Among the essays on the chapter, cf. in particular Seán Golden, 'Parsing Rhetorics: the Cad as Prolegomena to the Readings of *Finnegans Wake*', in Bernard Benstock (ed.), *The Seventh of Joyce: Selected Papers from the Seventh International James Joyce Symposium, Zurich, June 1979* (Bloomington: Indiana University Press, 1982), 173–7, which considers the linguistic and political meanings of the episode.

22 On the ballad's representation of Irish history cf. Catherine Whitley,

12 Giacomo Devoto, *Il linguaggio d'Italia* (Milan: Rizzoli, 1977), 251 (my translation, emphases added).

13 Bruno Migliorini, *Storia della lingua italiana* (Florence: Sansoni, 1962), 181 (my translation, emphases added).

14 For a useful description of Anglo-Irish (or Irish English, or Hiberno-English) cf. P. W. Joyce, *English as We Speak It in Ireland*, ed. T. P. Dolan (Dublin: Wolfhound Press, 1979–88, first published in 1910), and especially Dolan's introduction.

15 Laurent Milesi, 'L'idiome babélien de *Finnegans Wake*. Recherches thématiques dans une perspective génétique', in Claude Jacquet (ed.), *Genèse de babel: Joyce et la création* (Paris: CNRS, 1985), 155–215.

16 *Ibid.*, 163.

17 With the 'O' of 'Oriolopos', 'h . . . c . . . e' becomes an 'echo'. On the combination of the inversion of HCE's initials and the 'O', cf. Fritz Senn, 'Some Conjectures about Homosexuality in FW', *A Wake Newslitter*, 6, 5 (October 1969), 70–2.

18 Orion, who was blind, recovered his sight by looking at the rising sun, and then wandered on the earth looking for his foster father, the cause of his blindness, killing all the animals he met, until he died and was assumed in heaven as the constellation that bears his name.

19 In chapter ii.3, 'the bulkily hulkwight, hunter's pink of face, an oriel orioled' (*FW* 310.26–7) combines again hunter, giant and 'oriel' (suggesting also a clock or watch, cf. the Italian *oriuolo*).

20 The pervasive and very important alchemical subtext of this chapter and of the *Wake* in general is analysed at length by Barbara DiBernard in *Alchemy and Finnegans Wake* (Albany: State University of New York Press, 1980). Cf. in particular 12–30 and 126–38. Cf. also Ian MacArthur, 'Alchemical Elements of FW', *A Wake Newslitter* 12, 2 (April 1975), 19–23.

21 DiBernard explains that this refers to Thomas Norton's *The Ordinall of Alchimy*, included in Elias Ashmole's *Theatrum Chemicum Brittannicum* in 1652 and reprinted in 1893 in A. E. Waite's *The Hermetic Museum*, one of the books referred to in the *Wake*. See *Alchemy and Finnegans Wake*, 5, 134.

22 Cf. for instance Edward Gibbon's remark, 'My English text is chaste, and all licentious passages are left in the obscurity of a learned language.' *Autobiography* (London: Macmillan, 1930), 173–4. My thanks to Jane and Antony Everson for bringing this passage to my attention. Pieter Bekker showed me an early twentieth-century family edition of Boccaccio's *Decameron* in which the more daring passages are left in Italian in the text and translated on separate sheets that can be kept in a folder together with explicit illustrations of the tale, away from the women and children.

23 *My Brother's Keeper* (New York: Viking Press, 1958), 104.

24 Review of *Ulysses* in the *Sporting Times*, 34, 1 April 1922, quoted in Richard Brown, *James Joyce and Sexuality* (Cambridge: Cambridge Uni-

versity Press, 1985), 1. Brown lists a series of similar attacks on *Ulysses* (see n. 1, p. 165). In a letter to Joyce, H. G. Wells attributes Joyce's obsession with 'waterclosets' to his belief in 'chastity and purity' (*JJ*II 607–8).

25 Carole Brown, '*FW* 378: Laughing at the Linguists', *A Wake Newslitter*, Occasional Paper No. 2 (March 1983), 4–5: 4.

26 See *JJ*II 546.

27 And, of course, also to Bloom's reflections on 'art' as he goes to the toilet in *Ulysses*; cf. Susan Brienza, 'Krapping Out: Images of Flow and Elimination as Creation in Joyce and Beckett', in Phyllis Carey and Ed Jewinsky (eds.), *Re: Joyce'n'Beckett* (New York: Fordham University Press, 1992), 117–46; Vincent Cheng, ' "Goddinpotty": James Joyce and the Literature of Excrement', in Rosa Maria Bollettieri Bosinelli, Carla Marengo Vaglio and Christine van Boheemen (eds.), *The Languages of Joyce: Selected Papers from the Eleventh International James Joyce Symposium, Venice, 12–18 June 1988* (Philadelphia: Benjamins; Amsterdam: Benjamins Publishing Co., 1992), 85–99.

28 According to Ellmann the story was a favourite of Joyce's father, who told how Buckley, an Irish soldier in the Crimean war, having an opportunity to shoot a Russian general, did not have the heart to do it when the general, in a very human and helpless plight, lowered his trousers in order to defecate. But when the general wiped himself with a piece of grassy turf, Buckley's pity vanished and he fired. Ellmann adds that Joyce was at a loss as to how to use it in *Finnegans Wake*, and was offered the key by Samuel Beckett who, on being told the story, at the moment when the general wipes himself with the green turf, remarked, 'Another insult to Ireland' (*JJ*II 398, n.). In this regard, cf. Nathan Halper, 'Another Anecdote in Ellmann', *A Wake Newslitter* 5, 6 (1968), 90–3.

29 My thanks to Laurent Milesi for this piece of philological information.

30 For an interpretation of the story, cf. in particular Nathan Halper, 'James Joyce and the Russian General', *Partisan Review* 18 (1951), 424–31, and the essays by Rabaté and Milesi cited in notes 32 and 37 below.

31 Cf. also Breon Mitchell, 'The Newer Alchemy: Lord Rutherford and *Finnegans Wake*', *A Wake Newslitter* 3, 5 (1966), 96–102. Mitchell explains that the 'annihilation of the atom' involved is that of the atom-splitting experiment of 1919 conducted by Lord Rutherford.

32 Jean-Michel Rabaté, *James Joyce, Authorized Reader* (Baltimore and London: Johns Hopkins University Press, 1991), esp. 'Language of Earse', 132–49. On the episode and its political overtones see also Roland McHugh, *The Sigla of Finnegans Wake* (London: Edward Arnold, 1976), 81–6.

33 Rabaté, *James Joyce: Authorized Reader*, 140.

34 *Ibid.*, 141.

35 I shall discuss in chapter 4 how the mother becomes both life-giver and logos-giver.

36 Mary Reynolds has shown that Joyce's manuscript draft works into the description of sleeping Shem ('but you cannot see whose heel he sheepfolds in his wrought hand because I have not told it to you. O, foetal sleep!', *FW* 563.08–10) a verse from *Paradiso* xxv, 5 which portrays Dante's native Florence as 'the fair sheepfold where I slept as a lamb' ('il bello ovile ov'io dormi' agnello'). Cf. Reynolds, *Joyce and Dante: The Shaping Imagination* (Princeton: Princeton University Press, 1981), 30.

37 Besides the articles or chapters mentioned above, cf also chapter 6 of Rabaté's *James Joyce: Authorized Reader* ('Idiolects, Idiolex', 116–31); and Laurent Milesi, 'The Perversions of "Aerse" and the Anglo-Irish Middle Voice in *Finnegans Wake*', *Joyce Studies Annual* 4 (1993), 98–118.

38 Literally, 'small women', *Epistle to Can Grande*, §10. Toynbee translates it as 'women-folk', but Dante's word has a more depreciatory tone.

39 'The Language of Politics and the Politics of Language', in Giorgio Melchiori, *Joyce's Feast of Languages: Seven Essays and Ten Notes. Joyce Studies in Italy* 4, ed. Franca Ruggieri (Rome: Bulzoni, 1995), 107–14: 109–10.

40 Harry Levin, *James Joyce: A Critical Introduction* (London: Faber, 1960), 133.

41 In chemistry, 'the power or capacity of certain elements to combine with or displace a greater or lesser number of hydrogen (or other) atoms' (*OED*). In this context, the capacity of the word to combine with other ones in forming new significant phrasal or textual (often inter-linguistic) units, at the same time displacing the original standard meaning and resetting them in the new contexts thus created.

42 Laurent Milesi discusses the Pentecostal theme of the linguistic unity in '*Finnegans Wake*: The Obliquity of Trans-lation', in M. Beja and D. Norris (eds.), *Joyce in the Hibernian Metropolis* (Columbus: Ohio University Press, 1996), 279–89.

43 Cf. McHugh's *Sigla*, 113–21.

44 Adaline Glasheen tries to identify the 'characters' involved in her *Third Census of Finnegans Wake* (Berkeley and Los Angeles: University of California Press, 1977); cf. also Philip Graham, 'The Middlewhite Fair', *A Wake Newslitter* 6, 5 (October 1969), 67–9.

45 Cf. Marigo's note to *Dve* i.xvii.

46 *Summa Theologica* i, 39, 8c.

47 See Jacques Aubert, *The Aesthetics of James Joyce* (Baltimore and London: Johns Hopkins University Press, 1992), 11–23.

48 Umberto Eco, *The Middle Ages of James Joyce: The Aesthetics of Chaosmos* (London: Hutchinson Radius, 1989), footnote 17, p. 32.

49 Corinna del Greco Lobner, *James Joyce's Italian Connection: The Poetics of the Word* (Iowa City: University of Iowa Press, 1989).

50 *Ibid.*, 58–9.
51 On this, however, cf. also Hugh Kenner's discussion of the epiphany in *Dublin's Joyce* (second edn, New York: Columbia University Press, 1987), esp. the section 'Epiphany and the Intuition of Being', 147–8.
52 Lobner, *Joyce's Italian Connection*, 68–9.
53 But see also Jacques Aubert's discussion of the contribution of the Aristotelian concept of *anagnoresis* to the Aquinian basis of Joyce's (or Stephen's) theory, especially as regards the 'trivial' and commonplace nature of the epiphanic experience; *The Aesthetics of James Joyce*, 100–7. On the medievalism of Joyce's mind see Eco, *The Middle Ages of James Joyce*, and Lucia Boldrini (ed.), *Middayevil Joyce: Essays on Joyce's Medieval Cultures* (Amsterdam and Atlanta: Rodopi, forthcoming).
54 Giorgio Melchiori, 'Introduzione', *Finnegans Wake: H.C.E.* (Milan: Mondadori, 1982), xvi (my translation).
55 A. Walton Litz, *The Art of James Joyce: Method and Design in* Ulysses *and* Finnegans Wake (London: Oxford University Press, 1961), 36 (my emphasis).

4 FIGURES OF INEFFABILITY

1 'And so, figuring paradise, the sacred poem must leap.'
2 *The Vision: or Hell, Purgatory, and Paradise* was for instance the title by which Henry Francis Cary's early nineteenth-century translation of the *Commedia* was known.
3 Cf. e.g. Padoan, '"La mirabile visione" di Dante e l'epistola a Can Grande', in *Il pio Enea, l'empio Ulisse* (Ravenna: Longo, 1977).
4 Charles Singleton, 'The Irreducible Dove', *Comparative Literature* 9 (1957), 129.
5 Erich Auerbach, *Mimesis: The Representation of Reality in Western Literature* (New York: Doubleday Anchor Books, 1953), 164–5.
6 James S. Atherton, *The Books at the Wake* (Mamaroneck, NY: Appel, 1974), 79; see also *Letters* II 248.
7 The fifth canto of the *Inferno*, together with that of Conte Ugolino (*Inf* XXXI) is one of the most translated into English. See Gilbert Cunningham, *The Divine Comedy in English: A Critical Bibliography 1782–1900* (Edinburgh and London: Oliver & Boyd, 1965); and David Wallace, 'Dante in English', in Rachel Jacoff (ed.), *The Cambridge Companion to Dante* (Cambridge: Cambridge University Press, 1993), 237–58.
8 Atherton also identifies another allusion to *Inf* V nine pages before the beginning of II.2: 'Look at this passage about Gallilleotto' (Atherton quotes it as 'Look at this passage from Galilleotti'), which is alleged to come from 'the lingerous longerous book of the dark' (*FW* 251.24–5) (*Books at the Wake*, 80–1). Galahad or, in Italian, Galeotto, the go-between of Lancelot and Princess Guenevere, becomes in Dante the book itself which made Paolo and Francesca fall in love and kiss, and

thus commit adultery like the characters of the Arthurian cycle they were reading about. But in Joyce's text, as Mary Reynolds points out, Francesca's story is brought down to the level of a teacher seducing his pupil; see Reynolds, *Joyce and Dante: The Shaping Imagination* (Princeton: Princeton University Press, 1981), 216.

9 Atherton, *Books at the Wake*, 80.

10 'Triumphus Cupidinis', lines 1–3, in Francesco Petrarca, *Rime, Trionfi e Poesie Latine*, F. Neri, G. Martellotti, E. Bianchi and N. Sapegno (eds.) (Milan and Naples: Ricciardi Editore, 1951), 481.

11 *The Divine Comedy*, trans. and notes Charles S. Singleton, 6 vols. (Princeton: Princeton University Press, 1970–5).

12 Cf. Jean-Michel Rabaté, 'A Portrait of the Author as a Bogeyman', in *James Joyce, Authorized Reader* (Baltimore and London: Johns Hopkins University Press, 1991), 150–84.

13 In a very recent book, which I only read as I was putting the finishing touches to mine, Sam Slote has written extensively on the function of silence in Dante, Joyce and Mallarmé. Given the nature of our projects, we often analyse similar issues and passages from Dante's and Joyce's texts, but our two studies approach the topic in very different ways, and Slote's does not attempt a parallel reading of Dante and Joyce as I do in these pages, concentrating rather on the function and concept of silence in each of the three writers he has chosen. Especially interesting I find his discussion of the relationship between what he calls 'iterable' and 'initerable' languages in Dante, the former assuming that the experience of *Paradiso* is representable, the latter recognising that that experience is not accessible and is therefore apart from language. See Sam Slote, *The Silence in Progress of Dante, Mallarmé, and Joyce* (New York: Peter Lang, 1999).

14 On the 'Poetics of the New' cf. Teodolinda Barolini, *The Undivine Comedy: Detheologizing Dante* (Princeton: Princeton University Press, 1992), chapter 2, esp. 24–5.

15 This passage is discussed in Reynolds, *Joyce and Dante*, 86–7. See also Adam Piette, *Remembering and the Sound of Words: Mallarmé, Proust, Joyce, Beckett* (Oxford: Clarendon, 1996), 163–4.

16 Ernst Robert Curtius's classic *European Literature and the Latin Middle Ages* (London: Routledge and Kegan Paul, 1953) offers a useful discussion of the topos of inexpressibility in ancient and medieval literature; cf. esp. 159–62. Manuela Colombo, *Dai mistici a Dante: Il linguaggio dell'ineffabilità* (Florence: La Nuova Italia, 1987) is entirely devoted to the history of the topos, how it passed into Dante's works from the writings of the mystics, and its development in post-Dantean vernacular literature. I have found Peter Hawkins's 'Dante's *Paradiso* and the Dialectic of Ineffability', in Peter S. Hawkins and Anne Howland Schotter (eds.), *Ineffability: Naming the Unnamable from Dante to Beckett* (New York: AMS Press, 1984), 5–21, particularly stimulating.

17 Cf. Colombo, *Dai Mistici a Dante*, esp. 32–5.
18 Hawkins, 'Dante's *Paradiso* and the Dialectic of Ineffability', 7. See also Jeremy Tambling's subtle analysis of Dante's 'significar' and 'vo significando' in *Dante and Difference: Writing in the Commedia* (Cambridge: Cambridge University Press, 1988), esp. chapter 4, 96–128.
19 'Nam allegoria dicitur ab alleon graece, quod in latinum dicitur alienum, sive diversum' ('for the word "allegory" is so called from the Greek *alleon*, which in Latin is *alienum* or *diversum*', *Epistle to Can Grande*, in *Dantis Aligherii Epistolae*, ed. and trans. Paget Toynbee (Oxford: Clarendon, 1920), §7).
20 T. S. Eliot, 'The Metaphysical Poets', in *Selected Essays* (London: Faber, 1951), 289.
21 The metaphor of the 'book of memory' had already been used by Dante for the *Vita Nuova* (*VN* 1). Maria Corti discusses this image in Dante's works in relation to the poet's use of references and allusions in her fascinating *Percorsi dell'invenzione: Il linguaggio poetico e Dante* (Turin: Einaudi, 1993); see in particular chapter 2, '"Il libro della memoria" e i libri dello scrittore'.
22 On the relationships between memory and forgetting, poetry, silence and the final vision of the *Paradiso* see Giuseppe Mazzotta's *Dante, Poet of the Desert: History and Allegory in the Divine Comedy* (Princeton: Princeton University Press, 1979), chapter 6, esp. 260–9.
23 Barolini discusses Dante's insistence on the need to 'jump' in *Paradiso* in *The Undivine Comedy*; see esp. chapter 10, 'The Sacred Poem is Forced to Jump: Closure and the Poetics of Enjambement'.
24 Cf. e.g. *Purg* I, 1 ff.; *Par* II, 1; XXIII, 57.
25 Cf. e.g. *Inf* II, 8–9, but, further back, also the beginning of the *Vita Nuova*.
26 Cf. e.g. *Par* I, 135.
27 A fascinating and thorough treatment of this aspect is offered by John Bishop's *Joyce's Book of the Dark* (Madison: University of Wisconsin Press, 1987), in particular in the second chapter, significantly titled 'Nothing in Particular: On English Obliterature', in which Bishop emphasises the importance of void and of absence in the *Wake* and relates them to the loss experienced at night, in dream, during sleep, of the faculties that dominate waking life.
28 Cf. e.g. Phillip Herring, *Joyce's Uncertainty Principle* (Princeton: Princeton University Press, 1987). I shall come back to the gnomon later in this chapter.
29 Hart, *Structure and Motif in Finnegans Wake* (London: Faber, 1962), 30.
30 Cf. Henry James, Preface to *The Turn of the Screw* (Harmondsworth: Penguin, 1984).
31 *Pound/Joyce: The Letters of Ezra Pound to James Joyce, with Pound's Essays on Joyce*, ed. with Commentary Forrest Read (London: Faber, 1968), 228.
32 Cf. *Par* IX, 4–6 and XVII, 91–92.

33 Gaping Ghyl is a vertical shaft in Yorkshire. See Roland McHugh, *Annotations to Finnegans Wake* (Baltimore and London: Johns Hopkins University Press, 1980, 1991).

34 There are several instances in the *Divine Comedy* of the metaphor of 'untying the knot'; it often means to answer a question, explain something which is hard to understand (cf. e.g. *Par* VII, 54 and *Inf* X, 95). In the *Purgatorio* the knot is most often the sin from which the repentant souls will soon be freed, and 'solvere' thus means expiate; but cf. also *Purg* XXXIII, 46–50, where Beatrice promises that her obscure prophecy will soon be 'solved': 'solveranno questo enigma forte' ('will solve this hard enigma', *Purg* XXXIII, 50), which recalls ALP's words in her final monologue, 'Every letter is a hard but yours sure is the hardest crux ever' (*FW* 623.33–4).

35 I am relying here also on Laurent Milesi's subtle analysis of the intricacies of Issy's vowels and grammar in 'Italian Studies in Musical Grammar', in Claude Jacquet and Jean-Michel Rabaté (eds.), *Scribble 3: Joyce et L'Italie* (Paris: Minard, 1994), 105–53.

36 This essay by Rabaté and the one by Milesi mentioned in the note above offer the best and most extensive treatment of the relationship between language (letters) and identity or subjectivity, and I have refrained in many cases from covering ground already brilliantly explored by them.

37 See Milesi, 'Italian Studies', 135–44, and 'Toward a Female Grammar of Sexuality: The De/Recomposition of "Storyella as she is syung"', *Modern Fiction Studies: Feminist Readings of Joyce* 35, 3 (1989), 569–86.

38 Cf. Jacques Derrida, *Edmund Husserl's Origin of Geometry: An Introduction* (Lincoln and London: University of Nebraska Press, 1962).

39 Lucia Boldrini, 'The Artist Paring his Quotations: Aesthetic and Ethical Implications of the Dantean Intertext in *Dubliners*', in Rosa Maria Bollettieri Bosinelli and Harold F. Mosher Jr. (eds.), *ReJoycing: New Readings of Dubliners* (Lexington: University Press of Kentucky, 1998), 227–30.

40 Through an anagram no doubt made easier by the change of stress in Dante's line from the usual 'geòmetra' to 'geomètra' to preserve the rhythm of the endecasyllable.

41 Mary Reynolds, *Joyce and Dante*, 212.

42 The first version of the story can be read in Don Gifford, *Joyce Annotated: Notes for Dubliners and A Portrait of the Artist as a Young Man* (Berkeley, Los Angeles and London: University of California Press, 1982), 29–34 and 289–93. For an account of the development of 'The Sisters' from its earliest version to the published one, cf. Florence Walzl, 'Joyce's "The Sisters": A Development', *James Joyce Quarterly* 10 (1973), 375–421.

43 T. S. Eliot, 'Tradition and the Individual Talent', in *Selected Essays* (London: Faber, 1951), 17–18.

44 Cf. Conrad's 1920 preface to *The Secret Agent* (1907) (Harmondsworth: Penguin, 1990), 40.

45 On this cf. Ian F. A. Bell, *Critic as Scientist: The Modernist Poetics of Ezra Pound* (London and New York: Methuen, 1981), and in particular the first chapter, 'Poet as geometer', which discusses Pound's interest in James McNeill Whistler's art and in Cartesian analytic geometry for the development of his Vorticist theories.

46 This is a purely speculative hypothesis, as I know of no evidence that Joyce and Pound exchanged ideas about geometry. But Pound's use of circles and triangles in his criticism of Dante and Joyce's inscription of the 'geomater''s triangle in the circle in the *Wake*, as well as the literary friendship between the two in the second half of the 1910s, suggest that the possibility should not be discounted altogether. See also Ray Mines and Reed Way Dasenbrock's essays on mathematics in *Ulysses*, '"Nought Nowhere Was Never Reached": Mathematics in *Ulysses*', *James Joyce Quarterly* 35, 1 (Fall 1997), 25–36 and ' "Quella Vista Nova": Mathematics and the Ending of Ulysses', in Boldrini (ed.), *Middayevil Joyce: Essays on Joyce's Medieval Cultures* (Amsterdam and Atlanta: Rodopi, forthcoming).

47 E. Pound, 'Dante', in *The Spirit of Romance* (London: Peter Owen, 1952), 127.

48 Eight years later, in the preface to the catalogue of the Gaudier-Brzeska memorial exhibition, Pound found in the sculpture 'The Dancer' (though I suspect he referred more precisely to 'The Red Dancer') the occasion to return to the relations between triangles and circles in a way that goes beyond the purely analogic and sees geometry in the sculptor's work as part of the artistic exploration of forms. 'The Dancer' is for Pound 'almost a thesis of [Gaudier-Brzeska's] ideas upon the use of pure form. We have the triangle and the circle asserted, *labeled* almost, upon the face and right breast . . . life flows, the circle moves and elongates into the oval, it increases and takes volume in the sphere or hemisphere of the breast. The triangle moves toward organism it becomes a spherical triangle . . . We have the whole series of spherical triangles . . . The "abstract" or mathematical bareness of the triangle and the circle are fully incarnate, made flesh, full of vitality and of energy.' *Gaudier-Brzeska: A Memoir* (New York: New Directions, 1970), 137–8. Pound now clearly relates the geometrical figures to the human figure, and the (abstract) triangle and sphere are now concretised in the sculpture's sense of body, movement and energy.

49 Howard Helsinger, in one of the earliest essays focusing specifically on a comparison between Joyce and Dante, remarked on this geometrical image to convey Stephen's coldness towards women. Cf. 'Joyce and Dante', *English Language History* (1968), 603.

50 This definition can be found in any textbook of Euclidean geometry; I borrow the bibliographical reference from Fritz Senn, 'The aliments of jumeantry', *A Wake Newslitter*, 3, 3 (June 1966), 51–4, who relies on

Euclid's Elements, edited by Isaac Todhunter in 1862 and mentioned more than once in the *Wake*'s 'Geometry Lesson'. Senn's article is the earliest and still the most comprehensive demonstration of the extent of Joyce's reliance on 'the Euclid'.

51 My thanks to Fritz Senn for pointing out that the German for isosceles, *gleichschenklig* (literally, having equal thighs), supports the sexual meaning of the triangle even more explicitly.

52 Michael Murphy discusses the link between 'paternity' and the artist's craft in ' "Proteus" and Prose: Paternity or Workmanship?', *James Joyce Quarterly*, 35, 1 (Fall 1997), 71–81.

53 And it is striking that the younger self Stephen Dedalus looks back to while *hero*ically countering Dublin Platonist attitudes, is as much the D*aed*alus of *Stephen Hero* who had declaimed his theories to Cranly (mentioned four times in the Library chapter), as the *Artist* of *A Portrait* who recited them to Lynch.

54 Don Gifford lists Stephen's sources for this passage in *Ulysses Annotated* (Berkeley, Los Angeles and London: University of California Press, 1988), 26.

55 On Stephen's weavings and weaving as a metaphor, cf. also Murray McArthur, *Stolen Writings: Blake's Milton, Joyce's Ulysses, and the Nature of Influence* (Ann Arbor and London: UMI Research Press, 1988), 4, 88. David Weir traces Joyce's mediation through Aristotelian and Paterian aesthetics, self and work, weaving and unweaving, tying and untying in the introduction to his excellent *James Joyce and the Art of Mediation* (Ann Arbor: University of Michigan Press, 1996).

56 Jacques Aubert, *The Aesthetics of James Joyce* (Baltimore and London: Johns Hopkins University Press, 1992), 9.

57 *The Critical Writings of James Joyce*, ed. Ellsworth Mason and Richard Ellmann (London: Faber, 1959), 42.

58 John Freccero has analysed Dante's image of the veil of allegory in relation to the Pauline and Biblical traditions; interestingly for our argument, in the latter the veil was literally a covering for the radiant face of Moses, and figurally the relationship between the Old and the New Testament, in which the unveiling of the truth literally coincides with the *revelation* of Christ. John Freccero, *Dante: The Poetics of Conversion* (Cambridge, MA: Harvard University Press, 1986), 122; but cf. the entire chapter 7, 'Medusa: The Letter and the Spirit'. My thanks to Jennifer Fraser for reminding me of this excellent essay.

59 Virginia Woolf, *Orlando* (London: Grafton, 1977), 195.

60 Cf. also Jean-Michel Rabaté, 'A Shadow of Doubt: Bisexuality in *Finnegans Wake*', in *Joyce upon the Void: The Genesis of Doubt* (New York: St Martin, 1991), 154–80.

61 Elémire Zolla, *The Androgynous: Fusion of the Sexes* (London: Thames and Hudson, 1978).

62 Giordano Bruno, *De monade numero et figura* (Frankfurt, 1591). Image

reproduced by permission of the British Library, where the book is held (shelfmark 532.b.29 f25). The complete title and publication details read: *Iordani Bruni Nolani De Monade numero et Figura liber Consequens Quinque De Minimo magno & Mensura. Item De Innumerabilibus, immenso, & infigurabili; seu De Vniuerso & Mundis libri octo.* Apud i. Wechelum & P. Fischerum: Francofurti, 1591. 80.

63 Clive Hart has examined various symbolic figures and diagrams of *Finnegans Wake*. See *Structure and Motif in Finnegans Wake*, esp. chapters 4 and 5, on the circle and the cross respectively. Of the diagram of *FW* 293 Hart writes, recalling Leonardo's diagram in which genitals and navel are the centres of the square and the circle that circumscribe the two positions of the human figure: 'for Joyce navel and genitals are equivalent; they are contraries – the beginning and the end of birth – and so coincide. In the diagram on page 293 the navel and genitalia are respectively the upper and lower vertices of the central rhombus' (137–8).

64 Zolla, *The Androgynous*, 69.

65 In her *Eternal Geomater: The Sexual Universe of Finnegans Wake* (Carbondale and Edwardsville: Southern Illinois University Press, 1969), Margaret Solomon discusses the geometrical problems of *FW* ii.2 in the chapter 'Plain Geometry' (103–12). Her approach aims at showing how in each expression of the problem the *Wake* manages to include references to all the characters and their sexuality and how, therefore, each geometrical figure becomes an expression of completeness and all-inclusiveness. While I find some of Solomon's identifications and solutions convincing, her interpretation is often a rather mechanical list of correspondences between the sigla and the figures. My general understanding of the function of geometry in the *Wake* is, as will be made clearer in the discussion below, the exact opposite: while Solomon tends to solve all the problems through these identifications, it is my view that what matters is that the problems constructed in 1.6 and ii.2 cannot be solved in geometrical terms (of course, this does not mean that they may not include the configurations of the various sigla pointed out by Solomon).

66 Like the ones dismissed in the *Epistle to Can Grande*, §10, quoted in chapter 3 above.

67 Vicki Mahaffey suggests in her excellent study of authority in Joyce's work that the gnomon, with its emphasis on incompleteness, configures authority in *Dubliners* as 'female' rather then 'phallic', thus undercutting the more explicit association of power with patriarchy in the rest of the collection. See Mahaffey, *Reauthorizing Joyce* (Cambridge: Cambridge University Press, 1988), 32. Fritz Senn has recently argued that while the gnomon has traditionally been read as pointing to incompleteness, it can also be seen as producing a new shape, in fact two: the parallelogram with the piece missing, and the new, smaller parallelogram. See 'Gnomon Inverted', in *ReJoycing: New Readings of*

Dubliners, Bollettieri Bosinelli and Mosher (eds.), 249–57. In the light of what I have written above, I am tempted to interpret Senn's argument as pointing to a reproduction of the geometrical figure by parthenogenesis or hermaphroditic sexuality. It is also relevant that the gnomon appears in the context of a relation between pupil and teacher that has often been read as hinting at an unexpressed homosexuality – or, as Stephen says in 'Scylla and Charybdis' when talking about Shakespeare, at a 'love that dare not speak its name' (*U* 259) and for which therefore an alternative, 'figural' language has to be devised.

68 The 'isoscelating biangle' has been discussed, within the context of the genetic relation of 1.6 to 11.2, by Laurent Milesi in 'Killing Lewis With Einstein: "Secting Time" in *Finnegans Wake*', in Andrew Treip (ed.), *Teems of Times. European Joyce Studies* 4 (Amsterdam and Atlanta: Rodopi, 1994), 9–20.

69 As Solomon points out, the result, a T-shaped figure, would be the siglum for Issy (*Eternal Geomater*, 103–5).

70 Cf. *Purg* XXI, 97; XXX, 44, 52. See Robert Hollander's 'Babytalk in Dante's "Commedia"', in *Studies in Dante* (Ravenna: Longo, 1980), 120, which discusses in very subtle and persuasive terms the relationship between Latin and vernacular through Dante's treatment of babytalk from the *De vulgari eloquentia* to the *Divine Comedy*.

71 'Nel suo profondo vidi che s'interna, / legato con amore in un volume, / ciò che per l'universo si squaderna' ('In its depth I saw ingathered, bound by love in one single volume, that which is dispersed in leaves throughout the universe', *Par* XXXIII, 85–7).

72 Mazzotta relates Dante's image of the Sibyl to the Aristotelian and Augustinian conceptions of memory; cf. *Dante, Poet of the Desert*, 264–5.

73 Cf. Bell, *Critic as Scientist*, 12–13.

74 A stereoscope blends two pictures of an object into one image, so as to give an impression of solidity.

75 Also W, or w; but with the 'seeds', the W forms a 'WC'. See also Mahaffey's discussion of this passage, linking the visual, the sexual and the figural, in *Reauthorizing Joyce*, 37–8.

76 Mulligan calls Stephen 'the loveliest mummer of them all', *U* 4.

77 Laurent Milesi's 'Metaphors of the Quest in *Finnegans Wake*', in Geert Lernout (ed.), *Finnegans Wake: Fifty Years. European Joyce Studies* 2 (Amsterdam and Atlanta: Rodopi, 1990), shows how the question of the sources of the Nile (Nil) inevitably lead to a 'Noanswa' (Nyanza, no answer).

78 The Biblical Eden is also located between two rivers, like the 'cradle of Western culture', Mesopotamia, literally the land between the rivers. Rivers seem to enclose any dream or vision of a perfect, divine or semi-divine location, places sought for, the objects of a quest.

79 On the sweetness of the final vision, its relationship with the bitterness of the first canto of the *Inferno*, and the metaphor of the honeycomb for the tropological meaning in the tradition of Biblical exegesis, see Mazzotta, *Dante, Poet of the Desert*, 267.

Bibliography

WORKS BY DANTE AND JOYCE

DANTE

Vita Nuova. Ed. and Introduction Edoardo Sanguineti. Notes by Alfonso Berardinelli, Milan: Garzanti, 1977.

The Banquet (Il Convito) of Dante Alighieri. Trans. Katherine Hillard. London: Kegan Paul, Trench and Co., 1889.

Convivio. Ed. G. Busnelli and G. Vandelli. Introduction Michele Barbi. Second edition updated by Enzo Antonio Quaglio. Florence: Le Monnier, 1964.

De vulgari eloquentia. Ed., trans. and Introduction A. Marigo. Third edition updated by P. G. Ricci. Florence: Le Monnier, 1957 (first edn 1938).

De vulgari eloquentia. Ed. and trans. Stephen Botterill. Cambridge: Cambridge University Press, 1996.

De vulgari eloquentia. Ed. Pier Vicenzo Mengaldo. Padua: Antenore, 1968.

The De Vulgari Eloquentia. Trans. A. G. Ferrers Howell. London: Kegan Paul, Trench, Trubner & Co, 1890.

Epistola a Cangrande della Scala. In *Dantis Aligherii Epistolae*. Ed. and trans. Paget Toynbee. Oxford: Clarendon, 1920, 160–211.

La Commedia secondo l'antica vulgata. Ed. Giorgio Petrocchi. Società Dantesca Italiana. Milan: Mondadori, 1966–8.

The Divine Comedy. Trans. and notes Charles S. Singleton. 6 vols. Princeton: Princeton University Press, Bollingen Series, 1970–5.

JOYCE

Dubliners. 1914. New edition, with corrected text by Robert Scholes in consultation with Richard Ellmann. New York: Viking, 1967.

A Portrait of the Artist as a Young Man. 1916. Text, criticism and notes by Chester G. Anderson. Viking Critical Library. Harmondsworth and New York: Penguin, 1968.

Ulysses. 1922. London: Bodley Head, 1960.

Finnegans Wake. 1939. London: Faber, 1950.

Stephen Hero. 1944. Ed. with an Introduction by Theodore Spencer. Revised edition with additional material and a Foreword by John. J. Slocum and Herbert Cahoon. London: Paladin, 1991.

James Joyce Archive. Gen. ed. Michael Groden. 63 vols. New York: Garland, 1978.

Letters of James Joyce. Vol. I ed. Stuart Gilbert. London: Faber, 1957. Vols. II, III, ed. Richard Ellmann. London: Faber, 1966.

Selected Letters of James Joyce. Ed. Richard Ellmann. New York: Viking, 1975.

The Critical Writings of James Joyce. Ed. Ellsworth Mason and Richard Ellmann. London: Faber, 1959.

SECONDARY TEXTS AND OTHER WORKS CITED

Armour, Peter. 'The Theme of Exodus in the First Two Cantos of the Purgatorio'. In *Dante Soundings: Eight Literary and Historical Essays*, ed. David Nolan. Dublin: Irish University Press, 1981, 59–99.

Atherton, James S. *The Books at the Wake.* Mamaroneck, NY: Appel, 1974.

Attridge, Derek. 'Countlessness of Livestories: Narrativity in *Finnegans Wake*'. In *Joyce in the Hibernian Metropolis*, ed. M. Beja and D. Norris. Columbus: Ohio University Press, 1996, 290–6.

Attridge, Derek, ed. *The Cambridge Companion to James Joyce.* Cambridge: Cambridge University Press, 1990.

Attridge, Derek and Daniel Ferrer, eds. *Post-Structuralist Joyce: Essays from the French.* Cambridge: Cambridge University Press, 1984.

Aubert, Jacques. *The Aesthetics of James Joyce.* Baltimore and London: Johns Hopkins University Press, 1992.

'riverrun'. In *Post-Structuralist Joyce*, ed. D. Attridge and D. Ferrer. Cambridge: Cambridge University Press, 1984, 120–30.

Auerbach, Erich. *Mimesis: The Representation of Reality in Western Literature.* New York: Doubleday Anchor Books, 1953.

Studi su Dante. Milan: Feltrinelli, 1963.

Baranski, Zygmunt. 'Dante's Biblical Linguistics'. *Lectura Dantis* 5 (1989), 105–43.

'La lezione esegetica di Inferno I: Allegoria, storia e letteratura nella Commedia'. In *Dante e le forme dell'allegoresi*, ed. M. Picone. Ravenna: Longo, 1987, 79–97.

Barolini, Teodolinda. *The Undivine Comedy: Detheologizing Dante.* Princeton: Princeton University Press, 1992.

Barthes, Roland. *S/Z* (1970). Oxford: Blackwell, 1990.

'The Death of the Author' (1968). In *Image–Music–Text*, ed. and trans. Stephen Heath. London: Fontana, 1977, 142–8.

'From Work to Text' (1971). In *Image–Music–Text*, ed. and trans. Stephen Heath. London: Fontana, 1977, 153–4.

'Théorie du Texte'. *Encyclopedia Universalis*. France, 1977. Vol. xv, 1973, 1013–17.

Beckett, Samuel. 'Dante. . . Bruno. Vico. . Joyce'. In *Our Exagmination Round His Factification for Incamination of Work in Progress*, ed. S. Beckett et al. London: Faber, 1951, 3–22.

Beckett, Samuel et al. *Our Exagmination Round His Factification for Incamination of Work in Progress* (1929). London: Faber, 1951.

Begnal, Michael and Fritz Senn, eds. *A Conceptual Guide to Finnegans Wake*. University Park and London: Pennsylvania State University Press, 1974.

Beja, Morris and David Norris, eds. *Joyce in the Hibernian Metropolis: Essays*. Columbus: Ohio University Press, 1996.

Bekker, Pieter. 'Reading "Finnegans Wake"'. In *James Joyce and Modern Literature*, ed. W. J. McCormack and A. Stead. London: Routledge and Kegan Paul, 1982, 185–201.

Bell, Ian F. A. *Critic as Scientist: The Modernist Poetics of Ezra Pound*. London and New York: Methuen, 1981.

Benstock, Bernard. *Joyce-again's Wake*. Seattle: University of Washington Press, 1965.

Benstock, Bernard, ed. *The Seventh of Joyce: Selected Papers from the Seventh International James Joyce Symposium, Zurich, June 1979*. Bloomington: Indiana University Press, 1982.

The Augmented Ninth: Proceedings of the Ninth International James Joyce Symposium, Frankfurt 1984. Syracuse: Syracuse University Press, 1988.

Bishop, John. *Joyce's Book of the Dark*. Madison: University of Wisconsin Press, 1987.

Bloom, Harold. *The Anxiety of Influence: A Theory of Poetry*. Oxford: Oxford University Press, 1973.

A Map of Misreading. Oxford: Oxford University Press, 1975.

Boccaccio, Giovanni. *Vita di Dante e difesa della poesia*. Ed. Carlo Muscetta. Rome: Edizioni dell'Ateneo, 1963.

Boldrini, Lucia. ' "The Sisters" and the *Inferno*: An Intertextual Network'. *Style* 25, 3 (1991), 453–65.

'The Artist Paring his Quotations: Aesthetic and Ethical Implications of the Dantean Intertext in *Dubliners*'. In *ReJoycing: New Readings of Dubliners*, ed. Rosa Maria Bollettieri Bosinelli and Harold F. Mosher Jr. Lexington: University Press of Kentucky, 1998, 228–46.

Boldrini, Lucia, ed. *Middayevil Joyce: Essays on Joyce's Medieval Cultures*. Amsterdam and Atlanta: Rodopi, forthcoming.

Bolens, Guillemette. 'Milly's Dream, Bloom's Body, and the Medieval Technique of Interlace'. In *Middayevil Joyce: Essays on Joyce's Medieval Cultures*, ed. L. Boldrini. Amsterdam and Atlanta: Rodopi, forthcoming.

Booker, M. Keith. *Joyce, Bakhtin and the Literary Tradition. Toward a Comparative Cultural Poetics*. Ann Arbor: University of Michigan Press, 1995.

Boyde, Patrick. *Dante Philomythes and Philosopher: Man in the Cosmos*. Cambridge: Cambridge University Press, 1981.

Night Thoughts on Italian Poetry and Art: Inaugural Lecture Delivered before the University of Cambridge on 16 November 1983. Cambridge: Cambridge University Press, 1985.

Boyle, Robert, S.J. 'Swiftian Allegory and Dantean Parody in Joyce's "Grace"'. *James Joyce Quarterly* 7 (1969), 11–21.

'Miracle in Black Ink: A Glance at Joyce's Use of His Eucharistic Image'. *James Joyce Quarterly* 10, 1 (1972), 46–70.

James Joyce's Pauline Vision: A Catholic Exposition. Carbondale and Edwardsville: Southern Illinois University Press, 1978.

Brienza, Susan. 'Krapping Out: Images of Flow and Elimination as Creation in Joyce and Beckett'. In *Re: Joyce'n'Beckett*, ed. Phyllis Carey and Ed Jewinsky. New York: Fordham University Press, 1992, 117–46.

Brown, Carole. '*FW* 378: Laughing at the Linguists'. *A Wake Newslitter*, Occasional Paper No. 2 (March 1983), 4–5.

Bruno, Giordano. *De monade numero et figura.* Frankfurt, 1591.

Caesar, Michael, ed. *Dante: The Critical Heritage, 1314(?)–1870.* London: Routledge, 1989.

Campbell, Joseph and Henry M. Robinson. *A Skeleton Key to Finnegans Wake.* London: Faber, 1947.

Carugati, Giuliana. *Dalla Menzogna al Silenzio: La scrittura mistica della 'Commedia' di Dante.* Bologna: Il Mulino, 1991.

Cheng, Vincent. '"Goddinpotty": James Joyce and the Literature of Excrement'. In *The Languages of Joyce: Selected Papers from the Eleventh International James Joyce Symposium, Venice, 12–18 June 1988*, ed. Rosa Maria Bollettieri Bosinelli, Carla Marengo Vaglio and Christine van Boheemen. Philadelphia: Benjamins; Amsterdam: Benjamins Publishing Co., 1992, 85–99.

Cheng, Vincent J., Kimberly Devlin and Margot Norris, eds. *Joycean Cultures, Culturing Joyces.* Newark: University of Delaware Press; London: Associated University Presses, 1998.

Clayton, Jay and Eric Rothstein. 'Figures in the Corpus: Theories of Influence and Intertextuality'. In *Influence and Intertextuality in Literary History*, ed. J. Clayton and E. Rothstein. Madison: University of Wisconsin Press, 1991, 3–36.

Colombo, Manuela. *Dai mistici a Dante: Il linguaggio dell'ineffabilità.* Florence: La Nuova Italia, 1987.

Colum, Padraic. *Our Friend James Joyce.* New York: Doubleday, 1958.

Conrad, Joseph. *The Secret Agent* (1907; 'Preface', 1920). Harmondsworth: Penguin, 1990.

Contini, Gianfranco. *Varianti e altra linguistica. Una raccolta di saggi (1938–1968).* Turin: Einaudi, 1970.

Cooksey, Thomas L. 'The Central Man of the World: The Victorian Myth of Dante'. In *Medievalism in England. Studies in Medievalism* iv, ed. Leslie J. Workman. Cambridge: Brewer, 1992, 187–201.

Cope, Jackson. 'An Epigraph for *Dubliners*'. *James Joyce Quarterly* 7 (1970), 362–4.

Joyce's Cities: Archaeologies of the Soul. Baltimore and London: Johns Hopkins University Press, 1981.

Corti, Maria. *Percorsi dell'invenzione: Il linguaggio poetico e Dante*. Turin: Einaudi, 1993.

Cunningham, Gilbert. *The Divine Comedy in English: A Critical Bibliography 1782–1900*. Edinburgh and London: Oliver & Boyd, 1965.

Curran, Constantine P. *James Joyce Remembered*. London and New York: Oxford University Press, 1968.

Curtius, Ernst R. *European Literature and the Latin Middle Ages*. London: Routledge and Kegan Paul, 1953.

D'Alfonso, Rossella. *Il Dialogo con Dio nella Divina Commedia*. Bologna: Clueb, 1988.

D'Andrea, Antonio. ' "L'allegoria dei poeti". Nota a Convivio II.1'. In *Dante e le forme dell'allegoresi*, ed. M. Picone. Ravenna: Longo, 1987, 71–8.

D'Ovidio, Francesco. *Dante e la filosofia del linguaggio*. Naples: Tipografia della Regia Università, 1892.

Dasenbrock, Reed Way. *Imitating the Italians: Wyatt, Spenser, Synge, Pound, Joyce*. Baltimore and London: Johns Hopkins University Press, 1991.

Dasenbrock, Reed Way and R. Mines. ' "Quella vista nova": Dante, Mathematics and the Ending of *Ulysses*'. In *Middayevil Joyce: Essays on Joyce's Medieval Cultures*, ed. L. Boldrini. Amsterdam and Atlanta: Rodopi, forthcoming.

Derrida, Jacques. *Edmund Husserl's Origin of Geometry: An Introduction*. Lincoln and London: University of Nebraska Press, 1962.

Devoto, Giacomo. *Il linguaggio d'Italia*. Milan: Rizzoli, 1977.

Di Capua, Francesco. *Insegnamenti retorici medievali e dottrine estetiche moderne nel 'De vulgari eloquentia' di Dante*. Naples: Loffredo, 1945.

DiBernard, Barbara. *Alchemy and Finnegans Wake*. Albany: State University of New York Press, 1980.

Dionisotti, Carlo. *Geografia e storia della letteratura italiana*. Turin: Einaudi, 1967.

Dragonetti, Roger. 'La Conception du langage poétique dans le "De vulgari eloquentia" de Dante'. *Romanica Gandensia* 9 (1961), 9–77.

Dronke, Peter. *Dante and Medieval Latin Traditions*. Cambridge: Cambridge University Press, 1986.

Eco, Umberto. *Le poetiche di Joyce*. Milan: Bompiani, 1976.

'L'Epistola XIII e l'allegorismo medievale'. *Carte Semiotiche* 0 (1984), 13–31.

The Middle Ages of James Joyce: The Aesthetics of Chaosmos. London: Hutchinson Radius, 1989.

'The Perfect Language of Dante'. In *The Search for the Perfect Language*. Oxford: Blackwell, 1995, 34–52.

Eliot, T. S. 'Dante'. In *Selected Essays*. London: Faber, 1951, 237–77.

'The Metaphysical Poets'. In *Selected Essays*. London: Faber, 1951, 281–91.
The Complete Poems and Plays. London: Faber, 1969.
'What Dante Means to Me'. In *To Criticize the Critic and Other Writings*. London: Faber, 1965, 1978, 125–35.
Ellis, Steve. *Dante and English Poetry: Shelley to T. S. Eliot*. Cambridge: Cambridge University Press, 1983.
Ellmann, Richard. *James Joyce*. New and revised edition. Oxford: Oxford University Press, 1982.
Ferrante, Joan. 'A Poetics of Chaos and Harmony'. In *The Cambridge Companion to Dante*, ed. R. Jacoff. Cambridge: Cambridge University Press, 1993, 153–71.
Francini Bruni, Alessandro. 'Joyce Stripped Naked in the Piazza' (1922). In *Portraits of the Artist in Exile: Recollections of James Joyce by Europeans*, ed. Willard Potts. Portmarnock: Wolfhound Press, 1979, 7–38.
Frank, Nino. 'The Shadow That Had Lost Its Man' (1967). In *Portraits of the Artist in Exile: Recollections of James Joyce by Europeans*, ed. Willard Potts. Portmarnock: Wolfhound Press, 1979, 74–105.
Freccero, John. *Dante: The Poetics of Conversion*. Cambridge, MA: Harvard University Press, 1986.
Freccero, John, ed. *Dante: A Collection of Critical Essays*. Englewood Cliffs, NJ: Prentice-Hall, 1965.
Gibbon, Edward. *Autobiography*. London: Macmillan, 1930.
Gifford, Don. *Joyce Annotated: Notes for Dubliners and A Portrait of the Artist as a Young Man*. Berkeley, Los Angeles and London: University of California Press, 1982.
Ulysses Annotated. Berkeley, Los Angeles and London: University of California Press, 1988.
Gillet, Louis. *Claybook for James Joyce*. London and New York: Abelard-Schuman, 1958.
Glasheen, Adaline. *Third Census to Finnegans Wake*. Berkeley and Los Angeles: University of California Press, 1977.
Golden, Seán. 'Parsing Rhetorics: The Cad as Prolegomena to the Readings of *Finnegans Wake*'. In *The Seventh of Joyce: Selected Papers from the Seventh International James Joyce Symposium, Zurich, June 1979*, ed. B. Benstock. Bloomington: Indiana University Press, 1982, 173–7.
Gorni, Guglielmo. *Lettera nome numero: L'ordine delle cose in Dante*. Bologna: Il Mulino, 1990.
Gozzi, Francesco. 'Dante nell'inferno di Joyce'. *English Miscellany* 23 (1972), 195–229.
Graham, Philip. 'The Middlewhite Fair'. *A Wake Newslitter* 6, 5 (October 1969), 67–9.
Halper, Nathan. 'James Joyce and the Russian General'. *Partisan Review* 18 (1951), 424–31.
'Another Anecdote in Ellmann'. *A Wake Newslitter* 5, 6 (1968), 90–3.
Hart, Clive. *Structure and Motif in Finnegans Wake*. London: Faber, 1962.

A Concordance to Finnegans Wake. Minneapolis: University of Minnesota Press, 1963.

Hawkins, Peter. 'Dante's *Paradiso* and the Dialectic of Ineffability'. In *Ineffability: Naming the Unnamable from Dante to Beckett*, ed. Peter S. Hawkins and Anne Howland Schotter. New York: AMS Press, 1984, 5–21.

Heath, Stephen. 'Ambiviolences: Notes for Reading Joyce'. In *Post-Structuralist Joyce: Essays from the French*, ed. D. Attridge and D. Ferrer. Cambridge: Cambridge University Press, 1984, 31–68.

Helsinger, Howard. 'Joyce and Dante'. *English Literary History* (1968), 591–605.

Henke, Suzette. 'Exagmining Beckett & Company'. In *Reviewing Classics of Joycean Criticism*, ed. Janet Dunleavy. Urbana and Chicago: University of Illinois Press, 1991, 60–81.

Herring, Phillip. *Joyce's Uncertainty Principle*. Princeton: Princeton University Press, 1987.

Hoffmeister, Adolf. 'Portrait of Joyce'. In *Portraits of the Artist in Exile: Recollections of James Joyce by Europeans*, ed. Willard Potts. Portmarnock: Wolfhound Press, 1979, 127–36.

Hogan, Patrick Colm. *Joyce, Milton, and the Theory of Influence*. Gainesville: University Press of Florida, 1995.

Hollander, Robert. *Studies in Dante*. Ravenna: Longo, 1980.

Jacoff, Rachel, ed. *The Cambridge Companion to Dante*. Cambridge: Cambridge University Press, 1993.

James, Henry. *The Turn of the Screw* (1898). Harmondsworth: Penguin, 1984.

Jenaro-MacLennan, Luis. *The Trecento Commentaries on the Divina Commedia and the Epistle to Cangrande*. Oxford: Clarendon, 1974.

Joyce, P. W. *English as We Speak It in Ireland* (1910), ed. T. P. Dolan. Dublin: Wolfhound Press, 1979–88.

Joyce, Stanislaus. 'The Background to *Dubliners*'. *Listener* 60 (25 March 1954), 526.

My Brother's Keeper. New York: Viking, 1958.

Kenner, Hugh. *Dublin's Joyce*. Second edition. New York: Columbia University Press, 1987.

Lagercrantz, Olof. *From Hell to Paradise: Dante and His Comedy*. New York: Washington Square Press, 1966.

Lawrence, Karen. 'Paternity as Legal Fiction in *Ulysses*'. In *The Augmented Ninth: Proceedings of the Ninth International James Joyce Symposium, Frankfurt 1984*, ed. B. Benstock. Syracuse: Syracuse University Press, 1988, 233–43.

Levin, Harry. *James Joyce: A Critical Introduction* (1941). London: Faber, 1960.

Litz, A. Walton. *The Art of James Joyce: Method and Design in* Ulysses *and* Finnegans Wake. London: Oxford University Press, 1961.

Lobner, Corinna del Greco. *James Joyce's Italian Connection: The Poetics of the Word*. Iowa City: University of Iowa Press, 1989.

MacArthur, Ian. 'Alchemical Elements of FW'. *A Wake Newslitter* 12, 2 (April 1975), 19–23.

MacCabe, Colin. *James Joyce and the Revolution of the Word*. London and Basingstoke: Macmillan, 1978.

Magalaner, Marvin and Robert M. Kain. *James Joyce: The Man, The Work, The Reputation* (1956). Oxford, Plantin, 1990.

Mahaffey, Vicki. *Reauthorizing Joyce*. Cambridge: Cambridge University Press, 1988.

Manganiello, Dominic. *Joyce's Politics*. London, Boston and Henley: Routledge and Kegan Paul, 1980.

T. S. Eliot and Dante. Basingstoke and London: Macmillan, 1989.

Mazzeo, Joseph A. *Structure and Thought in the Paradiso*. Ithaca, NY: Cornell University Press, 1958.

Mazzocco, Angelo. *Linguistic Theories in Dante and the Humanists: Studies in Language and Intellectual History in Late Medieval and Early Renaissance Italy*. Leiden, New York and Cologne: E. J. Brill, 1993.

Mazzotta, Giuseppe. *Dante, Poet of the Desert: History and Allegory in the* Divine Comedy. Princeton: Princeton University Press, 1979.

McArthur, Murray. *Stolen Writings: Blake's* Milton, *Joyce's* Ulysses, *and the Nature of Influence*. Ann Arbor and London: UMI Research Press, 1988.

McCormack, William J. and Alistair Stead, eds. *James Joyce and Modern Literature*. London: Routledge and Kegan Paul, 1982.

McDougal, Stuart Y., ed. *Dante Among the Moderns*. Chapel Hill and London: University of North Carolina Press, 1985.

McGreevy, Thomas. 'The Catholic Element in *Work in Progress*'. In *Our Exagmination Round His Factification for Incamination of Work in Progress*, ed. S. Beckett et al. London: Faber, 1951, 117–27.

McHugh, Roland. *The Sigla of Finnegans Wake*. London: Edward Arnold, 1976.

Annotations to Finnegans Wake. Baltimore and London: Johns Hopkins University Press, 1980, 1991.

The Finnegans Wake Experience. Dublin: Irish Academic Press, 1981.

Melchiori, Giorgio. 'Introduzione'. In James Joyce, *Finnegans Wake. H.C.E.* Milan: Mondadori, 1982.

Joyce's Feast of Languages: Seven Essays and Ten Notes. Joyce Studies in Italy 4, ed. Franca Ruggieri. Rome: Bulzoni, 1995.

Mengaldo, Pier Vincenzo. 'Introduzione'. In Dante Alighieri, *De vulgari eloquentia*, ed. Pier Vincenzo Mengaldo. Padua: Antenore, 1968.

Linguistica e retorica di Dante. Pisa: Nistri-Lischi, 1978.

Migliorini, Bruno. *Storia della lingua italiana*. Florence: Sansoni, 1962.

Milbank, Alison. *Dante and the Victorians*. Manchester: Manchester University Press, 1998.

Milesi, Laurent. 'L'idiome babélien de *Finnegans Wake*: Recherches thématiques dans une perspective génétique'. In *Genèse de babel: Joyce et la création*, ed. Claude Jacquet. Paris: CNRS, 1985, 155–215.

'Toward a Female Grammar of Sexuality: The De/Recomposition of "Storyella as she is syung"'. *Modern Fiction Studies: Feminist Readings of Joyce* 35, 3 (1989), 569–86.

'Metaphors of the Quest in *Finnegans Wake*'. In *Finnegans Wake: Fifty Years.* *European Joyce Studies* 2, ed. Geert Lernout. Amsterdam and Atlanta: Rodopi, 1990, 79–107.

'Italian Studies in Musical Grammar'. In *Scribble 3: Joyce et L'Italie*, ed. Claude Jacquet and Jean-Michel Rabaté. Paris: Minard, 1994, 105–53.

'Killing Lewis With Einstein: "Secting Time" in *Finnegans Wake*'. In *Teems of Times. European Joyce Studies* 4, ed. Andrew Treip. Amsterdam and Atlanta: Rodopi, 1994, 9–20.

'*Finnegans Wake*: The Obliquity of Trans-lation'. In *Joyce in the Hibernian Metropolis*, ed. M. Beja and D. Norris. Columbus: Ohio University Press, 1996, 279–89.

Milton, John. *Paradise Lost*, ed. Alistair Fowler. London and New York: Longman, 1971.

Minnis, A. J. *Medieval Theory of Authorship: Scholastic Literary Attitudes in the Later Middle Ages.* Aldershot: Wildwood House, 1988.

Mitchell, Breon. 'The Newer Alchemy: Lord Rutherford and *Finnegans Wake*'. *A Wake Newslitter* 3, 5 (1966), 96–102.

Montgomery, Niall. 'The Pervigilium Phoenicis'. *New Mexico Quarterly* 23 (1953), 470–1.

Murphy, Michael. '"Proteus" and Prose: Paternity or Workmanship?'. *James Joyce Quarterly* 35, 1 (Fall 1997), 71–81.

Noon, William T. *Joyce and Aquinas.* New Haven: Yale University Press, 1963.

Norris, Margot. *The Decentered Universe of Finnegans Wake: A Structuralist Analysis.* Baltimore: Johns Hopkins University Press, 1974.

Olender, Maurice. *Les Langues du Paradis. Aryens et Sémites: un couple providentiel.* Paris: Seuil, 1989.

Padoan, Giorgio. *Il pio Enea, l'empio Ulisse.* Ravenna: Longo, 1977.

Pagani, Ileana. *La teoria linguistica di Dante.* Naples: Liguori, 1982.

Pépin, Jean. *Dante et la tradition de l'allégorie.* Montreal: Institut d'Etudes Médiévales; Paris: Librairie Vrin, 1970.

Petrarca, Francesco. *Rime, Trionfi e Poesie Latine.* F. Neri, G. Martellotti, E. Bianchi and N. Sapegno, eds. Milan and Naples: Ricciardi Editore, 1951.

Picone, Michelangelo. '*La Vita Nuova* fra autobiografia e tipologia'. In *Dante e le forme dell'allegoresi*, ed. M. Picone. Ravenna: Longo, 1987, 59–69.

Picone, Michelangelo, ed. *Dante e le forme dell'allegoresi.* Ravenna: Longo, 1987.

Piette, Adam. *Remembering and the Sound of Words: Mallarmé, Proust, Joyce, Beckett.* Oxford: Clarendon, 1996.

Potts, Willard, ed. *Portraits of the Artist in Exile: Recollections of James Joyce by Europeans.* Portmarnock: Wolfhound Press, 1979.

Poulet, Georges. 'The Metamorphoses of the Circle'. In *Dante*, ed. J. Freccero. Englewood Cliffs, NJ: Prentice-Hall, 1965, 151–69.

Pound, Ezra. 'Dante'. In *The Spirit of Romance* (1910). London: Peter Owen, 1952, 118–65.

Literary Essays of Ezra Pound, ed. T. S. Eliot. London: Faber, 1954.

Pound/Joyce: The Letters of Ezra Pound to James Joyce, with Pound's Essays on Joyce, ed. with commentary Forrest Read. London: Faber, 1968.

Gaudier-Brzeska: A Memoir. New York: New Directions, 1970.

Selected Prose 1909–1965, ed. William Cookson. London: Faber, 1973.

Rabaté, Jean-Michel. *James Joyce, Authorized Reader*. Baltimore and London: Johns Hopkins University Press, 1991.

Joyce upon the Void: The Genesis of Doubt. New York: St Martin, 1991.

Rajna, Pio. 'Il primo capitolo del trattato "De vulgari eloquentia" tradotto e commentato'. In *Miscellanea di studi in onore di A. Hortis*. Trieste: 1910.

Reichert, Klaus. ' "It's as semper as oxhousehumper". The Structure of Hebrew and the Language of *Finnegans Wake*'. In *Myriadminded Man: Jottings on Joyce*, ed. Rosa Maria Bosinelli and Paola Pugliatti. Bologna: Clueb, 1986, 235–50.

'The Theory of the Fourfold Meaning in Joyce'. Paper read at the Tenth James Joyce International Symposium, Copenhagen, June 1986.

'Close Reading of the Babel Episode in the Bible'. Paper read at the Eleventh James Joyce International Symposium, Venice, June 1988.

'The European Background to Joyce's Writing'. In *The Cambridge Companion to James Joyce*, ed. D. Attridge. Cambridge: Cambridge University Press, 1990, 55–82.

Reynolds, Mary T. *Joyce and Dante: The Shaping Imagination*. Princeton: Princeton University Press, 1981.

'The Dantean Design of Joyce's *Dubliners*'. In *The Seventh of Joyce: Essays from the 7th International James Joyce Symposium, Zurich, June 1979*, ed. B. Benstock. Bloomington: Indiana University Press, 1982, 124–30.

Riquelme, John Paul. *Teller and Tale in Joyce's Fiction: Oscillating Perspectives*. Baltimore and London: Johns Hopkins University Press, 1983.

Risset, Jacqueline. *Dante écrivain ou l'Intelletto d'amore*. Paris: Seuil, 1982.

'Joyce traduce Joyce'. In *Joyce: Poesie e Prose*, ed. Franca Ruggieri. Milan: Mondadori, 1992, 703–23.

Senn, Fritz. 'The aliments of jumeantry'. *A Wake Newslitter* 3, 3 (1966), 51–4.

'Some Conjectures about Homosexuality in FW'. *A Wake Newslitter* 6, 5 (October 1969), 70–2.

Joyce's Dislocutions: Essays on Reading as Translation, ed. John Paul Riquelme. Baltimore and London: Johns Hopkins University Press, 1984.

Settanni, Ettore. *James Joyce e la prima versione italiana del Finnegan's [sic] Wake*. Venice: Cavallino, 1965.

Singleton, Charles S. 'Dante's Allegory'. *Speculum* 25 (1950), 78–86.

'The Irreducible Dove'. *Comparative Literature* 9 (1957), 129–35.

' "In Exitu Israel de Aegypto" '. In *Dante*, ed. J. Freccero. Englewood Cliffs, NJ: Prentice-Hall, 1965, 102–21.

Slote, Sam. *The Silence in Progress of Dante, Mallarmé, and Joyce*. New York: Peter Lang, 1999.

Solomon, Margaret. *Eternal Geomater: The Sexual Universe of Finnegans Wake*. Carbondale and Edwardsville: Southern Illinois University Press, 1969.

Tambling, Jeremy. *Dante and Difference: Writing in the Commedia*. Cambridge: Cambridge University Press, 1988.

Theoharis, Theoharis Constantine. *Joyce's Ulysses: An Anatomy of the Soul*. Chapel Hill and London: University of North Carolina Press, 1988.

Toynbee, Paget. *Dante Alighieri: His Life and Works*. London: Methuen, 1910.

Verdicchio, Massimo. 'Exagmination Round the Fictification of Vico and Joyce'. *James Joyce Quarterly* 26, 4 (1989), 531–9.

Vico, Giambattista. 'Discovery of the True Dante'. In *Discussions of the Divine Comedy*, ed. Irma Brandeis. Boston: Heath, 1966, 11–12. Also in *Dante: The Critical Heritage*, ed. M. Caesar. London: Routledge, 1989, 352–5.

La Scienza Nuova. Trans. Thomas G. Bergin and Max H. Fish. Ithaca, NY: Cornell University Press, 1984.

Wallace, David. 'Dante in English'. In *The Cambridge Companion to Dante*, ed. R. Jacoff. Cambridge: Cambridge University Press, 1993, 237–58.

Walzl, Florence. 'Joyce's "The Sisters": A Development'. *James Joyce Quarterly* 10 (1973), 375–421.

Weir, David. *James Joyce and the Art of Mediation*. Ann Arbor: University of Michigan Press, 1996.

Welliver, Warman. *Dante in Hell: The* De vulgari eloquentia. *Introduction, Text, Translation, Commentary*. Ravenna: Longo, 1981.

Wilhelm, James J. *Dante and Pound: The Epic of Judgement*. Orono, ME: University of Maine Press, 1974.

Williams, William Carlos. 'A Point for American Criticism'. In *Our Exagmination Round His Factification for Incamination of Work in Progress*, ed. S. Beckett et al.. London: Faber, 1951, 173–85.

Woolf, Virginia. *Orlando* (1928). London: Grafton, 1977.

Zolla, Elémire. *The Androgynous: Fusion of the Sexes*. London: Thames and Hudson, 1978.

Index